CRITICAL INSIGHTS

Things Fall Apart

by Chinua Achebe

CRITICAL INSIGHTS

Things Fall Apart

by Chinua Achebe

Editor
M. Keith Booker
University of Arkansas

Salem Press
Pasadena, California   Hackensack, New Jersey

Cover photo: ©iStockphoto.com/Richard McDowell

Published by Salem Press

© 2011 by EBSCO Publishing
Editor's text © 2011 by M. Keith Booker
"The *Paris Review* Perspective" © 2011 by Petrina Crockford for *The Paris Review*

∞ The paper used in these volumes conforms to the American National Standard for Permanence of Paper for Printed Library Materials, Z39.48-1992 (R1997).

Library of Congress Cataloging-in-Publication Data
Things fall apart, by Chinua Achebe / M. Keith Booker, editor.
    p. cm. — (Critical insights)
  Includes bibliographical references and index.
  ISBN 978-1-58765-711-5 (v. 1 : alk. paper)
  1. Achebe, Chinua. Things fall apart. 2. Igbo (African people) in literature. 3. Nigeria--In literature. I. Booker, M. Keith.
  PR9387.9.A3T5369 2011
  823'.914—dc22
                                                                    2010030196

PRINTED IN CANADA

Contents_____

Resources_____

About This Volume

M. Keith Booker

This volume of the Critical Insights Series offers a diverse selection of criticism of Chinua Achebe's *Things Fall Apart*, one of the most important and influential works of world literature of the twentieth century. The volume is divided into three parts. The first contains some general introductory and contextual material for understanding the novel. The second, Critical Contexts, is composed of essays that were commissioned specifically for this volume to provide broad coverage of significant aspects of *Things Fall Apart* and its critical heritage. Finally, the Critical Readings section consists of previously published essays that not only continue to be valuable in themselves but also illustrate important trends in the critical history of Achebe's novel.

In the first part of the volume, the editor's introduction presents a number of basic issues to be considered in thinking about *Things Fall Apart* as a literary and cultural phenomenon. It is followed by a brief biography of Achebe by Norbert Mazari and by a brief statement of perspectives on *Things Fall Apart* by Petrina Crockford for *The Paris Review.* The Critical Contexts essays then begin with Joseph McLaren's discussion of some of the cultural and historical contexts of Achebe's novel, followed by Amy Sickels's survey of the critical history of the novel, which is crucial to the critical history of the African novel as a whole. Thomas Jay Lynn next addresses issues of language that are important to an understanding of *Things Fall Apart*, and Matthew J. Bolton concludes this section with an essay discussing important points of contact between Achebe's novel and the Western literary tradition, from the Greek epic to literary modernism.

The reprinted articles included in the third part of this volume begin with two general critical discussions of *Things Fall Apart* by Margaret Laurence and myself, followed by David Cook's slightly more focused, but still quite general, discussion of the ways in which the novel depicts the crisis in Igbo culture brought about by the advent of European colonization. The other essays treat more specific thematic issues related to Achebe's novel, beginning with David Hoegberg's discussion of the importance of violence, both literal and (especially) cultural, in Achebe's novel. Carey Snyder's essay also emphasizes the importance of respect for other cultures with its discussion of the way the narrative complexities of *Things Fall Apart* complicate ethnographic readings. The following two essays, by B. Eugene McCarthy and Richard Begam, also focus on aspects of the narrative structure of the novel.

The essays by Biodun Jeyifo and Ada Uzoamaka Azodo discuss the figuration of gender in *Things Fall Apart*, one of the most debated topics in recent criticism of the novel. The latter, in its treatment of masculinity in relation to the figuration of Okonkwo, the novel's protagonist, leads to the discussion of the role played by Okonkwo in the final two essays. These essays point toward the way in which Okonkwo's figuration in the book engages in familiar Western conceptions of heroism that date back to ancient Greece, while also introducing new aspects that have to do with the fact that the relationship between the individual and society in traditional Igbo culture is not necessarily the same as that in Western cultures. Finally, Patrick C. Nnoromele and Alan R Friesen discuss the tragic aspects of Okonkwo's character, his heroism, and his death.

The volume ends with some valuable resources for understanding *Things Fall Apart* and its context, including a useful chronology of Achebe's life and work that helps to place the novel within Achebe's overall career. Finally, a bibliography lists some of the more prominent pieces in the wide array of criticism and discussion that Achebe's first novel has attracted over the years.

THE BOOK AND AUTHOR

On *Things Fall Apart*

M. Keith Booker

Though, as I write this introduction, Chinua Achebe is not among the three African writers to have been awarded the Nobel Prize in Literature, Achebe is almost certainly the most important African writer to have yet entered the stage of world literature. His *Things Fall Apart* (1958) is almost certainly the most important African novel to date, as signaled by the recent inclusion of its entire text in the *Norton Anthology of World Masterpieces*, which is only one of several reasons *Things Fall Apart* is likely to be the first African novel encountered by readers outside of Africa. Achebe's first novel is one of the great literary successes of the past half century, so much so that it has paradoxically had the negative effect of diverting deserved attention away from other valuable works of African literature. At a time when most African novels, whatever their merit, still struggle to gain recognition from critics, especially outside of Africa, *Things Fall Apart* is one of those golden texts that continues to attract new critical praise and legions of new readers more than a half century after its publication.

Achebe himself is the author of four additional novels, each of which has considerable merit in its own right, yet none of which has gained anything like the critical praise and popular acclaim of his first novel. Indeed, it is probably telling that Achebe's second-best-known novel is *Anthills of the Savannah* (1987), the one that differs most from *Things Fall Apart* and thus may be the least overshadowed by it. Meanwhile, Achebe has also written children's books, short stories, and poems as well as some of the most important criticism and commentary about African literature ever produced. His series of acerbic assaults, beginning with the well-known "An Image of Africa" in 1977, on what he sees as the racist inclinations of Joseph Conrad's *Heart of Darkness*, has initiated a major new discussion of that canonical work, exercising an influence on criticism of the novel that might have made the careers of most literary critics. Yet it is still *Things Fall Apart* for which

Achebe is principally known and with which most who have only a casual acquaintance with his work would associate his name.

For example, one of the principal effects of Achebe's critical engagement with *Heart of Darkness* and other Western texts that purport to represent Africans and African culture is that his own fiction has come to be perceived as the default counter to such (mis)representations. Thus Gerald Graff, in his 1992 book *Beyond the Culture Wars*, suggests that an effective pedagogical strategy might be to teach *Heart of Darkness* and *Things Fall Apart* in tandem to create a productive dialogue between the two. This suggestion is, of course, an excellent one, but it also indicates the way in which, at least for those on the periphery of African literary studies, all roads lead to *Things Fall Apart*, making it into the emblem of African literature as a whole.

In short, *Things Fall Apart* has arguably gotten more than its fair share of attention worldwide relative to other African literature, including Achebe's other work. That said, however, it is also the case that the attention gained by Achebe's first novel was instrumental in making African literature one of the most dynamic forces in world literature in the decades after it was published. For one thing, the success of Achebe's first novel demonstrated to publishers that they could make a profit by publishing African literature, leading to (among other things) the founding of Heinemann's seminal African Writers Series, with Achebe himself as a consulting editor. The critical and commercial success of *Things Fall Apart* also exercised a major influence on subsequent African writers, who were encouraged to believe that they could not only get published but also gain global recognition. For such writers, *Things Fall Apart* has provided a suggestive model of the kind that was unavailable to Achebe himself when he began writing.

Works of literature are often described as "groundbreaking," but few authors in the history of world literature have had to plow through as much virgin soil as did Achebe when he wrote his first novel. Achebe had to steer largely without a map—and he had to steer through difficult terrain indeed. He was faced with a series of decisions and dilemmas that few other writers have had to face. For one thing, the very act of writing was, for an African, a political statement that challenged centuries of colonialist prejudice that assumed that Africans' ability to use written language was somehow inferior to that of Europeans, a prejudice rooted in the fact that most sub-Saharan African cultures relied on oral forms of language, and did not have written languages, at the time of their first contacts with Europeans. That Achebe chose to perform this act of writing within the genre of the novel was also a political statement and a potentially problematic one. After all, at the time the novel was not only the first major literary genre that began as a written genre but also generally regarded as the modern European genre par excellence. Thus, in writing a relatively conventional novel (rather than modeling his work on African oral forms, as had Amos Tutuola), Achebe was potentially acknowledging the superiority of Western cultural forms—though it was also a way of challenging Western cultural supremacy head-on, demonstrating that African literature could be a match for European literature, even on the latter's home turf.

To complicate things further, Achebe chose to write not just a novel but a novel in *English*, the language of Nigeria's colonial conquerors, even though his story is rooted very much in the traditional culture of the Igbo people. A written Igbo script existed by the time Achebe began writing *Things Fall Apart*, and he theoretically could have written his book in Igbo; yet, had he chosen to do so, he would have had virtually no audience outside of Nigeria and would, in fact, have had a much smaller audience in Africa and in Nigeria itself, where the literacy rate in English was far higher than that in Igbo. There is, after all, no *Nigerian* language (or people or traditional culture), and English serves in the country (and in just about all of formerly British Africa) as a lingua franca that enables communication between different peoples. In addition, Achebe was writing for a dual audience, hoping both to demonstrate to the world that Africans were not linguistically and culturally primitive and inferior and to provide Africans (especially Nigerians) with an important resource for the evolution of their own new post-colonial cultural identities. Had he written in Igbo, he would have reached few if any readers outside of Africa and could not have engaged Western literary traditions in the kind of subversive dialogue that he did.

To achieve his goals, Achebe was, in effect, forced to write a novel and to write in English, though he brilliantly negotiated the potential controversies inherent in these decisions by carefully enriching the novel form with elements derived from Igbo oral culture and by spicing his English with a number of terms and phrases from the Igbo language. In doing so, he was able to demonstrate the richness of Igbo linguistic and cultural traditions, which was no doubt important for African readers coming out of a colonial period in which they had been taught that their cultures and languages were simplistic and primitive in comparison to European ones. But this demonstration may have been even more valuable to Western readers, many of whom had little or no knowledge of African cultures outside of what they had gained from vastly distorted representations of the continent, like those portrayed in *Heart of Darkness* or in the *Tarzan* films.

In the same vein, *Things Fall Apart*'s most important contribution may have been its vivid and compelling account of precolonial Igbo culture. It provides useful information (though some gaps in the historical memory had to be imaginatively filled in by Achebe) about a culture not well known to outsiders and that was in many ways beginning to be forgotten by the Igbo themselves. However, what was perhaps more important than any details of precolonial Igbo culture and society was Achebe's reminder that the Igbo did at least *have* a well-developed culture and society before colonization, thus countering a long colonialist legacy that implied that Africans essentially lived in a state of primitive savagery before the arrival of Europeans brought civilization to the "dark" continent. Achebe acknowledges in *Things Fall Apart* that Igbo culture had its problems and its flaws even before the arrival of the European colonizers, but this acknowledgment only adds veracity to his portrayal of a complex and sophisticated Igbo culture that had been in place long before the advent of colonization. It is to the destruction of this culture by colonization that the novel's title refers, and Achebe's heartrending presentation of the tragedy inherent in this destruction effectively dismantles the colonialist myth that Africans were rescued from permanent primitivity by the arrival of European civilization.

By focusing in this way on an entire society as a sort of collective protagonist, Achebe challenges the individualist inclinations of the novel form and of modern Western society as a whole. On the other hand, what is perhaps Achebe's greatest achievement in *Things Fall Apart* is to make his narrative seem more real and more immediate by focusing in a compelling and realistic way on the downfall of an individual protagonist, Okonkwo, while at the same time making the tragic fate of this man an embodiment of the tragic fall of traditional Igbo culture. Okonkwo is not an average Igbo, perhaps not even a "good" Igbo; however, he is who he is as a result of his immersion in Igbo culture during a particular historical moment. While his story touches on a number of universal themes and ideas, ultimately he is who he is and experiences what he does only because he is an Igbo at the time of colonization. It is this historical specificity that gives *Things Fall Apart* its greatest power.

Biography of Chinua Achebe

Norbert Mazari

Chinualomagu (Albert) Achebe was born on November 16, 1930, in Ogidi, Nigeria, a large Ibo village in the rain forest lands not far from the banks of the Niger River. He was the second youngest of six children born to Isaiah Achebe, a teacher-catechist for the Church Missionary Society and one of the first people of his region to convert to Christianity. Achebe's family was distinguished, as his grandfather had acquired three of the four possible titles in the village. Although as a boy he was educated as a Christian, learning to admire all things European and to reject things that were African, Achebe was still able to find beauty in traditional African culture. Since his father did not sever connections with his non-Christian relatives, Achebe established a relationship with his people's traditional world.

Achebe began his education in the Christian mission school of his birthplace. He then won a scholarship to Government College Umahia and in 1948 was chosen to be one of the first students to study at University College, Ibadan (later the University of Ibadan). While attending university, Achebe rejected his given English name, Albert, and began to use the African Chinualomagu, shortened to Chinua, which implies the meaning "God will fight for me." He also dropped his planned study of medicine and instead chose to pursue a degree in literature, receiving his B.A. in 1953. At this time, Achebe began to write short stories and essays, some of which centered on the conflict between Christian and traditional African culture, a subject that would become the focal point for much of his later works. After graduation, Achebe taught secondary school for less than a year before joining the Nigerian Broadcasting Company as "talks producer" in 1954.

In his first novel, *Things Fall Apart* (1958), Achebe focused on the Nigerian experience of European colonialism and dominance, developing his major themes from an African viewpoint and portraying the many aspects of the communal life of the Ibo people of Umuafia in the late nineteenth century at both the societal and individual levels. The novel is short, utilizing a close-knit style that creates an effective picture of the clash between the Ibo and European cultures at a time when white missionaries and officials were first penetrating Eastern Nigeria. The story focuses on two closely intertwined tragedies—the public tragedy of the Ibo culture as it is eclipsed by the European culture and the individual tragedy of Okonkwo, an important man of Umuafia who sees his traditional world changing and collapsing and is powerless to stop it. *Things Fall Apart* was met with wide critical acclaim and has since been translated into forty-five languages.

Achebe's second novel, *No Longer at Ease*, was published in 1960. As with his first novel, Achebe took the novel's title from a poem, this time one by T. S. Eliot. This work examines African society in the era of independence and continues the saga of Okonkwo's family with his grandson Obi, an educated Christian who has left his village for a position as a civil servant in urban Lagos, Nigeria. The story deals with the tragedy of a new generation of Nigerians who, although educated and Westernized, are nevertheless caught between the opposing cultures of traditional Africa and urban Lagos.

In 1961, Achebe was appointed Director of External Broadcasting for Nigeria. This position required Achebe to travel to Great Britain as well as other parts of the world. The same year he married Christie Okoli, who also worked at the Nigerian Broadcasting Company. They would have four children over the next eight years. A year later, in 1962, a collection of Achebe's short stories titled *The Sacrificial Egg, and Other Short Stories* was published. In 1962, Achebe also became the first series editor of Heinemann's African Writers Series, which soon became an important publishing venue for African writers. He would hold the position until 1972. Two years later, Achebe completed *Arrow of God* (1964). In this, his third novel, Achebe once again painted a picture of cultures in collision, and once again his novel attracted much attention, which only added to the high esteem in which he was already held.

A Man of the People, which would be Achebe's last novel for more than two decades, was published in 1966. With this novel, Achebe continued to develop the urban themes that he had presented in *No Longer at Ease*, but this time with a satirical edge, examining corrupt politicians who used to their own advantage the political system that they inherited from the departed imperial power.

After a massacre of Igbos took place in Northern Nigeria in 1966, Achebe resigned his position with the Nigerian Broadcasting Service and moved to Nigeria's Eastern Region, where he intended to go into publishing. When the region declared its independence as the separate state of Biafra, however, Achebe became personally involved with the ensuing civil war, serving the Biafran government from 1967 to 1970. During this period of his life, Achebe produced only one piece of work, a children's book titled *Chike and the River* (1966).

In the years following the war, Achebe produced two collections of poetry: *Beware, Soul Brother, and Other Poems* (1971,1972; published in the United States as *Christmas in Biafra, and Other Poems*, 1973) and *Don't Let Him Die: An Anthology of Memorial Poems for Christopher Okigbo* (1978). In addition, Achebe was coeditor of *Aka weta: Egwu aguluagu egwu edeluede* (1982), an anthology of Igbo poetry. With this turn toward poetry as a medium for his creative talents, Achebe was able to distinguish himself as both a great novelist and a fine poet. During this period, he also wrote a collection of short stories titled *Girls at War, and Other Stories* (1983) and coedited another collection titled *African Short Stories* (1985). In addition, he produced three works of juvenile literature as well as a number of essays. In the 1980s, Achebe's *Things Fall Apart* was adapted for stage, radio, and television.

In 1971, Achebe accepted a post at the University of Nigeria in Nsukka. The following year, he and his family moved temporarily to the United States, where Achebe took a position with the University of Massachusetts, Amherst, as a professor in its Department of Afro-American Studies. In addition, during this period he taught at several

American institutions as a visiting professor. While in the United States, he was awarded an honorary doctor of letters degree from Dartmouth College. Additionally, Achebe shared, with a Canadian, the 1972 Commonwealth Prize for the best book of poetry with his *Beware, Soul Brother, and Other Poems*. In 1976, he returned to Nsukka, where he held the rank of professor and edited *Okike*, a literary journal.

The year 1987 saw Achebe return to the novel as an expression of his now world-renowned talents. His *Anthills of the Savannah* was very well received and earned a nomination for the Booker Prize. According to Charles R. Larson, writing for the *Chicago Tribune*, "No other novel in many years has bitten to the core, swallowed and regurgitated contemporary Africa's miseries and expectations as profoundly as *Anthills of the Savannah*."

In 1990 a serious car accident left Achebe confined to a wheelchair. Shortly thereafter he accepted a teaching position at Bard College in Annandale-on-Hudson, New York. In 2007, Achebe was awarded the Man Booker International Prize, and two years later he left Bard College for Brown University, where he is the David and Marianna Fisher University Professor and Professor of Africana Studies.

From *Dictionary of World Biography: The 20th Century*. Pasadena, CA: Salem Press, 1999. Copyright © 1999 by Salem Press, Inc.

Bibliography

Achebe, Chinua. "The Art of Fiction No. 139: Chinua Achebe." Interview by Jerome Brooks. *The Paris Review* 133 (Winter, 1994): 142-166. In this interview, Achebe discusses his schooling, work as a broadcaster, and views on other writers, as well as the nature of his writing process and the political situation in Nigeria.

_____. *Home and Exile*. New York: Oxford UP, 2000. An exploration, based on Achebe's own experiences as a reader and a writer, of contemporary African literature and the Western literature that both influenced and misrepresented it.

Bolland, John. *Language and the Quest for Political and Social Identity in the Afri-*

can Novel. Accra, Ghana: Woeli, 1996. This volume examines Achebe's novel *Anthills of the Savannah*, among others, and is valuable for its examination of African fiction and history, touching on themes found in Achebe's work.

Booker, M. Keith, ed. *The Chinua Achebe Encyclopedia*. Westport, CT: Greenwood Press, 2003. A helpful reference in an encyclopedia format.

Carroll, David. *Chinua Achebe: Novelist, Poet, Critic*. Rev. 2d ed. New York: Macmillan, 1990. Includes historical details concerning Africa, colonialism, and twentieth-century Nigerian political history. Contains a sizable bibliography and an index.

Ezenwa-Ohaeto. *Chinua Achebe: A Biography*. Bloomington: Indiana UP, 1997. A full-length biography of Achebe, this book benefits from its author's insights as a former student of Achebe, a native of Nigeria, and a speaker of Igbo. Ezenwa-Ohaeto examines Achebe's life and literary contributions and places them within their social, historical, and cultural contexts. Written with the cooperation of Achebe and his family, the book includes several rare and revealing photographs. Includes bibliographical references and an index.

Gikandi, Simon. *Reading Chinua Achebe: Language and Ideology in Fiction*. Portsmouth, NH: Heinemann, 1991. Analyzes Achebe's short stories and novels.

Innes, C. L. *Chinua Achebe*. New York: Cambridge UP, 1990. Innes gives a detailed analysis of each of Achebe's novels, showing how Achebe adapted what he found in Western fiction to create a new literary form—the Africanized novel. Includes a chapter on the critical and political writings, demonstrating how the Nigerian civil war changed Achebe's politics and his fiction.

Innes, C. L., and Bernth Lindfors, eds. *Critical Perspectives on Chinua Achebe*. Washington, DC: Three Continents Press, 1978. This collection of essays by twenty different critics offers a comprehensive overview of Achebe's work. Contains a brief introduction to Achebe's life and background, five general assessments of his fiction, commentaries on his first four novels and his poetry, and an extensive bibliography.

Iyasere, Solomon O., ed. *Understanding "Things Fall Apart": Selected Essays and Criticism*. Troy, NY: Whitston, 1998. Nine essays demonstrate the breadth of approaches taken by recent critics: They include a reading of Okonkwo as a tragic hero, a discussion of the rhythm of the novel's prose as it echoes African oral tradition, and a discussion of how Achebe successfully transformed the colonizers' language to tell the story of the colonized.

Joseph, Michael Scott. "A Pre-modernist Reading of 'The Drum': Chinua Achebe and the Theme of the Eternal Return." *Ariel* 28 (Jan. 1997): 149-66. In this special issue on colonialism, postcolonialism, and children's literature, Achebe's "The Drum" is discussed as a satirical attack on European colonial values and a text dominated by nostalgia for a lost Golden Age.

Lindfors, Bernth, ed. *Conversations with Chinua Achebe*. Jackson: UP of Mississippi, 1997. Twenty interviews with Achebe in which he discusses African oral tradition, the need for political commitment, the relationship between his novels and his short stories, his use of myth and fable, and other issues concerning being a writer.

Muoneke, Romanus Okey. *Art, Rebellion, and Redemption: A Reading of the Novels of Chinua Achebe*. New York: Peter Lang, 1994. Muoneke examines Achebe's role as a public chronicler of Nigeria's social, economic, and political problems, as a way of exploring the larger issues of the writer's redemptive role in society. Argues that Achebe's novels challenge colonialism and negritude, two forces that have distorted the African image.

Petersen, Kirsten Holst, and Anna Rutherford, eds. *Chinua Achebe: A Celebration*. Portsmouth, NH: Heinemann, 1991. A compilation of essays analyzing Achebe's work to honor his sixtieth birthday.

Wren, Robert M. *Achebe's World: The Historical and Cultural Context of the Novels of Chinua Achebe*. Washington, DC: Three Continents Press, 1980. A seemingly authoritative, well-documented presentation that clarifies issues for readers not familiar with the Nigerian context. Claims that Achebe's first four novels form an essentially truthful and reliable guide to the historical Nigeria. Includes an extensive glossary and a helpful bibliography.

The *Paris Review* Perspective_____

Petrina Crockford for *The Paris Review*

History is not static—it takes the shape given it by the historian and the storyteller. This gives stories their power, but it also makes them dangerous: what we understand as truth depends on our vision of the world. "There is that great proverb," Chinua Achebe told *The Paris Review*, "that until the lions have their own historians, the history of the hunt will always glorify the hunter. Once I realized that, I had to be a writer."

Things Fall Apart is the story of the lion. It tells of the first contact between the Igbo tribe and British colonialists in late nineteenth-century Nigeria. Published in 1958, it is the first novel written by a black African to achieve international recognition and acclaim. Before then, the continent was known in the West through the stories of writers such as Joyce Cary and Joseph Conrad, who co-opted the African experience and did not move far beyond the notion of Africa as "the dark continent." Achebe writes from the inside of the African experience, depicting the disorder that colonialism brought to the Igbo with an immediacy unavailable to an outsider.

There was no precedent to publish or purchase a novel by an African in 1958; certainly no one in London's publishing industry had heard of Chinua Achebe. When Achebe's manuscript arrived at the fiction department of London publisher Heinemann, the editors there hesitated: Would there be a market for a book about Africans written by an unknown African? The fiction department passed the manuscript on to the education department under the logic that the education department sold textbooks to Africa. Don Macrae, a professor of economics just back from West Africa—didn't this mean he knew about Africans?—read the manuscript and wrote a seven-word report for the publisher: "The best first novel since the war." Heinemann was half convinced: they printed only two thousand copies in the first run before letting the book fall out of print. Only after Heinemann editor Alan Hill convinced his colleagues to publish the novel in paperback in 1962, along with Achebe's second novel, *No Longer at Ease*, and two more titles by African writers, did the book have a chance at gaining widespread readership. The reissue launched Heinemann's famous African Writers Series, which introduced the British public, and eventually the world, to African literature.

Things Fall Apart has gone on to sell nearly 11 million copies worldwide. It has been translated into forty-five languages. In 2008, the novel celebrated its fiftieth anniversary in print. The book has evolved through many editions, some more fanciful in their conception of Africa than others: the 1976 Heinemann edition features a shirtless black man, presumably Okonkwo, holding a machete and screaming before the image of a burning cross. ("Has cross burning ever been a cultural phenomenon in Nigeria?" *Transition* magazine asked Chinua Achebe. "No, no . . . it is not known among us at all," he answered. "We wouldn't have done that, and we still don't.") Even the reception history of *Things Fall Apart* is a bit checkered: Selden Rodman reviewed the novel for the *New York Times* in 1959 and called the story a description of "primitive society"; the *Times* also referred to the author as "Miss Achebe" in a brief announcement of the book's forthcoming publication ("Books"). And in a review in the *Observer*, Angus Wilson incorrectly identified Okonkwo's tribe as the Obi. The mistake of Obi for Ibo, itself a colonial mispronunciation of Igbo, was printed on the back cover of numerous editions. Mistakes like these seem scandalous now but only in the context of the expanded literary landscape brought to the English-speaking world by writers like Achebe.

Things Fall Apart has survived fifty years of misinterpretations and reinterpretations and has had a remarkably lasting effect on literature for a single book. The literary series it helped launch gave African writers and the reading public a meeting place in which to reconsider the past, transform the present, and envision a new future. Achebe himself edited the series, without pay, for ten years. Revenue generated by sales of *Things Fall Apart* allowed Heinemann to continue to publish African writers whose sales would not have kept them in print.

"I think of that masquerade in Igbo festivals," Achebe told *The Paris Review.* "The Igbo people say, If you want to see it well, you must not stand in one place. The masquerade is moving through this big arena. Dancing. If you're rooted to a spot, you miss a lot of the grace. So you keep moving, and this is the way I think the world's stories should be told—from many different perspectives."

Works Cited

Achebe, Chinua. "The Art of Fiction No. 139: Chinua Achebe." Interview by Jerome Brooks. *The Paris Review* 133 (1994): 142-66.

_____. "A Conversation with Chinua Achebe." Interview by David Chioni Moore and Analee Heath. *Transition: An International Review* 100 (2009): 12-33.

_____. *Things Fall Apart.* 1958. London: Heinemann, 1986.

"Books Today." Announcement of publication of *Things Fall Apart. New York Times* 16 Jan. 1959.

Rodman, Selden. "The White Man's Faith." Rev. of *Things Fall Apart*, by Chinua Achebe. *New York Times Book Review* 22 Feb. 1959: 28.

CRITICAL
CONTEXTS

Things Fall Apart:
Cultural and Historical Contexts_____

Joseph McLaren

Things Fall Apart was first published in 1958 at a time when the most prevalent works of fiction about Africa were written primarily by Europeans. Achebe's novel appeared during the early years of the independence era in black Africa, a year after Ghana achieved its independence and two years before Nigeria secured its own nationhood. The cultural and historical contexts of the novel can be considered in a number of ways. The late 1950s can be viewed as a historical as well as literary cultural epoch that shaped Achebe's decision to write the novel. However, *Things Fall Apart* is a retrospective work, examining the social transitions that occurred in Igboland, Eastern Nigeria, around the end of the nineteenth century and into the first decade of the twentieth. In a 1984 interview with Somali novelist Nuruddin Farah, Achebe acknowledged that, in the 1950s, he was among a select few Africans who were writing their own stories. Achebe was a forerunner for African novelists, and in certain ways *Things Fall Apart*, of necessity, confronts certain European novels, films, and ethnographic studies that portrayed Africans stereotypically, as different, apart, and primitive. Furthermore, as Michael J. Echeruo informs us, novels portraying Africa by Western authors were written "for the education and entertainment of the author's native readers" and were only incidentally "about Africa in any important sense" (1, 26).

The Threshold of Independence:
Reversing African Images

In numerous statements, Achebe has given his rationale for writing *Things Fall Apart*. His goal was to write a work about his own ethnic group that would counter the general, stereotyped portrayals of Africans as voiceless. During his formative years, Achebe's educational

19

background involved what he called "foreign aspects of my upbringing," elements of his education that were "not about Igbo things" (*Home* 19). In school, he became aware of the kinds of images of Africa that had been projected in Western fiction, particularly in the novels of Joyce Cary, such as *Mister Johnson* (1939), and especially in Joseph Conrad's *Heart of Darkness* (1899). *Mister Johnson* depicts a young Nigerian civil servant, and, as Achebe scholar C. L. Innes comments, Cary's novel sought to "justify colonialism either as it was or as reformers thought it should be" (13). Still, it achieved a good degree of popularity when it was published, and years later an older Achebe would find it ironic that *Mister Johnson* had once been called by *Time* magazine "the best novel ever written about Africa" (*Home* 22).

In addition to *Mister Johnson*, one of the most popular novels set in Africa and read in the West was Joseph Conrad's *Heart of Darkness*. The nearly fifty-year-old novel was a "classic" when *Things Fall Apart* was published, but in a lecture he delivered at the University of Massachusetts, Amherst, in 1975 (and published in *Hopes and Impediments* in 1989), Achebe challenged Conrad's representations of Africa:

> *Heart of Darkness* projects the image of Africa as "the other world," the antithesis of Europe and therefore of civilization, a place where man's vaunted intelligence and refinement are finally mocked by triumphant bestiality. ("An Image" 3)

Furthermore, Achebe viewed Conrad's projected Africa as a "metaphysical battlefield devoid of all recognizable humanity." Also problematic was "Conrad's withholding of language from his rudimentary souls" ("An Image" 12, 19).

Popular fiction about Africa from earlier generations, such as H. Rider Haggard's novels, also presented stereotypes that persisted during the late 1950s. Haggard's adventure novel *King Solomon's Mines* (1885) depicted Africans in "tribal" characterizations, and Edgar Rice Burroughs did the same in *Tarzan of the Apes* (1914) and its numerous sequels.

Later, the characterizations again appeared in a series of *Tarzan* films, especially in those released after the 1930s and into the 1950s. These novels served as texts to write against, but Achebe also found in William Butler Yeats, the twentieth-century Irish poet, a concordant voice. Yeats, who supported Irish nationalism in the face of British colonialism, had described the collapse of a civilization in his 1919 poem "The Second Coming," and even though Yeats was referring to postwar Europe, Achebe found the poem's description to be equally apt for colonial Africa. In short, Achebe was a product of his educational experience, and he had no doubt read a significant number of British writers—as Kalu Ogbaa observes, *Things Fall Apart* even "may have taken a few hints from [Thomas] Hardy's *The Mayor of Casterbridge*" (5).

In addition to literary works, Achebe was more than likely familiar with ethnographic writings about the Igbo, though there is little evidence that he borrowed directly from ethnographic writings as background material for *Things Fall Apart*. He might have read anthropologist P. Amaury Talbot's *In the Shadow of the Bush* (1912) and missionary G. T. Basden's *Among the Ibos of Nigeria* (1921) and *Niger Ibos* (1938). But whether or not Achebe actually read these authors, he was very likely aware of the fact that the Igbo had been subject to outsiders' interpretations.

In addition to writing against European authors, Achebe was also writing alongside other emerging African novelists. These novels were beginning to paint a different image of Africa for those in the West who had not necessarily been exposed to works by Africans. By the mid-1950s, black writers from South Africa, Cameroon, Senegal, and Kenya had written novels. South African Peter Abrahams, whose *Mine Boy* was published in 1946, more than a decade before *Things Fall Apart*, would later write *A Wreath for Udomo* (1956) about a modernized African who sought national liberation. Camara Laye's *The Dark Child* (1954) had been given considerable attention by the Western press, and, like *Things Fall Apart*, it also reimagined traditional settings, though with more of an autobiographical direction. Ousmane

Sembene's *The Black Docker* was published in 1956, and the same year that *Things Fall Apart* was released novels were brought out by Guinea's Emile Cissé and Kenya's Mugo Gicaru.

Nor was Achebe the first Nigerian writer of the 1950s; he was predated by Cyprian Ekwensi, whose novels had been appearing since 1948 and who wrote for African as well as Western readers, and Amos Tutuola, whose *Palm-Wine Drinkard* (1952) is often overlooked in studies of the Nigerian novel. In 1959, Achebe's fellow Nigerian writer Timothy Aluko would publish *One Man, One Wife*. In addition, Onitsha Market literature, the moralistic novellas and pamphlets and pulp fiction sold in the marketplace of Nigeria's southeastern town of Onitsha, was another popular cultural literary form available to Achebe when he was writing *Things Fall Apart*.

During the 1950s, interest in African societies increased as the western and eastern blocs of the cold war sought to gain a foothold on the continent by winning over the rising nationalist movements. The African countries that were moving more toward socialism, such as Tanzania and Ghana, were of particular interest to the United States, for example. In the era of *Things Fall Apart*'s publication Nigeria, on its way to independence, was under a federal system that divided the country into northern, western, and eastern areas, with the Igbo principally in the East, the Yoruba in the West, and the Hausa and Fulani in the North. As Achebe was writing his novel, the push for independence was gaining momentum, "with the Eastern and Western regions in Nigeria asking for independence and the Northern region reluctant to take it" (Ezenwa-Ohaeto 60-61). In the eastern region, Nnamdi Azikiwe, who, along with longtime Nigerian nationalist Herbert Macaulay, had headed the National Council for Nigeria and Cameroons (NCNC), was at the forefront of the struggle for independence. Achebe sympathized with the movement and, as biographer Ezenwa-Ohaeto notes, a 1956 visit by Queen Elizabeth to Nigeria "highlighted for Achebe the ideas intrinsic to his status as a colonial subject and an African citizen" (60). *Things Fall Apart* was also published just as Pan-African ideas were gaining attention as a result of the political positions held by Ghana's Kwame Nkrumah and others. Still, despite all of the political changes that were taking place around him, Achebe chose not to set *Things Fall Apart* within the 1950s; instead, he intended the novel to be part of a trilogy that would include the later published novels *No Longer at Ease* (1960) and *Arrow of God* (1964) and span from the precolonial days of the late nineteenth century up through the 1950s.

As Simon Gikandi comments, Achebe may well have been one of the first African "writers to recognize the function of the novel not solely as a mode of representing reality, but one which had limitless possibilities of inventing a new national community" (3). He was most concerned with humanizing African characters by portraying their culture and historical context and with showing the inner workings of a particular ethnic group, in this case, the Igbo. Published not long before *Things Fall Apart*, Achebe's article "The Novelist as Teacher" indicated that his purpose was to assist African "society" in restoring a "belief in itself" by discarding "the complexes of the years of denigration and self-abasement" (qtd. in Turkington 7).

Writing during a period when historians were focusing on "African empires of the past," Achebe chose to depict the earlier days of the "isolated" Igbo, who did not then have a centralized system of government (Izevbaye 48-49). In an era in which Africans were being homogenized by the West, Achebe's portrayals of the Igbo provide a closer, more discriminating analysis, one that "forces us to see anew the fluidity of self-understanding as well as class alignments in a living African culture" (George 176).

More important, the late 1950s was still a period in which "primitivism" surfaced in discussions of traditional African society. For the *New York Times* reviewer, *Things Fall Apart* was among a "small company of sensitive books that describe primitive society from the inside," another of which was Camara Laye's *The Dark Child* (Rodman 28). In one sense, Selden Rodman correctly identified Achebe's purpose—to give an insider's view of an African society. However, the language of his praise also contains what has become, for contemporary critics, a problematic labeling of traditional African society. The word "primitive," so widely used before and after the 1950s, was often accompanied by similar terms, such as "native" and "tribe," all of which tend to relegate African ethnicities to positions of backwardness and savagery. These ideas were inheritances of the eighteenth century, passed down by such thinkers as the German philosopher Georg Wilhelm Hegel, who viewed African societies as outside of history, in a "completely wild and untamed state," and Africans as lacking "self-control," which prevented them from developing any culture (93, 98). Such ideas persisted well into Achebe's time and were echoed by the British historian Hugh Trevor-Roper, who, like Conrad, equated Africa with "darkness." During the 1960s, Trevor-Roper remarked, "Perhaps, in the future, there will be some African history to teach," though he thought that African history really only consisted of the history of "Europeans in Africa" (9). Achebe's task was to challenge these views.

Missionary and Colonial Activities in Igboland

Things Fall Apart is a corrective work that attempts to revise prevalent Western images of Africa, and one of Achebe's greatest concerns while writing the novel was how he could represent Africa to Western audiences. Well aware that many Western writers such as Conrad had universalized Africans, making them into an indistinguishable mass rather than distinguishing between individual Africans and particular African ethnic groups, Achebe chose to focus his novel on the specificity of the Igbo world. By portraying the cultural life of the Igbo as he saw it through his position as the son of a Christian missionary, Achebe was able to counter Western images of Africa. He reconstructed the Igbo world that had existed before his birth, and he reimagined this world by presenting the effects of colonialism on individual Igbo people, such as Okonkwo, and on the villages of Umuofia and Mbanta, which are replicas of actual Igbo villages.

Things Fall Apart is set during the close of the nineteenth century and the opening decade of the twentieth, when British colonial agents were making deeper inroads into Igboland and solidifying their colonial interests. As Toyin Falola explains in his *History of Nigeria*, by 1914 the British "were preoccupied with consolidating their gains and establishing a new political system" (67). Thus, though Achebe's Umuofia is a product of his imagination, it reflects historical and cultural actualities. The encroachment of the British colonial presence in Nigeria is reflected throughout the novel in particular events, such as the arrival of Christian missionaries and colonial government officials and the "pacification" of African villages.

Achebe's representation of Igbo spirituality is consistent with studies of Igbo religion. The Igbo spiritual worldview—which involves ancestors, gods and goddesses, priests and priestesses—is central to the novel. Achebe gives special attention to one particular deity, the Earth Goddess, who is identified as Ani but is also known in Igbo religion as Ala. By focusing on the Earth Goddess, Achebe is able to offer a dimension of the spiritual world of the Igbo without representing in detail all the Igbo deities, although the novel does make reference to the god of thunder, Amadiora or Amadioha, and Idemili, the river goddess.

In the novel, as in real life, the arrival of Christian missionaries to the region greatly impacts the Igbo's spiritual practices; as historian E. A. Ayandele writes, their activities represent a "potentially violent intrusion" (5). Roughly fifty years prior to the time frame of *Things Fall Apart*, missionaries began arriving in the coastal regions of modern day Nigeria, and their activities expanded with the 1841 Niger Expedition, a British effort to explore the Niger River, establish trade and treaties with African leaders, halt the slave trade, and scout for agricultural and commercial opportunities. Missionaries began appearing in Igboland as early as 1857, although, historically, they did not become a strong presence in the region until the early decades of the twentieth century. The Roman Catholic Mission of the Holy Ghost Fathers and the Church Missionary Society, both of which had plans for Igbo conversion, sponsored two of the more active missionary groups. The process of conversion was accompanied by a mission school education, "the method by which the missionaries secured new members of the new religion among the Igbo" (Njoku 61).

In the novel, Achebe depicts the complex interactions between Africans and missionaries in a variety of settings, including Umuofia, Mbanta, and Abame. As Achebe demonstrates in the novel, Christianity appealed to individuals of lower status, outcasts or *osu*, for example, who found within the religion an alternative to their marginalized positions within Igbo society. Furthermore, certain Igbos associated with Christianity in order to receive preferential treatment from "Government Expeditions," military expeditions that frequently harassed villagers, "seized their animals, and often destroyed or ravaged their farm crops" (Ekechi 103, 105). Significantly, Achebe uses the Umuofians' abandonment of the twins, which was a general practice among the real-life Igbo, and their sacrifice of Ikemefuna, a demonstration of reciprocal justice perhaps, to show Igbo culture's vulnerability or susceptibility to Christian conversion. Achebe also particularizes this vulnerability by drawing Okonkwo as a super masculine figure and by setting up the father-son conflict between him and Nwoye; it is because of this conflict, as well as his inability to understand why the twins are killed and why Ikemefuna is sacrificed, that Nwoye is vulnerable to conversion.

Achebe relied on memory rather than archival research to construct his novel and reimagined the places and events he knew as a youth. The village of Umuofia, though "not a true replica of it," is somewhat derived from Ogidi, Achebe's "hometown." Ogidi, like Umuofia, had been affected by contact with British missionaries and colonizers since 1892. It had a foreign court system and a District Commissioner, whom Achebe represents, at the end of his novel, with biting irony. The book to be written by the novel's District Commissioner—*Pacification of the Tribes of the Lower Niger*—reflects the larger colonial enterprise in Nigeria. As Robert M. Wren explains, from the colonialist perspective "'pacification' was the route to 'civilization,' and the Igbo were to be civilized by British standards and under British rule, using British imported goods, the English language, and the Anglican religion" (30). In one example of such "pacification," the Aro trading oligarchy was overrun by the British in 1902. Another of the historical markers of the novel, the killing of the white man in Abame, can be linked to "the murder of a white missionary in Ahiara in 1905," a Dr. J. F. Stewart, "who set off on his bicycle from Owerri" (Turkington 7; Wren 26).

Igbo Language

Besides the history of the Igbo people, Achebe also drew on their language. Although the novel is written in English, the Igbo of that period would have expressed themselves in Igbo. Achebe uses names such Umuofia, which means "people of the forest," and Ikemefuna, which refers to one's strength not being lost, to show how Igbo language can project a complex cultural subtext. And unlike Conrad in *Heart of Darkness*, Achebe gives language to his characters. Though their thoughts and speech and Achebe's narrative voice are rendered in Standard English, they are all given an Igbo flavor and Africanized with the injection of traditional proverbs. In a cultural sense, a storehouse of proverbs demonstrates an individual's linguistic abilities, just as a large barn of yams is a sign of wealth. Okoye, for example, in a conversation with Okonkwo's father, Unoka, delivers "the next half a dozen sentences in proverbs," to show his linguistic ability (7). Perhaps the most significant proverb in the novel, which demonstrates how important these devices were to the Igbo, is used by Achebe himself at this moment in the novel. It could be called a proverb on proverbs: "Proverbs are the palm-oil with which words are eaten" (7). This statement implies that expressions or statements are made more appetizing, more linguistically palatable, when they are made through proverbs. Although Achebe has disagreed with other African writers who have insisted that African novels must be written in African languages, he has maintained the spirit of the oral tradition by incorporating elements of it, like proverbs, into his novels.

Things Fall Apart in the Twenty-First Century

The continued relevance of *Things Fall Apart* relates both to its universality and its particularity, its humanized image of the Igbo. That *Things Fall Apart* remains significant fifty years after its publication is largely due to Achebe's desire to tell a different kind of story about Africa, to, as he put it in an interview that aired on PBS in May 2008, tell a story in which Africa would be "seen in all its grandeur and all its weakness." Though, as Michael Valdez Moses cautions, one should be careful not to read the novel through a "'universalist' approach that reimposes a set of Western cultural norms upon an African novel" (110), the novel still achieves universal relevance. *Things Fall Apart* is clearly Igbo-centric, but for Western readers, the Igbo can represent all Africans, and for readers from former colonized countries, the novel can reflect their experiences of oppression. To tell the story of his people, to humanize them, Achebe not only had to confront stereotypes of African masculinity but also had to be careful not to gloss over the faults of individuals or the particular weaknesses of Igbo culture. Cultural weaknesses are global, endemic to even the so-called developed societies. The way Achebe develops Umuofia's societal fissures can be related to present-day cultural fault lines, and the falling apart of Umuofia can have broader symbolic implications. As John Clement Ball explains, Achebe shows "certain limitations and structural problems that rendered the clan vulnerable" (87).

To this end, Achebe gives Okonkwo stereotypically masculine attributes, making him physically strong and a powerful warrior and skilled wrestler, and he shows him committing objectionable acts such as beating his wives. Further, he engages in acts that, though authentic parts of Igbo culture, would likely reinforce stereotypes about African "primitivism," such as this one:

In Umuofia's latest war he was the first to bring home a human head. That was his fifth head, and he was not an old man yet. On great occasions such as the funeral of a village celebrity he drank his palm-wine from his first human head. (10)

The effect of these unflattering representations of Igbo people and culture is to humanize them. In the face of the West's generally dehumanized images of Africans, Achebe offers flawed characters as a way to directly confront Western stereotypes. By avoiding one-dimensional figures of power, authority, and goodness, Achebe "sidesteps the temptation to idealize or romanticize that way of life" (Obiechina 37). Igbo warfare in that time included the act of taking human heads, and by alluding to it Achebe made his portrayal of Igbo society honest. In an effort to counter those prevailing negative stereotypes, Achebe chose to present the Igbo as "intelligent, vigorous, dignified and purposeful creators of their own world and unique history" (Githae-Mugo 29).

Such a detail might also challenge Western readers to compare Igbo trophy taking with the West's history of warfare, in which land, people, wealth, and even works of art have all been taken as trophies. Similarly, the localized conflicts described in *Things Fall Apart* and Okonkwo's hypermasculinity might spur readers to think about the far-reaching and broadly devastating results of Western wars and conflicts. Achebe realized the dualism in one's humanity, and by presenting "weakness" he also reflected an Ibgo proverb, "Wherever one thing stands, another thing will stand beside it."

On a political level, the early twentieth-century colonial interests portrayed in *Things Fall Apart* can be used to discuss the end of empire and the New World Order of the twenty-first century. The roots of certain global dilemmas affecting twenty-first-century Africa can also be found in *Things Fall Apart*, especially in the novel's depiction of the fracturing of an ethnic group. Current conflicts in Sudan and past ones in Rwanda have been linked to the aftermath of colonialism and the lingering divisions or interests fostered by former colonizers. Many of the problems threatening African countries' national solidarities are in part caused by the artificial national borders erected during the early twentieth century and before. However, Achebe's novel should not be used to blame Africa's current problems solely on colonial intrusion, for, in his later novels, Achebe confronted the neocolonial elements that arose in African nations after the independence period.

In addition to political implications, the religious oppositions in the novel can be used to open discussions of the religious tensions currently affecting Africa and other parts of the world, such as the Middle East. In today's Africa, the most prevalent religions are Christianity and Islam, which have nearly equal numbers of followers, with a much smaller percentage of people following traditional African religious practices and those of other religions. The Christian conversion process described by Achebe has had ongoing effects, and Christian evangelism in Nigeria and elsewhere is now on the rise.

Perhaps most important, *Things Fall Apart* effectively shows the dangers of stereotyping African people. Achebe's concern over images of Africa and its people may be even more important in the digital age, in which visual representations can easily be used to demean and elevate groups of people. Creating positive portrayals of Africans is especially challenging today, with the media bombarding audiences with images of African conflicts, hunger, and disease. Achebe's comments in his memoir *The Education of a British-Protected Child* (2009) show the consistency of his vision regarding the way people of differing ethnicities or races should be perceived: "Our humanity is contingent on the humanity of our fellows. No person or group can be human alone" (166).

Although the novel's subject, the advent of British colonialism and conversion, may seem to be issues from the distant past of Africa and Nigeria, *Things Fall Apart* continues to be relevant because of its underlying theme of African humanization. When Achebe was interviewed regarding the fiftieth anniversary of the publication of the novel, he was shown various jacket covers of *Things Fall Apart*, beginning with the 1958 edition. Asked what he predicted for Africans in 2058, he reiterated his 1958 rationale:

I think that where we're headed is the final realization that Africans are people: nothing more and nothing less. In another fifty years, I hope we would have gotten there, and that references to the exotic or the primitive or the *Other* will have gone—and that whatever is happening in Africa will be handled just as something happening in Australia, America or elsewhere. Because, actually, we've come a long way in a short time. ("Conversation" 33)

Works Cited

Achebe, Chinua. "Achebe Discusses Africa 50 Years After *Things Fall Apart*." Interview with Jeffrey Brown. PBS *News Hour*. 27 May 2008.

_____. *Arrow of God*. London: Heinemann, 1964.

_____. "A Conversation with Chinua Achebe." Interview by David Chioni Moore and Analee Heath. *Transition: An International Review* 100 (2009): 12-33.

_____. *The Education of a British-Protected Child*. New York: Alfred A. Knopf, 2009.

_____. *Home and Exile*. New York: Oxford, 2000.

_____. "An Image of Africa: Racism in Conrad's *Heart of Darkness*." *Hopes and Impediments: Selected Essays*. New York: Doubleday, 1988. 1-20.

_____. *No Longer at Ease*. London: Heinemann, 1960.

_____. *Things Fall Apart*. 1958. New York: Anchor, 1994.

Aluko, Timothy. *One Man, One Wife*. 1959. Ibadan: Heinemann, 1967.

Ayandele, E. A. *The Missionary Impact on Modern Nigeria, 1842-1914: A Political and Social Analysis*. New York: Humanities Press, 1967.

Ball, John Clement. *Satire and the Postcolonial Novel: V. S. Naipaul, Chinua Achebe, Salman Rushdie*. New York: Routledge, 2003.

Basden, G. T. *Among the Ibos of Nigeria*. Philadelphia: Lippincott, 1921.

_____. *Niger Ibos*. 1938. London: Cass, 1966.

Berman, Edward H. *African Reactions to Missionary Education*. New York: Teachers College Press, 1975.

Burroughs, Edgar Rice. *Tarzan of the Apes*. New York: Burt, 1914.

Cary, Joyce. *Mister Johnson*. 1939. New York: Harper, 1951.

Conrad, Joseph. *Heart of Darkness*. 1899. New York: St. Martin's Press, 1989.

Echeruo, Michael J. *Joyce Cary and the Novel of Africa*. London: Longman, 1973.

Ekechi, F. K. "Colonialism and Christianity in West Africa: The Igbo Case, 1900-1915." *Journal of African History* 12.1 (1971): 103-15.

Ezenwa-Ohaeto. *Chinua Achebe: A Biography*. Bloomington: Indiana UP, 1997.

Falola, Toyin. *The History of Nigeria*. Westport, CT: Greenwood, 1999.

George, Olakunle. *Relocating Agency: Modernity and African Letters*. Albany: State U of New York P, 2003.

Gikandi, Simon. *Reading Chinua Achebe: Language and Ideology in Fiction*. London: James Currey, 1991.

Githae-Mugo, Micere. *Visions of Africa: The Fiction of Chinua Achebe, Margaret Laurence, Elspeth Huxley, and Ngugi wa Thiong'o*. Nairobi: Kenya Literature Bureau, 1978.

Haggard, H. Rider. *King Solomon's Mines*. 1885. Ed. Benjamin Ivry. New York: Barnes & Noble, 2004.

Hegel, G. W. F. *The Philosophy of History*. Trans. John Sibree. London: Colonial Press, 1900.

Herdeck, Donald E. *African Authors: A Companion to Black African Writing*. Vol. 1: *1300-1973*. Washington, DC: Inscape, 1974.

Innes, C. L. *Chinua Achebe*. New York: Cambridge UP, 1990.

Izevbaye, Dan. "The Igbo as Exceptional Colonial Subjects: Fictionalizing an Abnormal Historical Situation." *Approaches to Teaching Achebe's "Things Fall Apart."* Ed. Bernth Lindfors. New York: Modern Language Association of America, 1991. 45-51.

Laye, Camara. *The Dark Child*. 1954. London: Collins, 1955.

Moses, Michael Valdez. *The Novel and Globalization of Culture*. New York: Oxford UP, 1995.

Njoku, John E. Eberegbulam. *The Igbos of Nigeria: Ancient Rites, Changes, and Survival*. Lewiston, NY: Mellen, 1990.

Obiechina, Emmanuel. "Following the Author in *Things Fall Apart*." *Approaches to Teaching Achebe's "Things Fall Apart."* Ed. Bernth Lindfors. New York: Modern Language Association of America, 1991. 31-37.

Ogbaa, Kalu. *Gods, Oracles and Divination: Folkways in Chinua Achebe's Novels*. Trenton, NJ: Africa World Press, 1992.

Omotoso, Kole. *Achebe or Soyinka? A Study in Contrasts*. London: Hans Zell, 1996.

Rodman, Selden. "The White Man's Faith." Rev. of *Things Fall Apart*, by Chinua Achebe. *New York Times Book Review* 22 Feb. 1959: 28.

Sembene, Ousmane. *The Black Docker*. 1956. London: Heinemann, 1987.

Talbot, P. Amaury. *In the Shadow of the Bush*. 1912. New York: Negro Universities Press, 1969.

Trevor-Roper, Hugh. *The Rise of Christian Europe*. New York: Harcourt, 1965.

Turkington, Kate. *Chinua Achebe: "Things Fall Apart."* London: Edward Arnold, 1977.

Tutuola, Amos. *The Palm-Wine Drinkard and His Dead Palm-Wine Tapster in the Dead's Town*. London: Faber, 1952.

Wren, Robert M. *Achebe's World: The Historical and Cultural Context of the Novels of Chinua Achebe*. Washington, DC: Three Continents Press, 1980.

Writers in Conversation: Chinua Achebe with Nuruddin Farah. Videocassette. Roland Collection, 1984.

The Critical Reception of *Things Fall Apart*_____

Amy Sickels

Before *Things Fall Apart* was published, most novels about Africa had been written by Europeans, and they largely portrayed Africans as savages who needed to be enlightened by Europeans. For example, Joseph Conrad's classic tale *Heart of Darkness* (1899), one of the most celebrated novels of the early twentieth century, presents Africa as a wild, "dark," and uncivilized continent. In *Mister Johnson* (1939), which in 1952 *Time* called "the best novel ever written about Africa" ("Cheerful" para. 15), Irishman Joyce Cary's protagonist is a semi-educated, childish African who, on the whole, reinforces colonialist stereotypes about Africans. In 1958, however, Chinua Achebe broke apart this dominant model with *Things Fall Apart,* a novel that portrays Igbo society with specificity and sympathy and examines the effects of European colonialism from an African perspective.

No one could have predicted that this novel, written by an unknown Nigerian, would one day sell nearly 11 million copies. Today *Things Fall Apart* is one of the most widely read books in Africa; it is typically assigned in schools and universities, and most critics consider it to be black Africa's most important novel to date. Further, the novel has been translated into more than fifty languages and shows up frequently on syllabi for literature, world history, and African studies courses across the globe. The first African novel to receive such powerful international critical acclaim, *Things Fall Apart* is considered by many to be the archetypal modern African novel.

Though Achebe went on to write numerous novels, short stories, poems, and essays, all of which have received critical attention, he is still best known as the author of *Things Fall Apart.* Of all of his works, it is the most widely read, and in the fifty years since its publication, the novel has generated a breadth of critical responses. *Things Fall Apart* has endured years of close examination through a variety of critical lenses as trends in literary criticism changed with the emergence of new insights and ideas. The novel continues to be a popular subject for critical studies even as it has become an African classic and won a place in the international literary canon.

To understand the impact that *Things Fall Apart* had on both the African and international literary worlds, it is useful to briefly examine the novel's historical context. England took control of Nigeria in the late nineteenth century and imposed upon the country a British-run government and educational system. Achebe, born in 1930 in the village of Ogidi in Eastern Nigeria, grew up under colonial rule. He lived in a Christian household, though his grandparents still followed traditional tribal ways, a tension that, as he once remarked in an interview with *Conjunctions*, "created sparks in my imagination" (para. 47). He attended the prestigious University College, Ibadan, on scholarship, first as a medical student then as a literature major, during a time in which more and more Africans were questioning colonial rule and the European justification of it as a way to bring enlightenment to the "dark continent." In his literature classes, Achebe read William Shakespeare, Samuel Taylor Coleridge, James Joyce, Ernest Hemingway, Joseph Conrad, William Wordsworth, and, as he notes in *Morning Yet on Creation Day*, "some appalling novels about Africa (including Joyce Cary's much praised *Mister Johnson*)" (123). Though Western critics had praised Cary for his sympathetic and convincing African protagonist, Mr. Johnson, Achebe and his classmates found the novel insulting and racist. Conrad's *Heart of Darkness* would similarly repulse them; in an interview with *Conjunctions*, Achebe described it as a story about "Europeans wandering among savages," adding, "In the beginning it wasn't clear to me that I was one of those savages, but eventually it did become clear" (para. 102). It was these two novels in particular that convinced Achebe that "the story we [Africans] had to tell could not be told for us by anyone else, no matter how gifted or well-intentioned" (*Morning* 123).

Achebe wanted his own story about Africa to show the complexity and sophistication of African society before European arrival and to reveal the deep wounds colonialism had inflicted on the country's social, cultural, and political fabric. Yet Achebe was uncertain of what he could expect for his novel; as he recalled in a 2009 interview with *The Atlantic*, "There was no African literature as we know it today. And so I had no idea when I was writing *Things Fall Apart* whether it would even be accepted or published. All of this was new—there was nothing by which I could gauge how it was going to be received" ("African" para. 6). Although today the majority of critics consider Achebe to be the founding father of the modern African novel, Achebe was far from the first African to publish a novel. Before *Things Fall Apart*, the best-known African novel was *The Palm-Wine Drinkard* by Amos Tutuola, who was also Nigerian. Published by the prestigious Faber and Faber in London in 1952, the novel was acclaimed in the West; however, some African scholars were wary of it, fearing that Tutuola's use of pidgin English and his depiction of a drunk would cast Nigerians in a negative light.

Throughout the 1950s, a decade of hope in which many African countries gained independence, many other authors published works that countered colonialist racist claims and celebrated African culture, history, and society. *Things Fall Apart*, which the London house Heinemann published in 1958 with a modest print run of two thousand copies, came at the end of an intense nationalist movement and preceded Nigeria's independence by two years. It also appeared just as a national artistic and cultural renaissance was beginning. Yet Achebe's novel stands out from all the other African novels that soon followed it, partly in the effectiveness with which it engages the European literary tradition, and partly because it established a model that so many African novels of the next few years followed, at least in part. For example, simply writing in the European genre of the novel was an important and politically charged strategic decision as was Achebe's choice to write in English, accented with elements derived from the spoken traditions of the Igbo. As Isidore Okpewho comments, "What marked Achebe's novel as a pioneering effort was the seriousness of purpose and the depth of vision contained in his reaction to the European novel of Africa" (7). *Things Fall Apart* rose as a symbol of the Nigerian and African renaissance, and it served as an inspiration for the next generation of African writers.

The first reviews for *Things Fall Apart* appeared in Britain, then the United States. Though a few of these early Western reviewers took a condescending or Eurocentric tone, for the most part they were positive and emphasized the novel's significance as an African's insight into the lives of Africans at the time of colonization. Three days after the novel's publication, a *Times Literary Supplement* review praised Achebe's ability to draw "a fascinating picture of tribal life among his own people" ("Centre" 341). Positive reviews also appeared in *The Observer* and *The Listener.* The UK-based journal *African Affairs* attested: "This powerful first novel breaks new ground in Nigerian fiction" (Mackay 242). In the United States, the *New York Times* called Achebe a "good writer," and claimed, "his real achievement is his ability to see the strengths and weaknesses of his characters with a true novelist's compassion" (Rodman BR28).

Many of these early reviews emphasized Achebe's Nigerian roots, and, while they often praised the subject matter and his description of the African society, they tended to pay less attention to the novel's literary qualities, often dismissing its narrative as "simple" ("Centre" 341). Reviewers dwelled on Achebe's vivid portrayal of the Igbo village and the "insider" quality of the work. The *New York Times* called it one of the "sensitive books that describe primitive society from the inside" (Rodman BR28), and the *Times Literary Supplement* claimed that "the great interest of this novel is that it genuinely succeeds in presenting tribal life from the inside" ("Centre" 341). *African Affairs* chimed in: "In powerfully realistic prose the writer sets out to write a fictional but almost documentary account of the day to day happenings in a small Nigerian village without evasion, sophistry or apology" (Mackay 243).

Although Achebe, who feels strongly that an author must be responsible to his own society, in part wrote his novel to tell the story of his people for his people, in the beginning *Things Fall Apart* received more recognition in England than it did in Nigeria. This was partly due to the facts that, at the time, only a tiny minority of Nigerian society was literate in English and that the book was quite expensive for most Nigerians; furthermore, since the book was published in England, its earliest audience was naturally made up of Europeans. However, shortly after Nigeria gained independence in 1960, a cheap paperback edition of the novel was printed and became widely available throughout Africa. In 1964, *Things Fall Apart* became the first novel by an African writer to be listed on the syllabi for African secondary schools throughout the continent. By the mid-1960s, sales of the novel in Nigeria far surpassed those in Britain.

During the same period that *Things Fall Apart* was published, African literary criticism was developing, and, though it was not until the 1960s that African critics wrote extensively about the novel, a few African scholars commented on it within a year of its publication. Nigerian Ben Obumselu, one of the founders of African literary criticism, was one of the book's first African reviewers. His review, which appeared in the journal *Ibadan* in 1959, provided a more nuanced reading than many of the early British reviews; while overall it is positive, Obumselu also pointed out what he considered to be problematic about the book:

> The form of the novel ought to have shown some awareness of the art of this culture. We do not have the novel form, of course, but there are implications in our music, sculpture and folklore which the West African novelist cannot neglect if he wishes to do more than merely imitate a European fashion. . . . I am in particular disappointed that there is in *Things Fall Apart* so little of the lyricism which marks our village life. (qtd. in Bishop 88)

Obumselu was prescient in two ways: he was one of the first critics to focus on the novel's language and one of the first to raise the question of whether Achebe's novel imitates or subverts European models. Both concerns would become major points of debate for latter critics.

Obumselu was also one of the first critics to analyze the novel from an African perspective. In their review, the majority of Western critics had tended to celebrate the novel's "otherness." For instance, the early British and U.S. reviews tended to take anthropological or sociological viewpoints when discussing Achebe's descriptions of African culture and the Igbo village. Similarly, the early scholarly responses to *Things Fall Apart* were informed by anthropology, and this approach dominated the scholarly criticism until the 1980s.

In a way, Achebe's novel invites anthropological interpretation, for one its major strengths is its vivid descriptions of the day-to-day village life of the Igbo. The best of these studies provide a strong contextual background for Achebe's writing and a close analysis of the text. Yet, as M. Keith Booker explains, these vivid descriptions of Igbo society and culture also make "the book particularly vulnerable to the kind of anthropological readings that have sometimes prevented African novels from receiving serious critical attention as literature rather than simply as documentation of cultural practices" (*African Novel* 65). Thus the more problematic pieces of anthropological criticism tend to generalize or read the text from a biased Eurocentric or Western perspective. Still, many of the anthropological studies published during these early years provided important jumping-off points for later Achebe studies.

Most tend to focus on Igbo culture and its presentation in *Things Fall Apart*; topics included Igbo religion, the meaning of Chi, and the cultural norms in Igbo society. Representative articles include: Austin J. Shelton's "The 'Palm-Oil' of Language: Proverbs in Chinua Achebe" (1969); Ernest N. Emenyonu's "Ezeulu: The Night Mask Caught Abroad by Day" (1971); Lloyd Brown's "Cultural Norms and Modes of Perception in Achebe's Fiction" (1972); Carolyn Nance's "Cosmology in the Novels of Chinua Achebe" (1971); John Johnson's "Folklore in Achebe's Novels" (1974); and Bernth Lindfors's "The

Palm Oil with Which Achebe's Words Are Eaten" (1968). One article that provoked particular controversy is "The Offended Chi in Achebe's Novels" (1964), in which Shelton, positioning himself as an anthropologist and professional student of African culture, criticizes Achebe for implying that it is the arrival of the Christian missionaries that causes the Igbo society to fall apart and complains that Achebe blames the Europeans for the society's collapse when, in fact, it is Okonkwo himself who causes it. Shelton writes, "[Achebe's] own motives perhaps are linked with his patent desire to indicate that outsiders can never understand the works of Igbo-speaking writers (whose novels are in English)" (37). On the other hand, Margaret Laurence, in her 1968 study of Nigerian literature, *Long Drums and Cannons*, criticizes Shelton's response, arguing, "It is plain . . . that the tragedy of Okonkwo is due to pressures from within as well as from the outside" (96). Laurence examines Achebe's presentation of Igbo traditional society by considering the novel from within its cultural and historical contexts and also praises Achebe's literary skills, writing that his "careful and confident craftsmanship, his firm grasp of his material and his ability to create memorable and living characters place him among the best novelists now writing in any county in the English language" (89).

As more scholars took interest in the novel, criticism grew deeper and more nuanced. For example, David Carroll's *Chinua Achebe* (1970), a significant addition to Achebe studies, provides a detailed introduction to European colonialism, Igbo history, and Igbo culture and dedicates a chapter to a close analysis of *Things Fall Apart*. Carroll, using both anthropological and literary approaches, examines Achebe's writing in relation to Nigeria's history of colonialism, independence, and political conflict and argues that Achebe resists European exoticism and stereotypes to raise questions about African identity and representation. Emmanuel Obiechina, too, largely takes an anthropological approach to the novel, though from an African perspective, in *Culture, Tradition, and Society in the West African Novel*. Examining the traditional beliefs and practices represented in *Things Fall Apart* and other West African novels, he seeks to show how African society and culture "gave rise to the novel there, and in far-reaching and crucial ways conditioned the West African novel's content, themes, and texture" (3). Another important work from this period is Robert M. Wren's *Achebe's World* (1980), a valuable guide to Igbo history, politics, religion, and society.

The best of the anthropological articles give a strong portrait of Igbo culture in relation to the novel and examine the historical context of the writing; however, a drawback to anthropological readings is their neglect of the literary qualities of the novel. Although a few critical works of the 1960s and 1970s examined the structural and narrative aspects of *Things Falls Apart*—such as Eldred D. Jones's "Language and Theme in *Things Fall Apart*" (1964), Karl H. Bottcher's "The Narrative Technique in Achebe's Novels" (1972), and G. D. Killam's *The Writings of Chinua Achebe* (1969), a groundbreaking work for its time that focuses on craft while also examining how African writers represented their world in literature—formalist (including New Critical) approaches, which focused on the literary qualities of the work, were much more popular in the 1980s.

Such approaches analyze the formal qualities of a text—such as narrative, characterization, and structure—while bracketing off any historical, biographical, or sociological factors that may have influenced it. As this critical focus became more popular throughout the 1980s and 1990s, it undoubtedly brought more attention to Achebe's literary achievement in *Things Fall Apart*. Among the many standout pieces of formalist criticism are B. Eugene McCarthy's "Rhythm and Narrative Method in Achebe's *Things Fall Apart*" (1985), Angel Smith's "The Mouth with Which to Tell of Their Suffering: The Role of the Narrator and Reader in Achebe's *Things Fall Apart*" (1988), and Emmanuel Ngara's *Stylistic Criticism and the African Novel* (1982). The collection of essays *Critical Perspectives on Chinua Achebe* (1978), edited by C. L. Innes and Bernth Lindfors, presents diverse essays that both contextualize Achebe's work and assess his literary achievement. Two important books that also broke with anthropological criticism were Innes's *Chinua Achebe* (1990) and Simon Gikandi's *Reading Chinua Achebe* (1991).

As more and more critics began analyzing the text itself, a strain of criticism developed around the relations between *Things Fall Apart* and Aristotelian or Greek tragedy. While investigating the novel's structure, plot, and characters, critics began debating whether Okonkwo can be called a classical tragic hero. In Greek tragedy, the tragic hero is a noble character who tries to achieve some much-desired goal but encounters obstacles. He often possesses some kind of tragic flaw, and his downfall is usually brought about through some combination of hubris, fate, and the will of the gods. One of the earliest articles on this theme is Abiola Irele's "The Tragic Conflict in the Novels of Chinua Achebe" (1967), in which Irele asserts, *"Things Fall Apart* turns out to present the whole tragic drama of a society vividly and concretely enacted in the tragic destiny of a representative individual" (14). This idea grew popular during the 1970s and 1980s and has endured as a typical way of defining Okonkwo's character—even the back cover of the 1994 Anchor edition of the novel claims that it "is often compared to the great Greek tragedies." Some of the articles published during the 1980s on this theme include Ian Glenn's "Heroic Failure in the Novels of Achebe" (1985), Roger Landrum's "Chinua Achebe and the Aristotelian Concept of Tragedy" (1970), and Afam Ebeogu's "Igbo Sense of Tragedy: A Thematic Feature of the Achebe School" (1983). G. D. Killam also wrote about the tragic elements of the novel, asserting that Okonkwo's story "is presented in terms which resemble those of Aristotelian tragedy" and that Okonkwo's death is the result of "an insistent fatality . . . which transcends his ability to fully understand or resist a fore-ordained sequence of events" (17). David Cook, in *African Literature: A Critical View,* which contains an important early formalist study of *Things Fall Apart,* provides a close reading of Okonkwo, claiming, "If *Things Fall Apart* is to be regarded as epic, then Okonkwo is essentially heroic. Both propositions are tenable" (66). He closely examines Okonkwo's actions, and, although Cook believes Okonkwo is similar, he concludes: "Okonkwo is unlike the prototype epic heroes of Homer and Virgil in one very important respect which has to do with circumstances rather than character. He is not a founding figure in the fabled history of his people, but the very reverse" (67). Harold Bloom does not consider the novel a traditional Greek tragedy, but he does compare Okonkwo to Shakespeare's Coriolanus, concluding in his introduction to his Modern Critical Interpretations volume on *Things Fall Apart*, "If Coriolanus is a tragedy, then so is *Things Fall Apart*. Okonkwo, like the Roman hero, is essentially a solitary, and at heart a perpetual child. His tragedy stands apart from the condition of his people, even though it is generated by their pragmatic refusal of heroic death" (3).

This critical shift from anthropological readings to formalist ones helped solidify Achebe's literary reputation. However, like the anthropological approaches, formalist readings also present drawbacks. Booker explains:

> Indeed, the formal strategies employed by *Things Fall Apart* are so complex and sophisticated that they do recall the works of Western modernism. As a result, however, Western critics are in danger of falling into old habits of formalist reading and thereby of failing to do justice to the important social and political content of Achebe's book. (*African Novel* 66)

Because Western critics have often looked to European literary standards as guidelines for critiquing *Things Fall Apart*, their criticism has, at times, been myopic. For instance, as Booker comments, Charles R. Larson, in *The Emergence of the African Fiction*, "tended to argue for the aesthetic value of African literature merely through the use of universalist arguments that claim that African literature is worth reading because it is often quite similar to European literature. Such arguments obviously fail to respect the differences of African cultural traditions" (*African Novel* 5). Still, as recently as 2002, Bloom commented that

Things Fall Apart is a successful novel because "Okonkwo's apparent tragedy is universal, despite its Nigerian circumstancing" (2). He argues: "Okonkwo could be a North American, a Spaniard, a Sicilian, and Eskimo. The end would be the same" (2).

This universalist lens continues to be a popular method for reading *Things Fall Apart*, but, with the growing popularity of postcolonial theory, criticism has again shifted toward reexamining the novel's historical and cultural contexts, albeit in a different light. As Ato Quayson in *Strategic Transformations in Nigerian Writing* (1997) argues, "The traditional culture portrayed in a work such as Achebe's *Things Fall Apart* is never mistaken for a Japanese one. It is not just that the novel mimetically invokes Igbo forms of oral discourse, it also imitates a general cultural discursivity" (15). In addition, Booker maintains that literature cannot be separated from its context and history:

> It is valuable for Western readers to study African literature because a sensitive reading of that literature makes it quite obvious that the different social and historical background of African literature leads to artistic criteria and conventions that differ from those of Europe or America. (*African Novel* 6)

African critics have voiced some of the strongest protests against universalist and New Critical readings. For instance, Chinweizu, Onwuchekwa Jemie, and Ihechukwu Madubuike's controversial book *Toward the Decolonization of African Literature* (1983) critiques and reviews work by Western critics such as Charles R. Larson "in order to reveal the assumption of Western cultural superiority that lies behind their work, even when they are ostensibly attempting to serve as advocates for the value of African literature" (Booker, *African Novel* 6). Achebe himself has argued against formalist and universalist readings, most notably in his essay "Colonialist Criticism." He bristles at Western critics who seem to think they know more about Africans than Africans. "To the colonialist mind it was always of the utmost importance to be able to say: *I know my natives*," he writes (*Morning* 6), arguing that this attitude often lingers in literary critics, and he finds universalist readings to be Eurocentric and often incomplete: "I should like to see the word *universal* banned altogether from discussions of African literature" (*Morning* 13).

Still, it is important to note that throughout the 1960s and into the 1980s, critics, theorists, and writers were trying to develop standards for analyzing the large amount of new African literature. Both African and non-African critics debated the standards of criticism and disagreed over universalist as well as African nationalist approaches. *Toward the Decolonization of African Literature*, which urged African writers to break away from their colonizers by reconnecting with their culture, emerged from this debate. Some critics and writers believed that this reconnection could be accomplished through rejection of the language of the colonizer. For example, in "The Dead End of African Literature" (1963), Obiajunwa Wali argued that writing in English would not do justice to African complexity and originality; he challenged writers and critics to turn away from European literature and critical methods: "The whole uncritical acceptance of English and French as the inevitable medium for educated African writing, is misdirected, and has no chance of advancing African literature and culture" (14). This essay started an intense debate among African writers and critics. Internationally acclaimed Kenyan author Ngugi wa Thiong'o also argued in *Decolonizing the Mind: The Politics of Language in African Literature* (1986) that African writers should renounce their ties with their colonizers; soon after, he began writing his own texts in Gikuyu and (to a lesser extent) Swahili.

That Achebe wrote and continues to write in English has caused some controversy. While both African and non-African critics agree that Achebe modeled *Things Fall Apart* on classic European literature, they disagree about whether his novel upholds a Western model or, in fact, subverts or confronts it. For instance, in *Achebe and the Politics of Representation* (2001), Ode Ogede questions whether Achebe can use the "colonizer's tongue" without "reproducing some of their stereo-types" (ix). Yet Achebe has continued to strongly defend his decision:

> English is something you spend your lifetime acquiring, so it would be foolish not to use it. Also, in the logic of colonization and decolonization it is actually a very powerful weapon in the fight to regain what was yours. English was the language of colonization itself. It is not simply something you use because you have it anyway; it is something which you can actively claim to use as an effective weapon, as a counterargument to colonization. ("African" para. 30)

Rand Bishop, however, summarizes the opinions of the majority of critics when he writes that Achebe "seemed to find the happy middle ground that critics wanted, somewhere between the Victorian English of the British colonial forms and the 'young English' of Tutuola. In fact, Achebe's use of English became widely accepted as a standard" (43). When Ben Obumselu reviewed *Things Fall Apart* in 1958, he praised the way Achebe handled the English language while also drawing on Nigerian oral tradition: "Such an experiment requires both imagination and originality. . . . His experiment is a very positive contribution to the writing of West African English literature, and I believe it will make the work of subsequent authors easier" (qtd. in Bishop 43). As Isidore Okpewho remarks: "Achebe transcended form and style for a more revisionist representation of the peculiar conditions and outlook of an African society in ways that the British authors could never have conceived" (8). As Booker explains, the "African novel is always a complex hybrid cultural phenomenon that combines Western and African cultural perspectives" (7), and a sizable number of African critics—such as Abiola Irele, Ernest N. Emenyonu, and Michael J. Echeruo—have closely examined *Things Fall Apart* as reflective both of a unique African cultural and historical context and of universal themes.

When Obumselu suggested in 1959 that Achebe's experiment with language would impact African literature, he was quite correct. The language of the novel continues to be a major focus for critical studies ranging from the anthropological to the postcolonial. Achebe's narrative voice incorporates spare, formal English prose and Igbo expressions, proverbs, and untranslated Igbo words. According to Ogede, the novel "replicates, evokes and simulates oral events in a raw form" (*Reader's Guide* 17), drawing on traditional Igbo oral culture. Many critics have examined Achebe's use of Igbo proverbs and the oral components of the text, but two are particularly helpful to students: Bernth Lindfors's "The Palm-Oil with Which Achebe's Words Are Eaten" (1968) argues that Achebe combines the modes of oral and written cultures, and Chinwe Christina Okechukwu's *Achebe the Orator: The Art of Persuasion in Chinua Achebe's Novels* (2001) examines how Achebe uses oratory and rhetorical devices to educate his readers about colonialism and its aftermath.

The language of the novel has not only intrigued critics but has also been a major factor in the emergence of the modern African novel. That Achebe wrote in English, portrayed Igbo life from the point of view of an African man, and used the language of his people in the text were innovations that greatly influenced the African writers who published soon after Achebe. Novelists such as Flora Nwapa, John Munonye, and Nkem Nwankwo, who broke into print in the late 1960s, all looked to Achebe as a guide, and even some more established or older Nigerian novelists were influenced by Achebe's use of the Igbo language. For example, Onuora Nzekwu, whose first novel was written in a stiff, formal English, wrote his third novel in an African vernacular style.

Today Achebe's fiction and criticism continue to inspire and influence African writers. African authors born in the late 1950s and in the 1960s and 1970s—including Helon Habila, Tsitsi Dangarembga, and Chimamanda Ngozi Adichie—have been particularly inspired or influenced by Achebe. Adichie, for instance, the author of the popular and critically acclaimed books *Purple Hibiscus* (2003) and *Half of a Yellow Sun* (2006), commented in a 2005 interview, "Chinua Achebe will always be important to me because his work influenced not so much my style as my writing philosophy: reading him emboldened me, gave me permission to write about the things I knew well" (para. 13).

Over the years, *Things Fall Apart* has been examined by a wide variety of critical schools. Although certain types of criticism have dominated discussions of the novel during different periods, they have also been interlaced with studies from a variety of other critical perspectives—such as Marxist, reader-response, psychoanalytic, historical, feminist, and cultural-studies approaches. Still, throughout the 1990s the dominant trend was postcolonialism, which at times also draws on Marxist and poststructuralist theories. Postcolonialist criticism focuses its critiques on the literature of countries that were once colonies of other countries. It arose during the 1980s, as many African countries were in political and economic crisis and theorists reexamined ideas about progress and development. As Simon Gikandi explains, "Instead of seeing colonialism as the imposition of cultural practices by the colonizer over the colonized, postcolonial theorists argued that the colonized had themselves been active agents in the making and remaking of the idea of culture itself" (*Encyclopedia* 125). In *Post-colonial Literatures in English: History, Language, Theory* (1998), Dennis Walder defines postcolonial literary criticism: "On the one hand, it carries with it the intention to promote, even celebrate the 'new literatures' which have emerged over this century from the former colonial territories; and on the other, it asserts the need to analyze and resist continuing colonial attitudes" (6). He explains that *Things Fall Apart* is a postcolonial text, as it rejects the assumption that the colonized can only be the subjects of someone else's story; it seeks to "by telling the story of the colonized . . . retrieve their history. And more than that: by retrieving their history to regain an identity" (7). In *Reading Chinua Achebe* (1991), Gikandi argues that, although *Things Fall Apart* cannot be regarded as representative of a "real Igbo culture," it is an example of strategic resistance, as Achebe writes back or takes back his story and culture from colonial representations. Earlier debates about authenticity and representation—and the complications inherent to writing in a colonizer's language—were early jumping-off points for later postcolonial approaches.

Feminist criticism of *Things Fall Apart* did not begin appearing until the 1990s, but, when it arrived, it made a strong impact and opened the novel up to new interpretations. One of the more groundbreaking arguments is that of Canadian feminist critic Florence Stratton, who argues in *Contemporary African Literature and the Politics of Gender* (1994) that Achebe gives men cultural roles that were actually occupied by women in traditional Igbo culture. Biodun Jeyifo's "Okonkwo and His Mother" is an analysis of the gender politics of *Things Fall Apart*, and Rhonda Cobham, in "Problems of Gender and History in the Teaching of *Things Fall Apart*" (1990), argues that *Things Fall Apart* reinforces dominant male Christian views of traditional Igbo society.

For more than fifty years, *Things Fall Apart* has offered critics rich material for thought and reflection. Readers seeking in-depth overviews and samplings of criticism may wish to turn to several important essay collections about and guides to Achebe's work. Solomon O. Iyasere's *Understanding "Things Fall Apart": Selected Essays and Criticism* (1998) and *Chinua Achebe: A Celebration* (1990), edited by Kirsten Holst Petersen and Anna Rutherford, are both key collections. Isidore Okpewho's *Chinua Achebe's "Things Fall Apart": A Casebook* (2003) contains essays exploring the diverse issues raised by critics of the novel. *Emerging Perspectives on Chinua Achebe* (2004) is a two-volume set, edited by Ernest N. Emenyonu, that grew out of the twenty-fourth annual conference of the African Literature Association; it is quite comprehensive and covers all of Achebe's works to date, with essays by scholars from Africa, Europe, and Canada. *The Chinua Achebe Encyclopedia* (2003), edited by M. Keith Booker, is a comprehensive guide to Achebe's life and writings and includes descriptions of major characters, historical places, and critical responses to Achebe's work. David Whittaker and Mpalive-Hangson Msiska's *Chinua Achebe's "Things Fall Apart"* (2007) provides a detailed chapter on the history of criticism of the novel, as does Ode Ogede's *Achebe's "Things Fall Apart": A Reader's Guide* (2007). Booker's *The African Novel in English* (1998) provides substantial historical and contextual background on African literature and contains a chapter dedicated to *Things Fall Apart*. The most comprehensive biography on Achebe to date is Ezenwa-Ohaeto's *Chinua Achebe: A Biography* (1997).

Over the span of his long and productive career, Achebe helped create what is now known as the modern African novel and contributed to the development of African literary criticism. His influence on other African writers cannot be stressed enough. In addition to providing African writers with a new model, Achebe also helped promote African literature. In 1962 Achebe became the first series editor of the Heinemann African Writers Series, which has been one of the most important publishing venues for African literature. According to Achebe, the series' launch "was like the umpires' signal for which African writers had been waiting on the starting line" (*Home and Exile* 51).

When *Things Fall Apart* was published, Achebe gave Africans their own story in print. As he told *Conjunctions* in 1991:

> The popularity of *Things Fall Apart* in my own society can be explained simply, because my people are seeing themselves virtually for the first time in the story. The story of our position in the world had been told by others. But somehow that story was not anything like the way it seemed to us from where we stood. So this was the first time we were seeing ourselves, as autonomous individuals, rather than half-people, or as Conrad would say, 'rudimentary souls.' (para. 90)

Just as *Things Fall Apart* made a large impact on Africans, it has also proven to be popular among international audiences. It is one of those rare novels that can be read and reread from many different perspectives and continues to generate many diverse interpretations. It continues to endure as an international classic.

Works Cited

Achebe, Chinua. "An African Voice." Interview by Katie Bacon. *Atlantic Unbound: The Atlantic Online.* 2 Aug. 2008. 10 June 2009. http://www.theatlantic.com/unbound/interviews/ba2000-08-02.htm.

_____. "Chinua Achebe." Interview by Bradford Morrow. *Conjunctions* 17 (Fall 1991). 10 June 2009. http://www.conjunctions.com/archives/c17-ca.htm.

_____. *Home and Exile.* New York: Oxford UP, 2000.

_____. *Morning Yet on Creation Day.* Garden City, NY: Anchor Press/Doubleday, 1975.

Adichie, Chimamanda Ngozi. Interview by Daria Tunca. The Chimamanda Ngozi Adichie Website. 27 Jan. 2005. 3 Feb. 2010. http://www.l3.ulg.ac.be/adichie.

Auayson, Ato. *Strategic Transformations in Nigerian Writing.* Bloomington: Indiana UP, 1997.

Bishop, Rand. *African Literature, African Critics.* New York: Greenwood Press, 1988.

Bloom, Harold. "Introduction." *Chinua Achebe's "Things Fall Apart."* Ed. Harold Bloom. Philadelphia: Chelsea House, 2002.

Booker, M. Keith. *The African Novel in English: An Introduction.* Portsmouth, NH: Heinemann, 1998.

_____, ed. *The Chinua Achebe Encyclopedia.* Westport, CT: Greenwood Press, 2003.

Bottcher, Karl H. "The Narrative Technique in Achebe's Novels." *Journal of the New African Literature and the Arts* 13/14 (1972): 1-12.

Brown, Lloyd. "Cultural Norms and Modes of Perception in Achebe's Fiction." *Research in African Literatures* 3.1 (Spring 1972): 21-35. Rpt. in *Critical Perspectives on Chinua Achebe.* Ed. C. L. Innes and Bernth Lindfors. Washington, DC: Three Continents Press, 1978. 22-36.

Carroll, David. *Chinua Achebe.* New York: Twayne, 1970.

"The Centre Cannot Hold." *Times Literary Supplement* 20 June 1958: 341.

"Cheerful Protestant." Rev. of *Prisoner of Grace*, by Joyce Cary. *Time* 20 Oct. 1952. 10 June 2009. http://www.time.com/time/magazine/article/0,9171,817167-1,00.html.

Chinweizu, Onsucheka J., Onwuchekwa Jemie, and Ihechukwu Madubuike. *Toward the Decolonization of African Literature.* Washington, DC: Howard UP, 1983.

Cobham, Rhonda. "Problems of Gender and History in the Teaching of *Things Fall Apart.*" *Matatu: Journal for African Culture and Society* 7 (1990): 25-39.

Cook, David. *African Literature: A Critical View.* London: Longman, 1977.

Ebeogu, Afam. "Igbo Sense of Tragedy: A Thematic Feature of the Achebe School." *Literary Half-Yearly* 24.1 (1983): 69-86.

Emenyonu, Ernest N. "Ezeulu: The Night Mask Caught Abroad by Day." *Pan-African Journal* 4 (Fall 1971): 407-19.

_____, ed. *Emerging Perspectives on Chinua Achebe.* 2 vols. Trenton, NJ: African World Press, 2004.

Ezenwa-Ohaeto. *Chinua Achebe: A Biography.* Bloomington: Indiana UP, 1997.

Gikandi, Simon. *Reading Chinua Achebe: Language and Ideology in Fiction.* Portsmouth, NH: Heinemann, 1991.

_____, ed. *Encyclopedia of African Literature.* London: Taylor & Francis, 2003.

Glenn, Ian. "Heroic Failure in the Novels of Chinua Achebe." *English in Africa* 12.1 (1985): 11-27.

Innes, C. L. *Chinua Achebe.* New York: Cambridge UP, 1990.

Innes, C. L., and Bernth Lindfors, eds. *Critical Perspectives on Chinua Achebe.* Washington, DC: Three Continents Press, 1978.

Irele, Abiola. "The Tragic Conflict in the Novels of Chinua Achebe." *Critical Perspectives on Chinua Achebe.* Ed. C. L. Innes and Bernth Lindfors. Washington, DC: Three Continents Press, 1978. 10-21.

Iyasere, Solomon O., ed. *Understanding "Things Fall Apart": Selected Essays and Criticism.* Troy, NY: Whitston, 1998.

Johnson, John. "Folklore in Achebe's Novels." *New Letters* 40.3 (1974): 95-107.

Jones, Eldred D. "Language and Theme in *Things Fall Apart.*" *Review of English Literature* 5.4 (1964): 39-43.

Killam, G. D. *The Writings of Chinua Achebe.* New York: Africana, 1969.

Landrum, Roger. "Chinua Achebe and the Aristotelian Concept of Tragedy." *Black Academy Review* 1 (1970): 22-30.

Laurence, Margaret. *Long Drums and Cannons.* New York: Praeger, 1968.

Lindfors, Bernth. "The Palm-Oil with Which Achebe's Words Are Eaten." *African Literature Today* 1 (1968): 3-18. Rpt. in *Critical Perspectives on Chinua Achebe.* Ed. C. L. Innes and Bernth Lindfors. Washington, DC: Three Continents Press, 1978. 47-66.

McCarthy, B. Eugene. "Rhythm and Narrative Method in Achebe's *Things Fall Apart.*" *Novel* 18.3 (1985): 243-56.

Mackay, Mercedes. Rev. of *Things Fall Apart*, by Chinua Achebe. *African Affairs* 57.228 (July 1958): 242.

Nance, Carolyn. "Cosmology in the Novels of Chinua Achebe." *The Conch* 3.2 (1971): 121-36.

Ngara, Emmanuel. *Stylistic Criticism of the African Novel: A Study of the Language, Art, and Content of African Fiction.* Exeter, NH: Heinemann, 1982.

Ngugi wa Thiong'o. *Decolonizing the Mind: The Politics of Language in African Literature.* London: J. Currey, 1986.

Obiechina, Emmanuel. *Culture, Tradition, and Society in the West African Novel.* New York: Cambridge UP, 1975.

Ogede, Ode. *Achebe and the Politics of Representation.* Trenton, NJ: Africa World Press, 2001.

_____. *Achebe's "Things Fall Apart": A Reader's Guide.* London: Continuum, 2007.

Okechukwu, Chinwe Christina. *Achebe the Orator: The Art of Persuasion in Chinua Achebe's Novels.* Westport, CT: Greenwood Press, 2001.

Okpewho, Isidore, ed. *Chinua Achebe's "Things Fall Apart": A Casebook.* New York: Oxford UP, 2003.

Petersen, Kirsten Holst, and Anna Rutherford. *Chinua Achebe: A Celebration.* Portsmouth, NH: Heinemann, 1991.

Rodman, Selden. "The White Man's Faith." *New York Times* 22 Feb. 1959: BR28.

Shelton, Austin J. "The Offended Chi in Achebe's Novels." *Transition* 13 (1964): 36-37.

_____. "The 'Palm-Oil' of Language: Proverbs in Chinua Achebe." *Modern Language Quarterly* 30.1 (1969): 86-111.

Smith, Angel. "The Mouth with Which to Tell of Their Suffering: The Role of Narrator and Reader in Achebe's *Things Fall Apart.*" *Commonwealth Essays and Studies* 11.1 (1988). Rpt. in *Understanding "Things Fall Apart": Selected Essays and Criticism.* Ed. Solomon O. Iyasere. Troy, NY: Whitston, 1998. 8-26.

Stratton, Florence. *Contemporary African Literature and the Politics of Gender.* New York: Routledge, 1994.

Walder, Dennis. *Post-colonial Literatures in English: History, Language, Theory.* Malden, MA: Blackwell, 1998.

Wali, Obiajunwa. "The Dead End of African Literature." *Transition* 10 (Sept. 1963): 13-16.

Whittaker, David, and Mpalive-Hangson Msiska. *Chinua Achebe's "Things Fall Apart."* New York: Routledge, 2007.

Wren, Robert M. *Achebe's World.* Washington, DC: Three Continents Press, 1980.

An Adequate Revolution:
Achebe Writing Africa Anew

Thomas Jay Lynn

> Here then is an adequate revolution for me to espouse—to help my society regain belief in itself and put away the complexes of the years of denigration and self-abasement. . . . For no thinking African can escape the pain of the wound in our soul. . . . I would be quite satisfied if my novels (especially the ones I set in the past) did no more than teach my readers that their past—with all its imperfections—was not one long night of savagery from which the first Europeans acting on God's behalf delivered them.
>
> —Chinua Achebe, "The Novelist as Teacher" (71-72)

Chinua Achebe's seminal contribution not only to African, English, and world literature but also to a generational shift in African and international perceptions of Africa is tied to his multifaceted use and representation of language. At both ends of the Nigerian author's first novel, *Things Fall Apart*, for example, are passages that foreground the role of language and that resonate within and beyond the confines of the book: a passage near the beginning evokes "the art of conversation" among the traditional Igbo people from whom Achebe descends, while in the novel's concluding passage a British officer contemplates writing a book about "the pacification" of various West African peoples. Whereas in the concluding scene Achebe represents Western modes of thinking and writing about Africa, the earlier scene introduces the linguistic methods by which he will challenge these modes. What Achebe's treatment of language in these and other passages affirms is the profound integrity of an African society; what it supports is the ongoing restructuring of a global vision of Africa.

As soon as he has discovered and given orders for the handling of the lifeless body of Okonkwo, the novel's protagonist, the unnamed British District Commissioner reflects on the book he is writing and the title that he already has in mind for it—*The Pacification of the Primi-*

tive Tribes of the Lower Niger. Okonkwo's suicide of course raises many questions in the minds of readers, but this scene also raises important concerns about the District Commissioner, who is partly responsible for precipitating Okonkwo's death, and his prospective book. Having followed the arc of Okonkwo's life over the course of an entire novel, a reader may be struck by the limited scope the officer proposes to give Okonkwo. He tells himself:

> The story of this man who had killed a messenger and hanged himself would make interesting reading. One could almost write a whole chapter on him. Perhaps not a whole chapter but a reasonable paragraph, at any rate. There was so much else to include, and one must be firm in cutting out details. (208-09)

Although the District Commissioner's book would be nonfiction, the way in which he proposes to treat his subject is suggestive of the features of European fiction about Africa that prompted Achebe to write *Things Fall Apart* in the first place.

A word about this literary background is in order before returning to the officer. In British literature of the colonial period, individual Africans—their inner lives and psychic complexities—were rarely explored. Rather, when they did appear in fiction set in Africa, they were routinely employed as secondary or background figures, adding piquancy to the African adventures of Europeans. As Jonathan Peters states, "Notions about a mysterious Africa . . . had held on for centuries and had been made popular in the colonial period through novelists like [Sir Henry Rider] Haggard, [Joseph] Conrad, and [Joyce] Cary" (15). The connection between adventurous travel and a fanciful notion of Africa is reflected in the dissemination by European "travel books" of "prejudices and myths about Africa" (Ezenwa-Ohaeto 44). As for novelists, focusing sustained psychological attention on individual Africans would spoil the mystery, and, in any case, one can scarcely escape the conclusion that these and other European writers considered

Africans to be not interesting enough for focused interrogation. Haggard's enormously popular novel *King's Solomon's Mines* (1885) includes dramatic scenes that hinge on African mysteries that fatefully draw European characters, and, although it does attempt to give certain Africans occasional prominence and dignity, it invariably falls back on denigrating stereotypes of their mental qualities. In addition, the language barrier discouraged Europeans from creating penetrating dramatizations of the lives of Africans.

In "An Image of Africa: Racism in Conrad's *Heart of Darkness*" (1975), which has had the greatest impact of any Achebe essay, the author shows the connection between, on the one hand, the habitual European view of Africans as lacking a human status equal to their own and, on the other, the ways in which the language barrier prevented Europeans from making more truthful presentations of Africans and justified their demeaning attitudes towards them. Joseph Conrad's widely read novella *Heart of Darkness* (1899) ostensibly sympathizes with the plight of Africans under the cruel colonial yoke, but, as Achebe indicates, by associating Africans with animalistic and savage imagery and by depriving them of anything approaching a profound or subtle language, it denies them a humanity equivalent to that of Europeans. Though Conrad was exceptionally proficient in European languages, he likely would not have had the training to render African dialogue credibly. But in *Heart of Darkness* the narrator, Marlow, does not concede that his lack of knowledge of an African language is a significant hindrance to his communication with Africans or is the reason that what Africans say to each other goes unreported. Rather, Africans appear to be the ones who are linguistically deficient, and this partly suggests that their thought patterns are shallow. Conrad's readers, and possibly Conrad himself, would not have been troubled by such distortions, since they would have been camouflaged by the already prevalent belief that African languages and views were rudimentary. In his essay on *Heart of Darkness*, Achebe elucidates Conrad's slanted treatment of African language and his resulting degradation of Africans:

It is clearly not part of Conrad's purpose to confer language on the "rudimentary souls" of Africa. In place of speech they made "a violent babble of uncouth sounds." They "exchanged short grunting phrases" even among themselves. But most of the time they were too busy with their frenzy. . . . Africa as setting and backdrop which eliminates the African as human factor. Africa as a metaphysical battlefield devoid of all recognizable humanity, into which the wandering European enters at his peril. Can nobody see the preposterous and perverse arrogance in thus reducing Africa to the role of props for the break-up of one petty European mind [the mind of the story's Mr. Kurtz]? But that is not even the point. The real question is the dehumanization of Africa and Africans which this age-long attitude has fostered and continues to foster in the world. (8, 12)

Achebe's critique of *Heart of Darkness* can help inform our understanding of the final passage of *Things Fall Apart*, in which the District Commissioner anticipates his paragraph about Okonkwo and reveals attitudes about Africans that will underlie the book he plans to write.

One may ask why "'one of the greatest men of Umuofia'" (208) is worth only a paragraph in the book. From the District Commissioner's perspective, a more probing treatment of a "primitive" mind would require unnecessary "details." Another question concerns the quality of insight that the book might be expected to demonstrate given, among other factors, the language barrier. Undoubtedly, the officer will have to rely on an interpreter, as he does in his dealings with people of Umuofia (193), despite the evident limitation of this method: "The Commissioner did not understand what Obierika [Okonkwo's best friend] meant when he said, 'Perhaps your men will help us'" (207). But since a man in his position might think of African languages as rudimentary, an interpreter would likely seem sufficient to him. Indeed, the narrative reveals a dismissive quality in the officer's attitude toward African speech: his initial reaction to that consequential remark by Obierika is to think, "One of the most infuriating habits of these people was their love of superfluous words" (206). Especially since his lack of understanding has helped bring about Okonkwo's death, we may ask, finally, why the District Commissioner feels qualified to write about Okonkwo at all. The officer sees African societies as inferior and sees himself as an emissary of an enlightened nation: "'We have brought a peaceful administration to you and your people so that you may be happy'" (194). He could well believe, therefore, that he has the capacity to understand "these people." As Achebe writes in the essay "Colonialist Criticism," "To the colonialist mind it was always of the utmost importance to be able to say: 'I know my natives,' a claim which implied . . . that the native was really quite simple" (71).

Haggard and Conrad, of course, were not the only prominent Western novelists to translate their experiences of colonial Africa into fiction. The Anglo-Irish writer Joyce Cary, for example, published *Mister Johnson* in 1939. This novel is an exception to numerous other British colonial novels in that it revolves around an African, specifically the Nigerian title character. For Achebe, however, it only contributed to his awareness of the inadequacy of European representations of Africa. He has said that his reading of *Mister Johnson* was a factor that played an influential role in the eventual composition of *Things Fall Apart*:

> I was quite certain that I was going to try my hand at writing, and one of the things that set me thinking was Joyce Cary's novel set in Nigeria, *Mister Johnson*, which was praised so much, and it was clear to me that this was a most superficial picture . . . and so I thought if this was famous, then perhaps someone ought to try and look at this from the inside. (Interview 4; see also "Named" 38)

Cary's protagonist, Johnson, a local agent for British colonial concerns, is juvenile and unscrupulous, and simply on the basis of his characterization one understands why Achebe would think a different story was needed. But also Achebe's remark that "perhaps someone ought to try and look at this from the inside" indicates that a crucial ingredient for a different story would be a teller who knew intimately an African society and its language.

But to discover an even fuller picture of the social and political currents related to language that motivated Achebe to embark on his first novel, one may turn to *No Longer at Ease* (1960), the sequel to *Things Fall Apart*, which is set in the 1950s and which Achebe originally meant to be part of the same volume as *Things Fall Apart*. Overlapping themes still bind the two novels, and *No Longer at Ease* rewards readers of *Things Fall Apart*. Its protagonist, Obi Okonkwo, is the grandson of the original Okonkwo; he earns an English degree at an English university and returns to modern Lagos, assuming a post in the British civil service of the late colonial period. Yet Obi still remembers a particularly painful experience he had in England involving African language: "When he had to speak in English with a Nigerian student from another tribe he lowered his voice. It was humiliating to have to speak to one's country man in a foreign language, especially in the presence of the proud owners of that language. They would naturally assume that one had no language of one's own" (57). Of course Obi knows the linguistic reality is altogether different, that the Igbo language and conversation of his birthplace, Umuofia, is rich and exquisitely nuanced, and this awareness touches him with particular force when he returns to Umuofia for the first time after his university studies: "He wished they [the proud owners of English] were here today to see. Let them come to Umuofia now and listen to the talk of men who made a great art of conversation. Let them come and see men and women and children who knew how to live, whose joy of life had not yet been killed by those who claimed to teach other nations how to live" (57).

Obi's reflections are replicated in a sense by Achebe himself at the conclusion of his *Heart of Darkness* essay. In the novel, Obi feels the sting of having his language judged by a proud people who are ignorant of it, but he finds at least a partial remedy in affirming to himself the value of his language and the people who speak it. In the essay, Achebe writes of an American newspaper article that, while using the word "language" to refer to Western languages such as Spanish and Italian, uses the word "dialects" to refer to the languages of India and Nigeria. He contends that "this is quite comparable to Conrad's withholding of language from his rudimentary souls. Language is too grand for these chaps; let's give them dialects!" Achebe continues, "In all this business a lot of violence is inevitably done not only to the image of despised peoples but even to words, the very tools of possible redress" (19). Obi Okonkwo recalls the humiliation that English ignorance of African language causes him, but he also finds a remedy in language, and a parallel notion is suggested at this point in the *Heart of Darkness* essay: "Violence is done. . . . words . . . the very tools of possible redress." Furthermore, in light of Achebe's own experience with Conrad, Cary, and other European authors who, when he was younger, had made it impossible for him to identify with African characters, who took him over to "the side of the white man" in opposition to "the savages [who] were after him" (qtd. in Gikandi, *Reading* 6), *Things Fall Apart*, too, may be regarded as a means of using language to heal damage caused by the West's ignorance of African language and society.

Not only does Achebe's narrator invoke much the same phrase early in *Things Fall Apart*—"Among the Igbo the art of conversation is regarded very highly" (7)—that is placed in Obi's thoughts in its sequel, but also the entire *Things Fall Apart* passage that includes the phrase, like most of the book, shares the spirit of Obi's celebratory response to hearing the language of his hometown. This passage tells of an encounter between a prosperous man named Okoye and Okonkwo's father, Unoka, who is a financial "failure" (6). Okoye seeks repayment of a loan he made to Unoka, who has no intention of repaying it. The verbal parrying between the two is both rich and subtle, employing a range of rhetorical flourishes and maneuvers:

"Thank you for the kola. You may have heard of the title I intend to take shortly."

Having spoken plainly so far, Okoye said the next half a dozen sentences in proverbs. Among the Ibo the art of conversation is regarded very highly, and proverbs are the palm oil with which words are eaten. Okoye was a great talker and he spoke for a long time, skirting round the subject and then hitting it finally. In short, he was asking Unoka to return the two hundred cowries he had borrowed from him more than two years before. As soon as Unoka understood what his friend was driving at, he burst out laughing. He laughed loud and long and his voice rang out clear as the *ogene*, and tears stood in his eyes. His visitor was amazed, and sat speechless.

Pointing to groups of markings on the wall of his hut, Unoka tells Okoye:

"Each group there represents a debt to someone, and each stroke is one hundred cowries. You see, I owe that man a thousand cowries. But he has not come to wake me up in the morning for it. I shall pay you, but not today. Our elders say that the sun will shine on those who stand before it shines on those who kneel under them. I shall pay my big debts first." And he took another pinch of snuff, as if that was paying the big debts first. Okoye rolled his goatskin and departed. (7-8)

Part of what a reader notices in this exchange is its varied texture, which, even more than fifty years after *Things Fall Apart*'s first publication, seems natural, fresh, and distinctive. Throughout the novel Achebe introduces untranslated Igbo words and phrases, translated Igbo speech and idioms, and traditional Igbo oral art such as proverbs, folktales, and songs. These devices, some of which are on display in the conversation between Okoye and Unoka, have since helped shape the form of African literature (Gikandi, "Invention" xvii). Here and elsewhere in the novel, the Igbo language is rendered in a "cadenced,

proverb-laden style . . . rich in images drawn from traditional rural life"
(Riddy 151; see also Jones, on whom Riddy draws for this observation). Oyekan Owomoyela indicates that, indeed, "traditional African
discourse tends to rely to a considerable degree on proverbs," and also
suggests that the dignified cadence in which Achebe represents Igbo
speech in his early novels arises from his preference for relatively simple words derived from Anglo-Saxon (358-59). This method, too, is
evident in the exchange above.

On the most general level, however, the method of *Things Fall
Apart* is that of a modern novel that, along with Achebe's other early
novels, was created, as Simon Gikandi observes,

> in response to a set of modern texts, most notably Conrad's *Heart of Dark-
> ness*, in which African "barbarism" was represented as the opposite of the
> logic of modern civilization. Since he was educated within the tradition of
> European modernism, Achebe's goal was to use realism to make African
> cultures visible while using the ideology and techniques of modernism to
> counter the colonial novel [on] its own terrain. (Foreword xiv)

If Conrad's portrayal of African "barbarism" partly relied on distortions of African language, it also gained traction because of the common Western stereotypes of Africans as savage and violent. Marlow's
narration supports these stereotypes by indicating that some of the Africans of his novel are cannibals, having others shoot arrows from a
jungle bank (from which a deadly spear is also used), and implicating
some in "unspeakable rites" (albeit the European Mr. Kurtz plays an
authorizing role in the attack from the bank and the "rites") (50). To be
sure, Achebe counters these stereotypes in the form of the novel, but
the most effective particular tool that he employs is dialogue. This is
glimpsed in the exchange between Okoye and Unoka. Although the
former wants the loan repaid so that he might take the prestigious and
expensive Idemili title, he does not verbally, much less physically, as-
sault or coerce Unoka. He deploys mostly indirect verbal gestures and,

in response, so does Unoka. The loan is not repaid, but no threats are offered; the exchange itself seems to disperse potentially destructive forces, and Okoye leaves.

A thorough consideration of *Things Fall Apart* leads to this conclusion: far more time and effort are expended by Igbo society on peace-keeping than on violence, and the level of violence that is committed by the Umuofians and their neighbors pales in comparison to the level of peace they maintain. Certainly violence occurs—it is part of the success of the novel that Achebe does not overlook it or disguise its nature (though some may feel that he leans rather too far in the direction of candor in the matter). The story speaks of various acts of violence that occur over numerous years in the Igbo region in which the story is set: people there murder a woman, ritually kill a young man in compensation for that murder, abandon infant twins, murder a missionary, unmask an *egwugwu*, burn down a church, and (in the case of two different men) beat wives; Okonkwo himself beats two wives and a child, murders a colonial messenger, and commits suicide. There is also reference to "two inter-tribal wars" of an earlier period, in which "incredible prowess" was displayed by Okonkwo, who killed a total of five men as a warrior (8, 10). Yet a variety of restrictions are imposed on the use of violence, though the scope of this discussion precludes their full description. The killing of Ikemefuna, the young man who is given to Umuofia by Mbaino in the aftermath of the murder of the Umuofian woman, appears to be part of a compensation for the spilling of innocent blood. This compensation, which is the outcome of a verbal exchange between the two towns, circumvents a war that would have occasioned a far higher level of bloodshed. In fact, though Umuofia is skilled in warfare and feared by all the surrounding towns, it observes a strict code designed to avoid war: "It never went to war unless its case was clear and just and was accepted as such by its oracle. . . . Their dreaded *agadi-nwayi* would never fight what the Ibo call *a fight of blame*" (12; emphasis in original). Okonkwo's impulsive violence, which causes his demise, is repeatedly condemned by leaders of Umuofia. The penultimate case of that violence, his sudden beheading of the District Commissioner's messenger, is partly a call to revolt against British-led abuses against Umuofia, but no Umuofian supports him.

The words of Umuofians are in fact the vehicle by which Achebe answers the claims by European writers that Africans are physically savage and verbally undeveloped. The words that encourage peace, that stem violence, occur in some form of dialogue. Though from the beginning of the novel Achebe's narrator connects Okonkwo's violent temper to a failure of language—"And he did pounce on people quite often. He had a slight stammer and whenever he was angry and could not get his words out quickly enough, he would use his fists" (4)—even Okonkwo finds that when no work is at hand, "talking was the next best" (69). Two other instances of dialogue cultivating peace are significant. One occurs at the *egwugwu* ceremony, in which village leaders wearing ancestral masks adjudicate disputes. The one to which the novel gives full attention is that between Mgbafo and her husband, Uzowulu, who beats her. Mgbafo has run away from her marriage to live with her brothers, and Uzowulu wants the brothers to return either his wife or the bride-price he gave to their family. A remark that underscores both the value placed on dialogue and the connection between dialogue and peacekeeping is made by the *egwugwu* leader when Uzowulu concludes his testimony: "'Your words are good. . . . Let us hear Odukwe [Mgbafo's brother]. His words may also be good'" (90). But while Achebe's Umuofians cultivate dialogue and peace, they are not idyllically peaceful in word or deed; analogous to the demands that Umuofia makes of Abame to avoid war, Odukwe proposes that Uzowulu resolve the standoff verbally but also threatens violence if Uzowulu resumes his beating of Mgbafo (which is called "madness"): "'If. . . . Uzowulu should recover from his madness and . . . beg his wife to return she will do so on the understanding that if he ever beats her again we shall cut off his genitals for him'" (92). Nevertheless, for the moment, peace prevails and words facilitate it: the *egwugwu* decree that Uzowulu, in addition to bringing his brother-in-laws wine, must speak to Mgbafo, must "'beg your wife to return to you. It is not bravery when a man fights with a woman'" (93).

The arrival of Christian missionaries and British colonial administrators to the region shakes Umuofia to its foundation, but the first British missionary to live among Umuofians, Mr. Brown, is explicitly a conversationalist and tolerant toward non-Christians. Through an interpreter, he holds long talks about religion with Akunna, one of the "great men" and a nonconvert (179). In the view of Russian theorist Mikhail Bakhtin, true dialogue allows for the productive interactions of different cultures. Although it must be conceded that Bakhtin is probably not considering so great a difference in power orders as that between colonizer and colonized, he finds that in "a dialogic encounter of two cultures . . . [the two] are mutually enriched" (qtd. in Morson and Emerson 56). In this vein, Achebe's narrator indicates that, while neither Akunna nor Mr. Brown "succeeded in converting the other . . . they learned more about their different beliefs" (179). More to the point, during Mr. Brown's tenure Umuofia enjoys peace between members of the traditional religion and Christian converts. Brown's successor, on the other hand, Mr. Smith, far from engaging in dialogue, takes a Manichaean approach to the encounter between the traditional and newly arrived religions of Umuofia: "He saw things as black and white. And black was evil. He saw the world as a battlefield in which the children of light were locked in mortal conflict with the sons of darkness" (184). It is precisely this approach that discourages conversation and accommodation and that leads to religious outrages against both groups: the unmasking of an *egwugwu* and the burning of the local church. The latter incurs the violent intervention of the District Commissioner.

Yet greater violence occurs earlier in the novel, with the arrival of the first missionary in the region, and, in this case, too, the outburst is associated with an absence of a common language. A lost missionary encounters some people of Abame who have never seen a European, who do not understand him, and who come to fear the European onslaught that he portends. They murder him, and some weeks later the town of Abame is virtually wiped out by a savage British reprisal. The incident is based on a similar one that occurred in 1905 when British forces massacred the people of Ahiara as retribution for the death of a missionary. What may be noted here is that the missionary does try to communicate with the people he encounters in Abame, but he is not understood; rather, they take him to represent a serious threat: "Their Oracle . . . told them that the strange man would break their clan and spread destruction among them" (138). Not all speech succeeds in bridging the gap between cultures or holding off an overwhelming force. In this case, the failure of communication is shared, and the death of the missionary is the responsibility of the people of Abame, while the massacre that follows represents a level of violence not seen elsewhere in the novel.

One form of speech in *Things Fall Apart* actually encourages violence, a form that parodies dialogue: the language of deceit. It appears in a cautionary and etiological folktale (narrated by Okonkwo's second wife, Ekwefi, to her daughter, Ezinma) about the "eloquent" Tortoise, who beguiles the initially suspicious birds into helping him appropriate most of a feast that was meant for them. Finding that they have been deceived by Tortoise's "sweet tongue," the birds reclaim the feathers they had given him, and Tortoise falls to the earth, cracking his shell when he crashes against the hard things that cover his compound (96-99). With false words Tortoise disarms the birds, then betrays them, and this pattern arises again toward the end of the novel when the District Commissioner sends "his sweet-tongued messenger" to invite Okonkwo and the other leaders of Umuofia to a peaceful dialogue (a "palaver") (193). When he "receive[s] them politely" they literally disarm (193). But all the fair words have been part of the trap he sets for the men, and, shortly after they are handcuffed, the proposed dialogue turns into the Commissioner's monologue of condescension and coercion: "We shall not do you any harm . . . if only you agree to cooperate with us. We have brought a peaceful administration to you and your people so that you may be happy" (194). Monologue, then, is the speech of violence, which is further confirmed when the Commissioner's aids treat the leaders brutally after he leaves (194-95). This is the treachery that is a catalyst for Okonkwo's murder of one of the Commissioner's officers—perhaps, indeed, the one possessing the "sweet tongue" (204).

In an article commemorating the fiftieth anniversary of the publication of *Things Fall Apart*, Hillel Italie refers to it as "a triumph of contradictions." Though Italie does not mention it, one of the contradictions, or at any rate one of the paradoxes, of the novel is that, while it deploys an array of devices and creative brilliance to validate African language and culture, it is nevertheless a novel written in English. Not long after *Things Fall Apart* was first published, an important and extensive debate, in which Achebe has occasionally participated, began over whether a literary work can be legitimately African if it is written in a colonial language. Though the present essay does not fully explore this debate, it may be suggested that what Achebe asserted long ago about the usefulness of writing in such a language in the postcolonial context still merits consideration. In one essay, for example, "The African Writer and the English Language," he affirms the value that English has in reaching a wide audience in Nigeria, in which a large number of African languages are spoken yet in which none has as widespread currency as English. He observes that, for the same reason, a colonial language is useful for communicating beyond a nation's boundaries: "The only reason why we can even talk about African unity is that when we get together we can have a manageable number of languages to talk in—English, French, Arabic" (95). What does seem fair to say is that *Things Fall Apart* is a masterful novel that has reached a very large audience in Nigeria, Africa, and the world and that in the process has influenced generations of other African writers. Although in the view of many *Things Fall Apart* and other fictional works by Achebe fall short because they do not enrich or sufficiently validate an African language, his intention has been to mount an "adequate" response to distorted portrayals of African language and society, to devise a literary method for conveying that response, and to celebrate the dignity of African people and their cultures. In these endeavors he has been more than successful.

Works Cited

Achebe, Chinua. "The African Writer and the English Language." *Morning Yet on Creation Day*. New York: Doubleday, 1975. 91-103.

_____. *Arrow of God*. 1964. New York: Doubleday, 1974.

_____. "Colonialist Criticism." *Hopes and Impediments: Selected Essays*. New York: Doubleday, 1989. 68-90.

_____. "An Image of Africa: Racism in Conrad's *Heart of Darkness*." *Hopes and Impediments: Selected Essays*. New York: Doubleday, 1989. 1-20.

_____. Interview by Lewis Nkosi. *African Writers Talking*. Ed. Dennis Duerden and Cosmo Pieterse. Portsmouth, NH: Heinemann, 1972. 1-5.

_____. "Named for Victoria, Queen of England." *Hopes and Impediments: Selected Essays*. New York: Doubleday, 1989. 30-39.

_____. *No Longer at Ease*. 1960. New York: Doubleday, 1994.

_____. "The Novelist as Teacher." *Morning Yet on Creation Day*. New York: Doubleday, 1975. 67-73.

_____. *Things Fall Apart*. 1958. New York: Doubleday, 1994.

Cary, Joyce. *Mister Johnson*. 1939. New York: New Directions, 1991.

Conrad, Joseph. *Heart of Darkness*. 1899. Ed. Robert Kimbrough. 3rd Norton Critical ed. New York: W. W. Norton, 1988.

Ezenwa-Ohaeto. *Chinua Achebe: A Biography*. Bloomington: Indiana UP, 1997.

Gikandi, Simon. "Chinua Achebe and the Invention of African Literature." *Things Fall Apart*. By Chinua Achebe. 1958. Portsmouth, NH: Heinemann, 1996. ix-xvii.

_____. Foreword. *The Chinua Achebe Encyclopedia*. Ed. M. Keith Booker. Westport, CT: Greenwood Press, 2003. vii-xii.

_____. *Reading Chinua Achebe: Language and Ideology in Fiction*. Portsmouth, NH: Heinemann, 1991.

Haggard, H. Rider. *King Solomon's Mines*. 1885. Ed. Benjamin Ivry. New York: Barnes & Noble, 2004.

Irele, Francis Abiola, ed. *The Norton Anthology of World Literature*. 2nd ed. Vol. F. New York: W. W. Norton, 2002.

Italie, Hillel. "After 50 Years: 'Things Fall Apart' by Chinua Achebe Is Hailed as Uniquely Influential." *The Reading Eagle*. Associated Press. 2 Mar. 2008. 14 Jan. 2010. http://readingeagle.com/article.aspx?id=8237.

Jones, Eldred. "Achebe's Third Novel." *Journal of Commonwealth Literature* 1 (1965): 176-78.

_____. "Language and Theme in *Things Fall Apart*." *A Review of English Literature* 5.4 (1964): 39-43.

Morson, Gary Saul, and Caryl Emerson. *Mikhail Bakhtin: Creation of a Prosaics*. Stanford, CA: Stanford UP, 1990.

Owomoyela, Oyekan. "The Question of Language in African Literature." *A History of Twentieth-Century African Literatures*. Ed. Oyekan Owomoyela. Lincoln: U of Nebraska P, 1993. 347-68.

Peters, Jonathan A. "English-Language Fiction from West Africa." *A History of Twentieth-Century African Literatures*. Ed. Oyekan Owomoyela. Lincoln: U of Nebraska P, 1993. 9-48.

Riddy, Felicity. "Language as a Theme in *No Longer at Ease*." *Critical Perspectives on Chinua Achebe*. Ed. C. L. Innes and Bernth Lindfors. Washington, DC: Three Continents Press, 1978. 150-59.

Wise, Christopher. "An Image of Africa: Racism in Conrad's *Heart of Darkness*." *The Chinua Achebe Encyclopedia*. Ed. M. Keith Booker. Westport, CT: Greenwood Press, 2003. 115-16.

"You Must Not Stand in One Place":
Reading *Things Fall Apart* in Multiple Contexts_____

Matthew J. Bolton

> The Igbo people say, If you want to see it well, you must not stand in one place. . . . this is the way I think the world's stories should be told—from many different perspectives.
>
> —Chinua Achebe, interviewed in *The Paris Review* (18)

Few American readers of Chinua Achebe's *Things Fall Apart* will first encounter the novel in the context of studying Nigerian literature and history. Instead, students will be assigned the novel in high school survey courses, college world literature courses, or graduate studies of postcolonial literature. Others will read it on their own initiative, taking it up at a friend's recommendation or choosing it at random from a library or bookstore shelf. For all of these readers, Achebe's novel will be encountered in a very different context from the one out of which it emerged. Perhaps this is fitting. After all, Achebe wrote in English rather than Igbo and wrote as much for a European or American audience as for a Nigerian or African one. As an English-language novel about the Igbo people and an African story cast into a European literary form, *Things Fall Apart* belongs to several cultures at once. It is a quintessential example of world literature; in fact, the novel is included in its entirety in *The Norton Anthology of World Masterpieces*. Yet at the same time, *Things Fall Apart* has a profound autonomy: it carries with it its own historical and cultural context, such that a reader need know little about Nigerian culture and European colonialism to understand and appreciate Achebe's novel.

Things Fall Apart therefore raises a series of questions not only about *what* we choose to read but also about *how* we choose to read. How should readers draw connections between *Things Fall Apart* and the other books that are important to them? Should the novel be read in relation to the English and American literary traditions, or does it somehow stand apart from them? If we instead consider it to be an example of world literature, with what texts, cultures, and languages are we putting it in dialogue? Such questions are particularly pressing for teachers who hope to incorporate *Things Fall Apart* into their courses. If students benefit from making comparisons across texts, then teachers must find ways to select and group books that will lend themselves to such comparisons. This means viewing literature through several different lenses, identifying commonalities of theme, form, or voice that allow for meaningful comparisons across cultures. To explore this mode of comparative literature, one might read *Things Fall Apart* in relation to works from several different times and cultures. Achebe has written that his own book is a corrective to English novelists' negative representations of African people; he singled out Joyce Cary's *Mister Johnson* and Joseph Conrad's *Heart of Darkness* as the two works he most explicitly wrote against ("An Image of Africa" 38; "Art of Fiction" 11). The relationship between *Things Fall Apart* and the Victorian or early twentieth-century novel has been well documented, but the novel's relationship to several other bodies of literature has been less studied. One might move beyond the easy comparison with Conrad by recontextualizing *Things Fall Apart* within the conventions and canons of three very different literary traditions: the Homeric epic, modernist poetry, and African American literature. Such an exercise not only allows one to develop a model for how to read world literature but also demonstrates the tremendous power and scope of Achebe's novel. As a modern classic, *Things Fall Apart* gains in force by being compared with other great works of literature.

Before comparing *Things Fall Apart* to other texts and periods, it is worth giving some thought to the dynamics of reading world literature itself. Doing so allows one to develop a theoretical framework for how to read works from other cultures. In his book *What Is World Literature?* David Damrosch offers a compelling definition of the field. He suggests that the term should refer not to "an infinite, ungraspable canon of works but rather . . . [to] a mode of circulation and reading"

(5). Damrosch's definition is a pragmatic and functional one: "I take world literature to encompass all literary works that circulate beyond their culture of origin, either in translation or in the original language" (4). This definition is broad enough to admit any text one reads that originates in a culture other than one's own. If *Things Fall Apart* originates in Igbo culture, and a particular reader is not Igbo, then the book becomes for that reader an example of world literature. Damrosch's formulation locates world literature not in a particular reading list or canon of texts but rather in a set of readerly practices. Such a formulation is useful in reading *Things Fall Apart*, for it calls on the novel's audience to acknowledge the transactional nature of reading a book from another culture. It is not so much the book itself that is an example of world literature but rather the relationship between the book and its reader.

One therefore should not take a reductive, checklist-oriented approach to literature, reading *Things Fall Apart*, for example, as being a singular representative of Africa, Nigeria, or the Igbo people. To do so is to diminish the power and relevance of the book, to somehow cordon it off from the other works one has read. The great work of literature is not a snapshot of the culture in which it was written but a reaching beyond that culture. In fact, readers themselves participate in this cross-cultural process by taking up a book that originated in a culture very different from their own. *Things Fall Apart* may be representative of a particular culture, but it also enters into dialogue with everything else a reader has encountered. In this way, literature spills beyond borders and across periods. Wai Chee Dimock, in her article "Literature for the Planet," proposes that literature "holds out a different map, a different scale, predating and outlasting the birth and death of any nation" (175). One must recognize literature's difference by treating it not as a gloss to history but as an alternative to history. A great book is not a static representation of the cultural norms of a place, time, and language but a challenge to those norms.

One more theoretical formulation may be of use in comparing

Things Fall Apart to works of other periods. In his 1919 essay "Tradition and the Individual Talent," T. S. Eliot proposed a model for how great literature works:

> What happens when a new work of art is created is something that happens simultaneously to all the works of art which preceded it. The existing monuments form an ideal order among themselves, which is modified by the introduction of the new (the really new) work of art among them. (5)

Most readers understand the first part of this formulation: they think of literature as a series of "existing monuments." This is the logic behind the canon, that theoretical shelf of great books. Canon building is grounded in the idea that readers should work their way through what Victorian poet and critic Matthew Arnold called "the best that has been thought and said." More challenging, however, is the concept that an author who creates a "really new work of art" changes everything that has come before it. Eliot's model rejects the idea of a static body of great books. Instead, reading and writing are dynamic processes. A great author's engagement with the existing order can produce a text that forever modifies that order. Virgil changes how we read Homer, Dante changes how we read Virgil, Eliot changes how we read Dante, and Achebe changes how we read Eliot. Eliot's model licenses the reader to draw connections between and among any and all of the books he or she has read. Dimock's "different map" and Eliot's "ideal order" give precedence to the reader's consciousness as an organizing principle. Eliot's argument makes it valid to compare books simply on the basis of one's having read them.

Eliot's model of an "ideal order" is particularly applicable to reading world literature and postcolonial authors. If a reader is alive to the process by which writers transform and appropriate existing forms, he or she is in a better position to understand the hybrid nature of literature emerging from a postcolonial context. In *Things Fall Apart*, Achebe melds elements of Greek tragedy, the Western bildungsroman, modernist sensibilities, and the traditions of Igbo culture. The clash between traditional Nigerian culture and English colonialism animates not merely its theme and plot but the actual structure and language of the novel. *Things Fall Apart* is therefore not wholly representative of either African or English culture; instead, it constitutes a *tertium quid*, an act of cultural synthesis that exists in the text rather than in the world. As a great work of literature, *Things Fall Apart* possesses a culture distinct unto itself.

One might locate Achebe's novel among the "existing monuments" of literature by reading it in light of Homer's great epics the *Iliad* and the *Odyssey*. Like Homer before him, Achebe gives written form to the long oral tradition that he has inherited. The novel is full of parables, idioms, and proverbs culled from the Igbo oral culture. Like the Homeric epics, *Things Fall Apart* sets out to record and present the history and culture of a people. Achebe is writing not about his contemporaries but about his ancestors, and like Homer he must construct a language that will evoke this bygone age. Homer's epic verse was an act of synthesis, a borrowing from different Greek dialects and regions to create a new literary form of the language. Robert Fagles explains Homer's language this way: "It is not a language that anyone ever spoke. It is an artificial poetic language—as the German scholar Witte puts it 'The language of the Homeric poems is an invention of epic verse'" (12). Homer created a new form of the Greek language that would both allow him a full range of expression and accommodate itself to the dictates of the hexameters in which he wrote.

Achebe faces a challenge of a different caliber: he is attempting to tell the story of the Igbo people in the language of their colonizers. There were some risks inherent to this choice, for Achebe's use of English language might itself have "colonized" Igbo culture, remaking it according to its own set of implicit values. Achebe comes up with a powerful solution: he writes in a clear, elegantly understated English that is studded with Igbo words, phrases, and proverbs. His general approach is to use Igbo words for anything that has no ready equivalent in

English culture and the English language. Take Achebe's representation of traditional African religion as an example. Chielo is referred to as a "priestess," a word that accurately conveys her role in the village. The god she consults is called an "oracle"—again, a familiar concept. But English has no word for a religious ritual in which villagers don masks representing their ancestors. These masked men are therefore referred to as the *egwugwu*. The Igbo term represents a whole set of concepts and traditions that would be lost or warped were Achebe to reach for an English description of this role. *Things Fall Apart* and its glossary of Igbo words therefore serves as a primer of Igbo culture: Achebe records and preserves words and proverbs that are specific to his ancestral tribe and for which English proves inadequate.

Homer's epic and Achebe's novel not only set down in written form some of the essential elements of their respective cultures but also proved powerful forces in shaping those cultures. Great literature serves as what cultural anthropologist Pierre Bourdieu calls a *habitas*, or "structuring structure." Literature is not merely the product of a particular culture but also a producer of that culture. In writing the novel, Achebe drew on oral culture and history, but in publishing it, he disseminated this culture. President Barack Obama, in his 1995 memoir *Dreams from My Father*, recalls traveling through Kenya with a well-educated cousin, Sayid, who had a habit of quoting proverbs. "When two locusts fight, it is always the crow who feasts," Sayid says at one point (382). Obama is taken with the proverb, and inquires about its origins:

> "Is that a Luo expression?" I asked. Sayid's face broke into a bashful smile.
> "We have similar expressions in Luo," he said, "but actually I must admit that I read this particular expression in a book by Chinua Achebe. The Nigerian writer. I like his books very much. He speaks the truth about Africa's predicament. The Nigerian, the Kenyan—it is the same. We share more than divides us." (382)

Things Fall Apart, along with Achebe's other work, has helped give Africa back some of the cultural and linguistic heritage that colonialism stripped from it. This process illustrates why literature is more than a passive reflection of a given culture's norms or of a given point in history. As William Faulkner argued in his Nobel Prize acceptance speech, "The poet's voice need not merely be the record of man, it can be one of the props, the pillars to help him endure and prevail" (650). Achebe's novel serves as one of these pillars for the Igbo people, Nigeria, and Africa itself.

Like Homer, Achebe writes a story that centers on a great warrior and a great man: Okonkwo. He is a man whose bellicose sensibilities might make him feel at home on the fields of Troy, fighting alongside Homer's Greek heroes. He is reminiscent of Achilles, another proud and brooding warrior, or of Ajax, slow of speech and quick to anger. Like Agamemnon, he sacrifices his child to the gods for what he thinks is the good of his people. And, like Odysseus, he will be forced into exile, returning to his native land years later to find that strangers have usurped his place and broken his family. Yet because Achebe is in a position to read the whole scope of Greek literature, from Homer's epics to the plays of Sophocles, Euripides, and their contemporaries, his novel is infused with a tragic sensibility that had not yet been developed in Homer's own time. The great Athenian dramatists of the fifth century transmuted the materials of Homer's epics into something more austere and rigorous. Achebe draws on the work of both eras, and as such creates a novel that has the range of the epic but the intensity and pathos of a tragedy.

In the *Odyssey*, Odysseus is able to rout the suitors from his house and restore order: everything that has fallen apart in his absence can be put back together again. This kind of victory simply isn't available to Okonkwo, for the legal and military force behind the English colonization of Nigeria was too overwhelming for any man, no matter how great a warrior he may be, to overcome. Okonkwo cannot prevail against the Christians and the District Commissioner's men, and his tragic defeat stands in sharp contrast to the triumphant conclusion of the *Odyssey*. Like Oedipus and other tragic heroes of the Athenian playwrights, Okonkwo is a flawed man. Yet he is destroyed not so much by these flaws as by broad and impersonal forces of history. He has the misfortune to subscribe wholeheartedly to Igbo culture at a time when this culture was being dismantled and abandoned. And whereas the death of a Greek tragic hero serves to restore social order and to write large the values that were central to the Greek people, Okonkwo's death has no such resonance. In taking his own life, Okonkwo breaks one of his own tribe's taboos and will be buried not by his friends but by the District Commissioner's men. In his prime, Okonkwo embodied the ideals of Ibo culture, and his death serves not to restore the values of his culture but to hasten their demise.

Achebe's sense of history is therefore fundamentally different from that of the Greek writers of the eighth or fourth centuries. For Homer as for the tragedians, the stories of Agamemnon, Achilles, and their contemporaries reside in a timeless, anterior past that is largely disconnected from the present day in which they wrote. There is no attempt to draw a direct historical connection between these figures from the Age of Heroes and the present. Writing in the middle of the twentieth century, Achebe has a very different understanding of historical processes. The story of Okonkwo—and by extension the story of European colonialism in Africa—is one that has far-reaching effects that can be traced to Achebe's own time. Stories of traditional Ibo life cannot exist in isolation, as did Greek stories of the Olympian gods or of the heroes of the Trojan War. When Achebe writes of Ibo culture, he always sees it in flux, changing across time and under the pressure of European colonialism.

This modern sense of history informs Eliot's contention that literature consists of an "ideal order . . . which is modified by the introduction of the new (the really new) work of art among them." Literature, like history, consists of long chains of causation, influence, and association. According to Eliot's formulation, Achebe's novel can therefore change the way we read Homer's epics. Classical Greek literature was a powerful influence on Achebe, but in writing his book he in turn exerts a power over this body of literature. *Things Fall Apart* might prompt one to reconsider some of the assumptions on which Homer's epics and the epic tradition are grounded. Take, for example, Odysseus's account of his voyages in books 9-12 of the *Odyssey*. Beaching his ships on a little island just offshore of the larger island of the Cyclops, Odysseus describes both the islands and the Cyclops' lack of culture and technology:

> No flocks browse, no plowlands roll with wheat;
> Unplowed, unsown forever—empty of humankind—
> The island feeds just droves of bleating goats.
> For the Cyclops have no ships with crimson prows
> No shipwrights there to build them good trim craft
> That could sail them out to foreign ports of call
> As most men risk the seas to trade with other men.
> Such artisans would have made this island too
> A decent place to live in . . . no mean spot,
> It could bear you any crop you like in season . . .
> The land's clear for plowing. Harvest on harvest,
> A man could reap a healthy stand of grain—
> The subsoil's dark and rich.
>
> (9.135-147)

Here, some two thousand years before the English colonization of Africa, Odysseus gives voice to the colonial impulse and logic that would justify one people seizing the land and resources of another. Odysseus looks at the island and sees not what is present but what is absent. With a string of negating words and prefixes, he identifies what the Cyclops and their land have failed to produce: "*no* flocks . . . *no* plowlands . . . *un*plowed, *un*sown . . . the Cyclops have *no* ships . . . *no* shipwrights." He has a similar attitude toward the culture that has failed to produce ships, agriculture, and the other developments that Odysseus and Homer consider the markers of civilization. The Cyclops are "lawless brutes" who have "no meeting place for council, no laws either" (9.120, 127). Odysseus looks on this land and its people with the acquisitive gaze of the colonist, seeing about him resources that have not been put to their proper use. His logic seems to be that since the Cyclops are not properly taking advantage of their land and do not know how to govern themselves, someone else should to it for them. Keep in mind that Odysseus is telling his tale in the palace of the Phaecians, a seagoing people. His description of the Cyclops' island soon becomes speculative and promissory: "It could bear you any crop you like in season." Odysseus is only the first in a long line of explorers returning to Europe with stories of the riches available to those willing to venture to other lands.

So while it is valid and important to read Okonkwo as an inheritor of the epic mantle of Achilles and Odysseus, we should also see his story as a meditation on the colonial impulse that prompts Odysseus to explore one strange island after another. Okonkwo may have as much in common with Polyphemus the Cyclops as he does with Odysseus the colonialist. A teacher or student writing about or studying both texts might use Odysseus's encounter with the Cyclops as a point of entry into *Things Fall Apart*. If the *Odyssey* is the first book in Western culture, it is telling—and perhaps damning—that it already contains within it the logical fallacy by which the Europeans would justify the colonization of Africa.

Achebe's interest in Greek literature is not surprising given his relationship to the post-World War I literary movement known as modernism. Pound, Joyce, Eliot, Yeats, and other modernists were all preoccupied with the classics. After all, the seminal novel of the movement—and perhaps of the century—is Joyce's *Ulysses*, which borrows its structure from Homer's *Odyssey*. Pound's cycle of poems *The Cantos* owes a similar debt to Homer, while Eliot's *The Waste Land* is studded with classical references and epigraphs. Despite the appellation given them, the modernists were fascinated with history—and with literary history in particular. In choosing a title and epigraph for his novel, Achebe allies himself with the modernist project and invites comparisons with Yeats, Eliot, and the other writers of the generation that preceded him.

The title *Things Fall Apart* is taken from William Butler Yeats's poem "The Second Coming." Achebe uses the first four lines of the poem as an epigraph:

> Turning and turning in the widening gyre
> The falcon cannot hear the falconer;
> Things fall apart; the center cannot hold;
> Mere anarchy is loosed upon the world.
>
> (1-4)

Yeats's stanza encapsulates the process by which the Igbo culture is destroyed. It has an apocalyptic weight and heft to it, framing Achebe's story in Yeats's concept of history as a series of brutal cataclysms. Yeats saw the two-thousand-year reign of Christianity as coming to an end, and his narrator ponders, at the conclusion of "The Second Coming," "what rough beast, its hour come round at last/ slouches towards Bethlehem to be born" (21-22). Achebe's title therefore seems to equate the destruction of the Igbo way of life with Yeats's speculations about the end of Christian Europe. This is a fascinating act of appropriation, for Achebe's epigraph not only borrows from Yeats's poem but also comments on it. If the narrator of "The Second Coming" really wants to know what the collapse of his civilization will look like, he need only ask a Nigerian. The Igbo people have already lived through the sort of historic and cultural cataclysm that Yeats's narrator can only imagine.

Nor is *Things Fall Apart* the only title Achebe will draw from the modernist canon. His next novel, *No Longer at Ease*, takes its title from Eliot's poem "Journey of the Magi," in which the kings who visited the infant Jesus return to their native lands only to find themselves estranged from the cultures that were once their own. Achebe's use of modernist titles and epigraphs serve several purposes. With *Things Fall Apart*, his first novel, the choice of title may have been a strategy for establishing his own work's relevance to European and American audiences. By taking his title and epigraph from Yeats, Achebe insists that his novel be read in the context of the Western canon and of the modernist tradition. This may be a novel about Africa, the title seems to imply, but it is also a part of English literature. By invoking Yeats, Achebe creates for himself a place in the English canon and lays claim to his own inheritance as an English writer.

Like so many of the modernists of the generation before him, Achebe is concerned with the relationship between history and the present day. Toward the end of T. S. Eliot's *The Waste Land*, a voice declares, "These fragments I have shored against my ruins" (431). The line suggests that all of the quotations and references that have preceded it represent a process of salvage and salvation. Eliot attempts to construct a new historical and cultural context for his work and for that of his contemporaries out of the ruins of the past. Achebe, too, is involved with an Eliotic process of shoring fragments against his ruins. These fragments are found not in the Western canon, as Eliot's were, but in the threatened oral culture of the Igbo people. In *Things Fall Apart*, he gathers the words, proverbs, fables, songs, concepts, and traditions that were essential parts of Igbo culture. His novel preserves and reorders these fading elements of traditional life, creating a new structure that will save them from ruin. Like *The Waste Land*, *Things Fall Apart* serves as Bourdieu's *habitas*: it not only reflects the culture of its author but also serves as a force for reshaping and transmitting this culture. Obama's anecdote certainly illustrates the degree to which Achebe's writing has become a touchstone in African culture. Achebe's interest in using literature to reorder the fragmented histories and cultures available to him allies the novelist with Eliot and his contemporaries. If the modernist literature of the 1920s was born in part out of the trenches of World War I, Achebe's own strand of late modernism is born out of the ruptures and fissures that the legacy of English colonialism left on his native Nigeria.

Yet modernism itself owes a significant debt to African culture, and Achebe's invocation of modernist poetry in his titles and epigraphs represents a movement coming full circle. In his essay "An Image of Africa," Achebe, like many art historians before him, cites Gauguin, Matisse, and Picasso's interest in African masks as one of the catalysts of modernism. Gauguin's turn-of-the-century trip to Tahiti and his subsequent interest in African art "marked the beginning of cubism and the infusion of new life into European art that had run completely out of strength" (16). The relationship between African and European art is therefore a reciprocal one: Achebe may be influenced by modernism, but modernism in turn is indebted to traditional African art and culture.

The purpose of reading *Things Fall Apart* in the classical and modernist traditions is not to permanently embed the novel within these canons of texts and authors but rather to demonstrate that a great work of art has significance in multiple, shifting contexts. If literature, as Dimock puts it, "holds out a different map" than does history or geopolitics, then one may use literature to draw connections between disparate times, places, and cultures (175). In *Things Fall Apart*, Achebe has created a work that documents both traditional Igbo culture and the disintegration of that culture under colonial rule. As such, the novel has a fascinating relationship with African American literature, for it views the African Diaspora from the vantage point of those who stayed behind rather than those who were enslaved and sent to America. The slave trade has a distinct, if muted, presence in *Things Fall Apart* that links the novel explicitly to the African American experience. Moreover, in the District Commissioner's and Mr. Smith's attitudes toward and treatment of the Igbo people one sees at work the same logic that justified slavery in America and other parts of the world.

Visiting Okonkwo in his exile, Obierika brings his friend news of the white men who have begun to visit villages in the areas. Obierika tells of how one village killed the first white man to visit it and in reprisal was massacred by a group of white soldiers. He says: "I am greatly afraid. We have heard stories about white men who made the powerful guns and the strong drinks and took slaves away across the seas, but no one thought the stories were true" (141). Okonkwo's uncle, Uchendu, replies: "There is no story that is not true" (141). News of the slave trade has already reached the Igbo people, but the institution has not yet directly affected them. Okonwko and his contemporaries will face not enslavement and forced deportation but colonialism and subjugation at home. Yet Obierika's glancing reference to the slave trade reminds the reader that the enslaved African American people who worked the fields of Virginia and Mississippi—or, for that matter, worked the fields of New York and Massachusetts generations before—emerged from cultures like that of the Igbo. *Things Fall Apart* has a direct relevance to the African American experience because it offers a glimpse into the culture and language that was lost or transformed beyond recognition in the Diaspora.

Many African American authors, particularly in recent years, have explored the period of history when African identity gave way to African American identity. In her 2008 novel *A Mercy*, Toni Morrison sets some scenes in Africa itself, where one of her protagonists is first sold into slavery. In doing so, Morrison widens the scope of her own treatment of African American history and culture, making an explicit connection between the culture of colonial and postcolonial America and that of Africa itself. *A Mercy* helps to locate other of Morrison's characters, such as Sethe in *Beloved*, in the larger context of the African Diaspora. August Wilson, in his play *The Gem of the Ocean*, likewise focuses on the generations that lived both in Africa and in America—those who witnessed one culture fall apart while another emerged to take its place. The play culminates with its twentieth-century protagonist having a vision of himself as being transported on a slave ship. Because Wilson wrote his ten "century plays," each of which focuses on a different decade of the twentieth century, out of sequence, *The Gem of the Ocean* is one of the final plays he wrote but is set in the first decade of the century. The direct connection to African culture is a topic that Wilson drew closer toward as he continued to explore the course of the twentieth century as manifested in African American life.

Achebe's *Things Fall Apart* therefore serves as an important touchstone for writers and students not only of African literature but also of African American literature. In addition to re-creating life in a traditional African village, and hence showing the sort of culture out of which the enslaved African people were taken, in its portrayal of the District Commissioner it writes large the logic of enslavement and subjugation. When Okonkwo and his men accept the District Commissioner's invitation to parley, they are set upon and handcuffed. For three days, the men are kept imprisoned. Mocked and beaten by their jailors, the warriors emerge humiliated, their fighting spirit broken. In ordering Okonkwo and his men to be shackled, the District Commissioner makes clear the connection between colonial rule in Africa and the slave system in America. For three days and nights, Okonkwo and his men suffer a kind of bondage that links them to their fellow Africans who were sold into slavery.

In a 1994 interview with *The Paris Review*, Chinua Achebe reflected on his work as an author by quoting a traditional proverb: "The Igbo people say, If you want to see it well, you must not stand in one place. . . . this is the way I think the world's stories should be told—from many different perspectives" (18). One might *read* the world's stories in this way, too, looking at a single story or novel from multiple perspectives. Relocating *Things Fall Apart* in a series of different literary contexts reminds one that reading is not a passive act but a transformative one. By drawing connections between works from different times and places, the reader expands his or her own sense of history and culture. Reading Achebe's novel allows one to bring the experience of the Igbo people—and by extension the larger forces of colonialism—into dialogue with everything else one has read. In this respect, literature can serve not just to record the flux of culture and history but also to reshape it.

Works Cited

Achebe, Chinua. "The Art of Fiction No. 139: Chinua Achebe." Interview by Jerome Brooks. *The Paris Review* 133 (Winter 1994): 142-66.

_____. "An Image of Africa: Racism in Conrad's *Heart of Darkness*." *Hopes and Impediments: Selected Essays*. New York: Doubleday, 1988. 1-20.

_____. *Things Fall Apart*. New York: Doubleday, 1959.

Bourdieu, Pierre. *Outline of a Theory of Practice*. New York: Cambridge UP, 1977.

Damrosch, David. *What Is World Literature?* Princeton, NJ: Princeton UP, 2003.

Dimock, Wai Chee. "Literature for the Planet." *PMLA* 116 (Jan. 2001): 173-88.

Eliot, T. S. "Tradition and the Individual Talent." *Selected Essays: 1917-1932*. New York: Harcourt, Brace, 1932. 5-19.

_____. *The Waste Land: The Complete Poems and Plays: 1909-1950*. New York: Harcourt, Brace & World, 1962.

Faulkner, William. "Address upon Receiving the Nobel Prize for Literature." *The Portable Faulkner*. Ed. Malcolm Cowley. New York: Penguin, 1946. 649-50.

Homer. *The Odyssey*. Trans. Robert Fagles. New York: Penguin Classics, 1996.

Joyce, James. *Ulysses*. New York: Vintage, 1986.

Mack, Maynard, ed. *The Norton Anthology of World Masterpieces*. 6th expanded ed. New York: W. W. Norton, 1997.

Morrison, Toni. *A Mercy*. New York: Alfred A. Knopf, 2008.

Obama, Barack. *Dreams from My Father*. New York: Three Rivers Press, 1995.

Wilson, August. *The Gem of the Ocean*. New York: Theater Communications Group, 2006.

Yeats, William Butler. "The Second Coming." *Selected Poems and Two Plays*. New York: Collier, 1962. 91.

CRITICAL READINGS

Things Fall Apart

Margaret Laurence

Achebe's first novel, *Things Fall Apart*, re-creates the first impact of European invasion upon the old Ibo society. Okonkwo is an important and respected man in Umuofia, in the days immediately prior to the European colonisation, that is, the late 1800's. He has been driven on to achievement by shame at his father's failure. His father, Unoka, was a gentle but irresponsible man who loved playing the flute but who could not succeed because he did not work hard enough and did not care enough about the values of his intensely competitive society, a society in which a livelihood was hard to get from the soil and the man of status was the man who had a flourishing yam crop. Unoka never took a title. Among the Ibo, to take a title—especially that of *ozo*—was a means of proving one's status within the community, for the title with its accompanying staff of office was bought at considerable expense from the closed group who already held titles. Although the Ibo did not have kings or chiefs, the establishment had worked out ways to perpetuate itself. Okonkwo has always tried twice as hard as most men, and has been renowned as a great wrestler. He has built his farm into a wealthy one, and has three wives and two titles. But he is a very severe man who cannot express his affection lest anyone think he is weak. His *chi* or personal god is said to be good—'But the Ibo people have a proverb that when a man says yes his *chi* says yes also.' Because of Okonkwo's determination he moulds his own fate—or for a time appears to.

The nine villages of Umuofia send Okonkwo as an emissary of war to a neighbouring village where an Umuofia woman has been killed. Okonkwo returns with two hostages, one a boy of fifteen, Ikemefuna, who is given by the elders into Okonkwo's care and goes to live in Okonkwo's compound. Okonkwo's son, Nwoye, becomes friends with the young stranger, and begins a relationship which will in the end change the whole course of Nwoye's life.

After Ikemefuna has been living in Okonkwo's compound for three years, the Oracle of the Hills and the Caves ordains the boy's death as a sacrifice to the gods. An elder advises Okonkwo to have nothing to do with the boy's death, because Ikemefuna calls Okonkwo 'father'. But when the village men reluctantly lead the boy along the forest path, Okonkwo is among them, and when the moment comes, Okonkwo is trapped by his own obsession, the need to appear absolutely strong. The death of Ikemefuna is one of the most moving passages in the novel. The boy has been told not that he is to be sacrificed but that he is being taken back home to his own village.

> 'Eze elina, elina!
> Sala
> Eze ilikwa ya
> Ikwaba akwa oligholi
> Ebe Danda nechi eze
> Ebe Uzuzu nete egwu
> Sala'

He sang it in his mind, and walked to its beat. If the song ended on his right foot, his mother was alive. If it ended on his left, she was dead. No, not dead, but ill. It ended on the right. She was alive and well. He sang the song again, and it ended on the left. But the second time did not count. The first voice gets to Chukwu, or God's house. That was a favourite saying of children. Ikemefuna felt like a child once more. It must be the thought of going home to his mother.

One of the men behind him cleared his throat. Ikemefuna looked back, and the man growled at him to go on and not stand looking back. The way he said it sent cold fear down Ikemefuna's back. His hands trembled vaguely on the black pot he carried. Why had Okonkwo withdrawn to the rear? Ikemefuna felt his legs melting under him. And he was afraid to look back.

As the man who had cleared his throat drew up and raised his matchet, Okonkwo looked away. He heard the blow. The pot fell and broke in the sand. He heard Ikemefuna cry, 'My father, they have killed me!' as he ran towards him. Dazed with fear, Okonkwo drew his matchet and cut him down. He was afraid of being thought weak.

Dazed with fear—in such a way can an appalling act take place. This may be the nature of many murders; it is certainly the nature of Okonkwo's. Okonkwo's tragedy is that he can never explain himself. There is never any human being who can understand his anguish over the death of Ikemefuna, and even if he might have lessened his pain by sharing it—with, for example, his close friend Obierika—Okonkwo's main flaw, the need to appear publicly strong and absolutely certain, prevents his ever bringing out his sorrow. His son Nwoye does not understand Okonkwo's motivations any more than Okonkwo understood those of Unoka, his father. Nwoye, in a tragic but inevitable pattern, becomes increasingly severed from Okonkwo and from his entire family. Obierika, Okonkwo's great friend, reproaches him for the death of Ikemefuna, but Okonkwo—needing to believe himself right, even against his own feelings, which he sternly casts aside—rejects the reproach and will not listen. Okonkwo is unable to accept the values of love and gentleness—he fears them too much, fears that they may weaken him in his own eyes and in the eyes of the community.

Yet Okonkwo is never presented as a man in whom warmth is lacking. The love and concern are there, but are held firmly suppressed. When Okonkwo's young daughter, Ezinma, becomes ill, he is so anxious and upset that he goes to the *obi* or hut of Ekwefi, the child's mother, and prepares medicine himself for the girl. Ezinma is feared to be an *ogbanje*, 'one of those wicked children who, when they died, entered their mothers' wombs to be born again'. This is comparable to the Yoruba *abiku*, the child born with death in its soul, and in a country in which infant mortality was so high, it is not surprising that this belief grew up—the children who died were always the same children, born again and again, fated to die again and again, eternal bringers of anguish to each new set of parents. Ezinma has survived to the age of ten, and Okonkwo and Ekwefi are beginning to hope she may mean to stay after all. When the child recovers from the illness, however, Okonkwo cannot show his emotion.

Ezeudu, one of the elders, dies—this was the same elder who warned Okonkwo not to have anything to do with Ikemefuna's death. At Ezeudu's funeral, Okonkwo's dane-gun goes off accidentally and kills the dead man's son. Because the killing of a clansman is a crime against the earth, Okonkwo is banished from Umuofia for seven years. The neighbours, including his friend Obierika, help him to pack during the night. But when dawn comes, they can no longer raise a hand to help him. They come back, like avenging furies compelled into this ritual destruction. They set fire to his houses and kill his animals, for they are 'cleansing the land which Okonkwo had polluted with the blood of a clansman'. They are acting correctly in their own eyes, and with every social sanction. Their feelings as individuals have become subservient to the group mystique. They are doing what is expected of them and what they expect of themselves.

Thus, through an accident, Okonkwo loses everything he has worked so hard to obtain. Yet—was it entirely an accident that the boy whom Okonkwo killed was the son of the elder whose warning to Okonkwo had once been fatally ignored? Achebe makes it possible to interpret Okonkwo's act in a variety of ways and to see his downfall as being at least partly caused by forces of destruction and fear within himself. Okonkwo, having moved to his mother's village, is in despair and feels that his *chi*—the god within—is to blame.

> His life had been ruled by a great passion—to become one of the lords of the clan. That had been his life-spring. And he had all but achieved it. Then everything had been broken. He had been cast out of his clan like a fish on to a dry, sandy beach, panting. Clearly his personal god or *chi* was not made for greater things. A man could not rise beyond the destiny of his *chi*. The saying of the elders was not true—that if a man said yes his *chi* also affirmed. Here was a man whose *chi* said nay despite his own affirmation.

But Okonkwo may misunderstand his own deepest nature. In suppressing any gentleness and any acknowledgement of love, may he not have done some violence to himself? Far from Okonkwo saying *yes* while his *chi* said *no*, it may have been that the god within wanted to affirm the values of human contact, while Okonkwo out of fear and out of anxiety about the community's appraisal of him, said his hidden *no*.

The whole question of the *chi* is one which comes into much of Achebe's writing, and perhaps it is worthwhile to try to see what the *chi* is. The Ibo have many gods, and the Supreme Being is Chukwu. Apart from the whole pantheon of gods, however, is the *chi*, which Margaret Green in *Ibo Village Affairs* (Frank Cass & Co., London, 1964) defines as 'the personal spirit which everyone has and which is in the nature both of a creating and a guardian spirit'. Some critics have described the *chi* as the 'Conscience' but this word—essentially Christian—does not seem very accurate. The term *chi* appears to be closer to a concept of the unconscious mind or perhaps to the Ijaw idea of the *teme*, the steersman of the soul, the deepest inner nature, the part of the human spirit that decides a man's fate before his birth. But where John Pepper Clark's Ijaw characters fulfil their violent destinies in ways which remain mysterious to themselves, and where Wole Soyinka's Yoruba characters are sometimes compelled to act in dark ways which may go contrary to their conscious desires, Achebe seems to be showing with the character of Okonkwo a man whose inner god prompts a gentleness which is always ignored. Okonkwo is constantly racked by anxiety, obsessed with his own publicly proclaimed strength and his own standing in the community. As such, he is a true representative of the Ibo of that period, living in villages which regarded one another with a mutual suspicion born of insecurity, a highly individualistic society which did not acknowledge inherited rulers but in which the wealthy became the virtual rulers. It hardly needs pointing out, however, that Okonkwo's spiritual afflictions are not limited to the Ibo society of the last century. Any city in America or Europe could provide Okonkwo's counterparts—a different language, a different background, a different way of earning one's living, a different set of beliefs, but the same anxieties which can cause a man to do violence to his own spirit.

When at last Okonkwo is able to return to Umuofia, he knows that the village will have changed but he does not realise quite how much. He has lost his place among the nine masked spirits, the *egwugwu* who wear the ancestral masks and act as a judicial council in cases which cannot be settled amicably by the councils of men. He has lost his chance to lead his people, and lost the years when he might have taken high titles. Nevertheless he plans to rebuild his compound and to initiate his sons into the *ozo* society, the members of which are the highest title-holders.

But Umuofia has changed beyond recognition. The new Christian mission has claimed many, including Okonkwo's son Nwoye. The government of the English is now established, and the court 'where the District Commissioners judged cases in ignorance'. Court messengers have been appointed to interpret and act as go-betweens, and although they are Africans and even Ibo, they are foreigners to Umuofia. The courts and the English district officers do not understand the status of the village elders and the men of title. Okonkwo is appalled. 'What is it that has happened to our people?' Obierika's reply sums up the cruel inevitability of the situation.

'The white man is very clever. He came quietly and peaceably with his religion. We were amused at his foolishness and allowed him to stay. Now he has won our brothers, and our clan can no longer act like one. He has put a knife on the things that held us together and we have fallen apart.'

Okonkwo's son Nwoye is now called Isaac. Achebe draws an unforced and unexplained but deeply ironic parallel here between Okonkwo and the Biblical patriarch Abraham, and the son Isaac who was once offered up as sacrifice, and we are reminded of the now shadowy figure of Okonkwo's other 'son', Ikemefuna, who was in fact sacrificed and whose death Okonkwo never recovered from and Nwoye never forgave.

The tension and misunderstanding mount. A mission convert tears off the mask of an ancestral spirit, exposing the human face and the man whose sacred duty it is to wear the mask and bear the possession by the spirit. This act, which amounts to the killing and defiling of an ancestral spirit, so infuriates the elders that they demand the mission head to leave. Acting out of his own very different concepts, not understanding their views any more than they understand his, the English missionary bravely refuses to go. The villagers then, completely understandably, burn the church. A number of the elders are arrested, among them Okonkwo. When finally they are released, after the village has paid a fine, they hold a meeting of all the men of the village. Once more the great rallying cry is heard—*Umuofia kwenu!* But the government court messengers arrive to break up the meeting. Okonkwo, his deep pride mingling with his desire to be strong and to be seen to be strong, draws his matchet and kills one of the messengers. But he knows that the days of his power and the days of Umuofia's power are over. He knows that Umuofia will not go to war against the strangers. He returns to his compound and hangs himself.

Suicide is an offence against the earth, and in a bitter scene Okonkwo's great friend Obierika has to ask the District Commissioner and his men to cut Okonkwo down and bury him, for he can only be buried by strangers. In a last passionate outcry, Obierika tries to express Okonkwo's tragedy.

'That was one of the greatest men in Umuofia. You drove him to kill himself; and now he will be buried like a dog—'

But the D.C. does not understand. He goes away thinking that Okonkwo's story may possibly make quite a good short paragraph in a book he is writing, entitled *The Pacification of the Primitive Tribes of the Lower Niger.*

In an article on Achebe's first two novels, in *Transition*, no. 13, 1964, Austin J. Shelton suggests that in a way it was Okonkwo himself who made things fall apart—as though Achebe were totally unaware of this interesting possibility. Shelton is of the opinion that 'Achebe makes a vainglorious attempt . . . to ascribe all the evils which occurred in Ibo society to the coming of the white men. But he stacks the cards in the novels, hinting here and there at the truth, yet not explaining fully the substratum of divine forces working to influence the characters. His own motives perhaps are linked with his patent desire to indicate that outsiders can never understand the works of Igbo-speaking writers (whose novels are in English). . . .'

In fact, Achebe specifically does not blame 'all the evils which occurred in Ibo society' on the white man. It is plain throughout *Things Fall Apart* that the tragedy of Okonkwo is due to pressures from within as well as from the outside. Okonkwo is a man who is very greatly damaged by the external circumstances of his life. He is also a man who commits violence against the god within. In the same way, the old Ibo society is destroyed, as Achebe makes quite clear, both by inner flaws and outer assaults.

The picture of Ibo village life in *Things Fall Apart* is splendidly realised, and each of the characters takes on a life of his own. There are no stereotypes. The relationship and conflict between the villagers and the missionaries is shown—probably for the first time—for the heartbreakingly complicated affair it must have been.

'You say that there is one supreme God who made heaven and earth,' said Akunna on one of Mr Brown's visits. 'We also believe in Him and call Him Chukwu. He made all the world and the other gods.'

'There are no other gods,' said Mr Brown. 'Chukwu is the only God and all others are false. You carve a piece of wood . . . and you call it a god. But it is still a piece of wood.'

'Yes,' said Akunna. 'It is indeed a piece of wood. The tree from which it came was made by Chukwu, as indeed all minor gods were. But He made them for His messengers so that we could approach Him through them. . . .'

In a sense each man is right, but they understand one another scarcely at all. Naturally Achebe's sympathies are weighted on the side of his ancestors, for it was the Christian missions which came uninvited and which in the end managed to sever two entire generations of Africans from their past and to cause untold psychological harm. Nevertheless, Achebe never condemns Christianity and he does not even condemn individual missionaries. He recognises their devotion to their own beliefs, and their at times considerable courage. What he deplores is their total ignorance of the people to whom they were preaching, their uninformed assumption that Africans did not have any concept of God, and their lack of any self-knowledge which might have made them question something of their own motives in desiring to see themselves as bringers of salvation.

Okonkwo remains, until his death, enclosed within his own fears and his unhappy desire for status. Nwoye turns into Isaac and is cut off forever from his father. Neither can speak to the other with any words which will bridge their separation. The villagers and the missionaries impinge upon each other's lives, but there is no comprehension between them. Achebe portrays this failure of communication at both a personal and a social level, in a prose which is plain and spare and at all times informed with his keen sense of irony.

From *Long Drums and Cannons: Nigerian Dramatists and Novelists, 1952-1966* (2001), pp. 91-97. Copyright © 2001 by University of Alberta Press. Reprinted with permission of the University of Alberta Press.

Works Cited

Achebe, Chinua. *Things Fall Apart*. London: Heinemann, 1958; Heinemann African Writers Series, 1962.

Green, Margaret. *Ibo Village Affairs*. 2nd ed. London: Cass & Co., 1964.

Shelton, Austin J. "The Offended Chi in Achebe's Novels." *Transition*, 13 (1964): 36-37.

Chinua Achebe:
*Things Fall Apart*_____

M. Keith Booker

Things Fall Apart (1994b) is almost certainly the African novel that
is most often read by Westerners and most often taught in British and
American classrooms. Not only is it a staple of college courses in African literature, but it is also widely taught in courses in world literature.
It is also frequently taught in courses on African culture, society, and
history as an introduction to the workings of a precolonial African
community. As a result, Achebe's book is frequently the first African
novel encountered by its Western readers, and rightfully so. Not only is
it one of the earliest African novels (it was first published in 1958), but
it also exemplifies many of the fundamental issues that face Western
readers of African novels. For most readers, the most memorable part
of the book is its vivid evocation of Igbo society in the early twentieth
century, at the time of the first major incursions of British colonialism.
Achebe has made it clear that his principal purpose in the book was to
give African readers a realistic depiction of their precolonial past, free
of the distortions and stereotypes imposed in European accounts. The
Africans of Achebe's book live not in primitive savagery, but in a sophisticated society

> in which life is rounded and intricate and sensitively in correspondence
> with a range of human impulses. It admits both the aristocratic and the
> democratic principles. It is a life lived by a dignified clan of equals who
> meet together in an Athenian way. (Walsh 1970, 49)

Achebe's reminders that precolonial African societies functioned in
such sophisticated ways are, of course, valuable to both African and
Western readers. On the other hand, the detailed depiction of the workings of Igbo society in *Things Fall Apart* makes the book particularly
vulnerable to the kind of anthropological readings that have sometimes

prevented African novels from receiving serious critical attention as literature rather than simply as documentation of cultural practices. Ato Quayson (1994) argues that much of the published criticism on the book is typical of criticism of African literature as a whole: it treats the text as a transparent and direct representation of reality without paying sufficient attention to the book's aesthetic dimensions, especially those related to African oral traditions.

However, *Things Fall Apart* is such an intricately crafted work of fiction that many critics have acknowledged its aesthetic merits, while noting the importance of its reminders that precolonial African societies were complex and sophisticated structures bearing little relationship to European myths of African savagery and primitivism. Thus, even the "anthropological" material in the book has a strong aesthetic dimension. As Obiechina points out, "the integrative technique in which background and atmosphere are interlaced with the action of the narrative must be regarded as Achebe's greatest achievement" in works such as *Things Fall Apart* and *Arrow of God* (Obiechina 1975, 142).

Noting the critical acclaim for Achebe's depiction of traditional Igbo society, Solomon Iyasere argues that it fails to do justice to the novel's complexity. "On closer examination, we see that it is provocatively complex, interweaving significant themes: love, compassion, colonialism, achievement, honor, and individualism" (Iyasere 1978, 93). Donald Weinstock and Cathy Ramadan, noting this same structural complexity, argue that Achebe blends realistic and symbolic modes of writing in a manner akin to that employed by novelists such as Joseph Conrad, James Joyce, and D. H. Lawrence (Weinstock and Ramadan 1978, 126-27). Indeed, the formal strategies employed by *Things Fall Apart* are so complex and sophisticated that they do recall the works of Western modernism. As a result, however, Western critics are in danger of falling into old habits of formalist reading and thereby of failing to do justice to the important social and political content of Achebe's book.[1] By circumscribing Achebe's book within European aesthetic traditions, such readings are in danger of perpetuating precisely the colonialist gestures that the book is designed to surmount. *Things Fall Apart* thus illustrates particularly well Achebe's warning that the Western critic of African literature "must cultivate the habit of humility appropriate to his limited experience of the African world and be purged of the superiority and arrogance which history so insidiously makes him heir to" (Achebe 1975, 8).

Readers and critics of Achebe's novel must pay close and careful attention not only to the style and the content of the book, but also to the intricate relationships between them. The content of the first part of the book is striking for its depiction of traditional Igbo society; the style and structure of the entire book are striking for the way in which they incorporate elements of Igbo oral traditions. Many critics have remarked on the sophistication with which Achebe wove traditional oral forms into his written text. According to Obiechina (1993), for example, the way embedded forms—such as proverbs and folk tales—contribute directly to the impact of Achebe's main narrative is similar to the way they are used in African oral epics. Indeed, Iyasere (1978) notes that much of the complexity of Achebe's narrative technique arises from his effective use of strategies derived from Igbo oral culture. Similarly, JanMohamed, while emphasizing the fundamental differences between oral and written—or chirographic—cultures, concludes that *Things Fall Apart* manages to achieve an impressive combination of the two modes and to remain "delicately poised at the transition from the epic (oral) to the novel (chirographic)" (JanMohamed 1984, 34).

The very existence of Achebe's text as a written, bound book places it in dialogue with the Western novelistic tradition, even as it draws heavily upon Igbo oral traditions for its style and content. Moreover, it is important to note that Achebe wrote the book in direct reaction to the demeaning and objectionable depictions of Africans in novels such as Joseph Conrad's *Heart of Darkness* and Joyce Cary's *Mister Johnson*. Innes discusses the way in which Achebe not only responds to Cary's stereotypical vision of Africans, but also shows that Cary's "African" figure Mr. Johnson is a purely European creation many of whose characteristics (such as his individual isolation and lack of contact with family or relatives) are almost unimaginable from an African point of view (Innes 1990, 21-41). In keeping with its integration of style with content, of atmosphere with narrative, and of written with oral forms, *Things Fall Apart* is itself a complex cultural hybrid that is a product not only of the Igbo cultural traditions it so vividly portrays, but also of the encounter between those traditions and the culture of the West.

On the other hand, Achebe's book is a striking demonstration of Fanon's observation that "the colonial world is a Manichean world" (Fanon 1968, 41). In the book, European and African societies come together in a mode of radical difference. The resulting encounter between the two cultures (in an atmosphere of mutual misunderstanding) leads to cataclysmic results for the African society, which is no match for the Europeans in terms of military and economic power. Of course, depictions of Africans and African society as strange and incomprehensible to Westerners can be found in many examples of Africanist discourse, including literary works like *Heart of Darkness*. One of the most valuable aspects of *Things Fall Apart*, for Western readers at least, is its presentation of the estrangement between European and African cultural traditions from an African perspective: it reminds us that there are two sides to this story of encounter between alien cultures. Achebe presents Igbo society in a way that makes its workings perfectly comprehensible, carefully weaving Igbo customs and Igbo words into his narrative in a way that makes them accessible to Western readers. Meanwhile, the Europeans of Achebe's book are depicted as peculiar, incomprehensible, and even vaguely ridiculous—as when a white missionary has his translator speak to the people of Mbanta in Igbo, not realizing that the translator speaks a different dialect from the audience. The translator's words seem strange (and sometimes comical): he continually says "my buttocks" whenever he means to say "myself" (p. 144).[2] Such reversals from the norm of British literature (in which Africans or Indians struggle, often comically, with the English language or English customs) make a powerful statement about the importance of point of view in confrontations between foreign cultures and thoroughly undermine the Western tendency to think of our values as absolute and universal.

On the other hand, *Things Fall Apart* establishes numerous points of contact between European and African cultures, and Achebe is careful to avoid depicting African society as totally foreign to Western sensibilities. For example, many critics have observed the parallels between Achebe's precolonial Umuofia and ancient Greece. Achebe himself has acknowledged these parallels in an interview with Charles Rowell, arguing (in a mode reminiscent of the work of Martin Bernal (1987) and Cheikh Anta Diop (1974)) that the similarities may arise because Greek culture was itself heavily influenced by African culture (Achebe 1990). *Things Fall Apart* as a whole has often been compared to Greek tragedy.[3] Michael Valdez Moses notes the "strikingly Homeric quality" of the book and compares its protagonist Okonkwo to Homer's Achilles (Moses 1995, 110). Okonkwo also resembles Oedipus: he is banished from Umuofia for the accidental killing of a fellow clansman, thus recalling Oedipus's punishment for the inadvertent murder of his father. In this vein, Rhonda Cobham argues that Achebe has chosen to present "those aspects of Igbo traditional society that best coincide with Western-Christian social values," thereby establishing a worldview that is not limited to the precolonial past but can speak to the postcolonial present as well (Cobham 1991, 98). As Achebe himself has put it, a point that is "fundamental and essential to the appreciation of African issues by Americans" is that "Africans are people in the same way that Americans, Europeans, Asians, and others are people" (Achebe 1991, 21).

Achebe does an excellent job of presenting characters whose humanity Western readers can recognize. However, as Florence Stratton points out, the complex characters of the book tend to be male, while the female characters are depicted in vague and superficial ways (Stratton 1994, 29). Okonkwo's wives have virtually no identities outside their domestic roles. His daughter Ezinma is the strongest female character, yet her strength is repeatedly attributed to her more masculine characteristics. Moreover, she essentially disappears late in the narrative, determined to pursue a conventional role as wife and mother. The patriarch Okonkwo dominates the text. If *Things Fall Apart* is first a story of the disintegration of a traditional African society, it is also the personal tragedy of a single individual, whose life falls apart in the midst of that same process. Indeed, Okonkwo unites these communal and individual elements. Obiechina, for example, emphasizes Achebe's achievement in presenting Okonkwo both as embodiment of certain traditional Igbo cultural values and as a distinct "individual with obvious personal weaknesses" (Obiechina 1975, 204).

A careful consideration of Achebe's presentation of Okonkwo as both an individual and as an allegorical representative of his entire society provides a fruitful framework within which to read Achebe's novel. For example, the initial section of the book is devoted principally to a description of everyday life at the end of the nineteenth century in Umuofia, a group of nine villages in the Igbo area of what is now southeastern Nigeria. This section also introduces the protagonist Okonkwo, one of the leaders of the village of Iguedo in Umuofia. We learn a great deal about Okonkwo's background, including his struggle to overcome what he regards as the legacy of weakness and lack of achievement left him by his father Unoka. This section describes the hard work and dedication that have made it possible for Okonkwo to rise from humble beginnings to a position of prominence in his village. We also learn of Okonkwo's physical prowess and of the way he became famous as the greatest wrestler in Umuofia by defeating the champion Amalinze the Cat in what has become a near-legendary match. This section also provides details about Okonkwo's family life. We learn, for example, that he has three wives and eight children. We also learn something of the texture of the everyday life in Okonkwo's household, which consists of a compound that includes Okonkwo's private hut and separate huts for each wife and her children.

Okonkwo rules this household "with a heavy hand," and the first part of *Things Fall Apart* presents not only extensive descriptions of his sometimes harsh treatment of his wives and children, but also detailed background on the causes behind his rather authoritarian personality (p. 13). Okonkwo's major motivation (and the principal reason for his domineering behavior) is his determination to succeed where his musician father (whom he regards as cowardly and effeminate) failed. Okonkwo thus goes out of his way to behave in what he considers to be a staunchly masculine manner and to demonstrate his strength in every way possible. This strength, however, arises from a kind of weakness. "His whole life," the narrator tells us, "was dominated by fear, the fear of failure and weakness. . . . It was the fear of himself, lest he should be found to resemble his father" (p. 13).

Achebe, a master storyteller, dramatizes this aspect of Okonkwo's personality in a number of ways, especially in the story of Ikemefuna, a boy from the neighboring village of Mbaino. Ikemefuna and a young girl are sent to Umuofia to compensate for the killing of an Umuofian woman in Mbaino. The girl is given as a replacement wife to the dead woman's husband, while Ikemefuna goes to live in the household of Okonkwo until the boy's final fate can be determined. Ikemefuna lives with Okonkwo for three years and becomes like a member of the family, growing especially close to Okonkwo's eldest son, Nwoye. Then, however, the Oracle of the Hills and Caves decrees that Ikemefuna must be killed as a sacrifice. Okonkwo, as a leader of Umuofia, knows that he must abide by this decision. However, he does more than simply accept the fact that Ikemefuna must die. Although warned by the elder Ogbuefi Ezeudu not to participate in the killing, Okonkwo himself strikes the fatal blow, cutting the boy down with his machete because "he was afraid of being thought weak" (p. 61). Okonkwo, in seeking to meet his society's standards of admirable conduct, performs a deed that is considered reprehensible by many in that society, including his good friend Obierika, who is horrified by Okonkwo's participation in Ikemefuna's killing, even though he himself regards that killing to be justified. "If the Oracle said that my son should be killed,"

Obierika tells Okonkwo, "I would neither dispute it nor be the one to do it" (p. 67).

The episode of the killing of Ikemefuna is pivotal for a number of reasons. This sacrifice dramatizes aspects of Igbo society that seem harsh, cruel, or even savage by modern Western standards and thus illustrates Achebe's determination to provide a realistic description of traditional Igbo society and his refusal to romanticize that society to impress a Western audience. As Oladele Taiwo puts it, "Besides the strengths in tribal society he gives the weaknesses. We therefore have a true and complete picture in which the whole background is fully realised" (Taiwo 1976, 112). It is important to recognize, though, that the killing of Ikemefuna, however startling by Western standards, does not necessarily demonstrate a weakness in Igbo society. This act has a genuine justification from the Igbo point of view. Moses thus notes that the ritual killing of Ikemefuna (who had nothing to do with the original crime) "is cruel and violates liberal norms of justice," but the sacrifice "does serve to prevent a war between the two clans and therefore helps to ensure the long-term security of both villages." This action, for Moses, "suggests not the absence of ethical standards among the Igbo people, but the existence of a strict premodern morality that values the welfare of the clan and tribe above that of the individual" (Moses 1995, 115). In this way, the episode serves not only to provide a striking illustration of Okonkwo's personality but also to make an important point about the differences between Igbo social values (which place the good of the community above that of any single person) and Western liberal standards of individualism.

One of the most important aspects of *Things Fall Apart* is its delineation of a society that operates on principles quite different from the individualistic notions that shape most Western ideas of social justice. The book thus asks us to challenge our assumption that individualism is an absolute and universal good. Achebe achieves this goal in a number of ways. Much of the description of Igbo society focuses on presenting the crucial role played by communal activities such as the

Week of Peace and the Feast of the New Yam. And many of the book's more dramatic scenes (such as the killing of Ikemefuna or Okonkwo's exile from Umuofia after he accidentally kills Ezeudu's son during Ezeudu's funeral) are built around confrontations between the good of the community and what Westerners would regard as the "rights" of individuals. But this aspect of Achebe's book is built into the text in more profound ways as well. For example, Innes notes that the narrative voice of the text is itself a sort of amalgam of traditional Igbo voices, in contrast to modern Western expectations that the narrator of a story will be a distinct individual (Innes 1990, 32).

By problematizing Okonkwo's relationship to the values of his society, the killing of Ikemefuna calls attention to the book's central focus on the relationship between the individual and the community in Igbo society. It is clear that Okonkwo can, to a certain extent, function as an allegorical stand-in for traditional Igbo society as a whole.[4] Walsh sees Okonkwo's downfall as a marker of the destruction of traditional Igbo society "because of the way in which the fundamental predicament of the society is lived through his life" (Walsh 1970, 52). JanMohamed, influenced by Jameson's work, follows Walsh in suggesting that Achebe makes "his heroes the embodiments of the fundamental structures and values of their cultures" (JanMohamed 1983, 161). On the other hand, the relationship between Okonkwo and his society is complex and problematic. It comes as no surprise, then, that the implications of the relationship between Okonkwo and his society have been the object of considerable critical disagreement. Eustace Palmer, for example, agrees that Okonkwo is "the personification of his society's values." Thus, "if he is plagued by a fear of failure and of weakness it is because his society puts such a premium on success" (Palmer 1972, 53). For Palmer, then, Okonkwo's ultimate tragedy results from weaknesses that are the direct result of flaws in Igbo society. For other critics, Okonkwo's fall results not from the characteristics of Igbo society but from the destruction of this society by British colonialism. Killam thus agrees that Okonkwo consolidates "the values most admired by

Ibo peoples," but concludes that his fall occurs because colonialism disrupts these values and not from shortcomings in the values themselves (Killam 1977, 16).

Killam's reading is clearly more consonant with the overall theme of *Things Fall Apart* than is Palmer's. For one thing, Palmer (though himself an African) obviously reads the text from a purely Western, individualistic perspective. From this point of view, which privileges strong individuals who are willing to oppose conventional opinion, it is clearly a flaw for an individual to embody the mainstream values of his culture. On the other hand, Killam's reading is undermined by the fact that Okonkwo already seems headed for trouble even before Umuofia is aware of the British presence, perhaps because, in his quest for personal success, he is already more individualistic than most of his fellow villagers. Several times Okonkwo breaks fundamental rules of his society and then must be punished, culminating in his banishment from Umuofia at the end of the first part of the book.[5] Many critics argue that Okonkwo's fall occurs not because he embodies the values of his society, but precisely because he deviates from his society's norms of conduct. Biodun Jeyifo, for example, argues that Okonkwo is "doomed because of his rigid, superficial understanding—really misrecognition—of his culture" (Jeyifo 1991, 58). Similarly, Carroll believes that Okonkwo's successes are largely achieved through an inflexible focus on his goals, a focus that eventually sets him at odds with a society "remarkable for its flexibility" (Carroll 1990, 41). Finally, critics such as Ravenscroft and Ojinmah note that the Igbo society depicted by Achebe is characterized by a careful balancing of opposing values (particularly of masculine and feminine principles), while Okonkwo focuses strictly on the masculine side of his personality and thus fails to achieve this balance (Ravenscroft 1969, 13; Ojinmah 1991, 15-16).

Such gendered readings of Okonkwo's characteristics are central to many critical discussions of *Things Fall Apart*. Much of JanMohamed's discussion of Okonkwo's typicality focuses on the way Okonkwo "becomes an emblem of the masculine values of Igbo culture." But

JanMohamed emphasizes that the culture itself balances masculine with feminine values. Okonkwo's rejection of the feminine aspects of his culture thus make him seem "rigid, harsh, and unfeeling in his pursuit of virility" (JanMohamed 1983, 164). Innes also emphasizes the balance between masculine and feminine values in Igbo culture, arguing that Okonkwo's tendency to categorize various activities as either masculine or feminine is typical of his society, but again pointing out that Okonkwo has less respect for feminine values than does his society as a whole (Innes 1990, 25-26). Several feminist critics, however, have pointed out that the society itself, at least as depicted by Achebe, is heavily oriented toward masculinity. While some value is placed on feminine virtues and activities, the values labeled by the society as masculine are consistently valued more highly than those labeled as feminine. In addition, the power structure of Igbo society, while decentered and in many ways democratic, is entirely dominated by males. Okonkwo's domination of his household thus becomes a microcosm of the domination of the society as a whole by patriarchal figures.

It is certainly the case that the leaders of Umuofia are all male. Moreover, these leaders are often shown exercising power directly over women. In one of the book's key demonstrations of the workings of justice in Umuofia, the village elders meet to adjudicate a marital dispute in which the woman Mgbafo has fled the household of her husband, Uzowulu, because he has repeatedly beaten her (sometimes severely) for nine years. The proceedings are restricted to males, and no women (including Mgbafo) are allowed inside the hut where they occur. Indeed, we are told that no woman has ever participated in such proceedings and that women know better than even to ask questions about them (p. 88). Uzowulu presents his case, asking that Mgbafo be ordered to return to him. Then, Mgbafo's brother argues that she should be allowed to remain with him and her other brothers apart from her abusive husband. The elders (some of whom seem to regard the case as too trivial to be worthy of their attention) order Uzowulu to offer a pot of wine to Mgbafo's brothers in restitution. They then order the brothers to return Mgbafo to her husband, refusing to cast blame on the abusive husband.

Stratton grants that Achebe's "masculinization" of Igbo society serves the positive function of countering the feminization of Africa so typical of narratives like those of Cary, Conrad, H. Rider Haggard, and other colonial writers. On the other hand, she also argues that Achebe may undermine colonialist racial stereotypes only at the expense of perpetuating gender stereotypes (Stratton 1994, 37). One could, of course, argue that Achebe, is simply being realistic in his depiction of Igbo power relations, but Stratton is probably correct that he could have done more to question these relations in terms of gender.[6] After all, Achebe does an excellent job of deconstructing the hierarchical relationship between the races in colonial Africa, but Stratton is probably justified in suggesting that, while Achebe effectively dismantles "racial romances" such as Cary's *Mister Johnson*, he does little to prevent his book from becoming a sort of "gender romance" (Stratton 1994, 36). The decision in this marital dispute, for example, is not challenged in any way in the text and could even be taken as an example of the smooth, almost utopian, functioning of Umuofian society before the intrusion of colonialism. Indeed, Achebe's book sometimes suggests that one of the negative effects of colonialism was its disruption of the clear hierarchy of gender relations in Umuofia. For example, when the men of the village discuss the strange customs of some of their neighbors, Okonkwo mentions that some people are so peculiar that they consider children the property of their mothers rather than their fathers, as in any properly patriarchal society. His friend Machi responds that such a practice would be as inconceivable as a situation in which "the woman lies on top of the man when they are making the children." Obierika then links this reversal of gender roles to the arrival of Europeans. He suggests that such a sexual inversion would be "like the story of white men who, they say, are white like this piece of chalk" (p. 74).

It may also be significant in this regard that Okonkwo, when exiled from Umuofia in Part Two of *Things Fall Apart*, is sent to the home of his mother's family as punishment. And it is precisely in this locale, which for Okonkwo has clearly feminine resonances, that European culture makes its first significant intrusions into traditional Igbo life. The second part of the book also details the increasing inroads made by Christian missionaries, thus further increasing Okonkwo's sense of crisis about his own identity. Importantly, one of the converts won by the missionaries is Okonkwo's son Nwoye, whom Okonkwo comes to regard as degenerate and effeminate—that is, as a throwback to his grandfather Unoka. Christianity is thus linked to femininity, again suggesting that the European impact on Igbo society included a disruption in the traditional gender hierarchy. Achebe suggests that it is typical of Igbo culture to view all aspects of life in terms of gendered categories. Recognizing this tendency can help Western readers understand the significance of Okonkwo's exile, just as an appreciation of the communal nature of Igbo society can help us to see why Okonkwo's exile is so difficult for him. In Igbo society, individual identity is connected far more closely to participation in a community than it is in the West. Therefore, Okonkwo's separation from his community is far more difficult and traumatic for him than a similar separation might be for a Western character.

This part of the book ends on a high note as Okonkwo prepares to return to Umuofia and hosts a feast to thank his kinsmen for their kindness during his seven years of exile. This communal event presents traditional Igbo society at its best, but it is undermined by the reader's recognition that this way of life is already being eroded by the incursions of Christianity and Western individualism. One of the elders of the clan ends the feast on a sad note, thanking Okonkwo for his hospitality, but gloomily acknowledging that the younger generations of Igbo are already losing their appreciation for the traditional bonds of kinship:

You do not know what it is to speak with one voice. And what is the result? An abominable religion has settled among you. A man can now leave his father and his brothers. He can curse the gods of his fathers and his ancestors, like a hunter's dog that suddenly goes mad and turns on his master. I fear for you; I fear for the clan. (p. 167)

The obvious accuracy of this somber prediction adds a tragic irony to Okonkwo's attempts in Part Three of the book to rebuild his life in Umuofia and to regain his status as a leader of the community: the traditional life of the community is already doomed. In this part of the book, the Christian missionaries are joined by soldiers and bureaucrats as British colonial rule is established in Nigeria. This process culminates in Okonkwo's impulsive killing of a messenger sent by the British to order the break-up of a meeting of Umuofia's leaders. The leaders are trying to decide upon a response to the recent detention and abuse of several elders of the community—including Okonkwo himself—by the British District Commissioner. The Commissioner then arrives with soldiers to arrest Okonkwo, only to find that Okonkwo (in radical violation of Igbo tradition) has hanged himself. Okonkwo, in this final example of the breakdown of Igbo communal life as a result of British colonialism, dies alone—and in a manner so repugnant to his fellow villagers that tradition does not allow them to bury him. That task must fall to the British. The Commissioner concludes that Okonkwo's story should make interesting reading, and might be worthy of a chapter, or at least a paragraph, in the book he himself is writing. Because this book, *The Pacification of the Primitive Tribes of the Lower Niger*, tells Okonkwo's story from the Commissioner's point of view, it serves as an emblem of the Africanist discourse Achebe seeks to overcome with *Things Fall Apart*, which tells Okonkwo's story in an African voice.

Achebe's novel stands as a direct refutation of Africanist discourse like the Commissioner's *Pacification* report and makes it clear that colonialism brought not civilization but chaos and destruction. In its depictions of the British colonial administration and the missionary Smith (far more strident and uncompromising than his predecessor Brown) Achebe's book is sharply critical of the colonialism that shattered traditional Igbo life. Ernest Emenyonu calls attention to this aspect of Achebe's work when he argues that, "no matter how couched in proverbs, images and innuendoes, the intense virulence of Achebe's indictment of colonial diplomatic tactlessness and absurd human highhandedness cannot be lost on the perceptive reader" (Emenyonu 1990, 83-84). This critical side of Achebe's project is achieved through a variety of complex strategies and goes well beyond mere description of the damage done by British colonialism to Igbo society. By situating itself in opposition to the depiction of relationships between Africa and Europe in such texts as *Heart of Darkness* or *Mister Johnson, Things Fall Apart* opens a complex literary dialogue that challenges not only the content of such texts, but also the fundamental rationalist, individualist, and historicist assumptions upon which those texts are constructed. Margaret Turner thus argues that "Chinua Achebe's trilogy, *Things Fall Apart, Arrow of God,* and *No Longer at Ease,* refutes Western standards of literature and Western ideology, in this case Hegel's universal and homogeneous state, by showing that both constitute aspects of the new colonialism" (Turner 1990, 32).

As Moses points out, sharp though his critique of colonialism may be, Achebe ultimately accepts the historical inevitability of modernization in a mode that shows a fundamental agreement with "the historicist legacy of Hegel's thinking" (Moses 1995, 108). Achebe's approach is again extremely complex. Just as he points out negative aspects of traditional Igbo society (such as the killing of twins and the treatment of certain members of the community—the *osu*—as total outcasts), so too does he suggest potentially positive developments related to the coming of Christianity and European civilization.[7] Indeed, in many cases the positive aspects of Westernization amount to direct reversals of abuses in Igbo society. Ultimately, however, *Things Fall Apart* demonstrates that even the negative aspects of Igbo society were part of an organic whole and that the disruptions brought about by their removal led to a collapse of the entire social structure. The book thus raises a number of profound questions not only about the nature and function of literature, but also about the nature of human societies and human cultural practices and the extent to which aspects of a given society are interwoven in complex and interdependent ways.

Historical Background

Nigeria, with a population of over ninety million (1993 estimate), is the most populous nation in Africa. It is also one of the largest, covering an area of approximately 357,000 square miles—somewhat larger than France and Great Britain combined. The Niger-Benue river system divides the country into three physically diverse sections. The hot, dry north is a heavily cultivated area of rolling savannahs located roughly fifteen hundred feet above sea level. Lake Chad, in the northeast, is one of the few large, permanent, standing bodies of water in the country, though its size varies with seasonal changes in rainfall. The southwest region contains both low-lying coastal plains and upland areas. The southeast region, consisting primarily of the delta of the Niger River, is largely covered by dense tropical forest. Nigeria's rich petroleum reserves are also located principally in this region. The new city of Abuja (designed and built beginning in the mid-1970s and located almost exactly in the middle of the country) became the capital in late 1991. The population of Abuja in 1992 was about 300,000, though it was growing rapidly. The largest city in Nigeria is the southwestern coastal city of Lagos, the former capital, with a population (1992 estimate) of over 1.3 million. Lagos is still the administrative and economic center of the country. The nearby city of Ibadan, with a population (1992 estimate) of nearly 1.3 million, is also a major commercial and intellectual center.

English is widely used in Nigeria in government, commerce, and education. In their everyday activities many of the inhabitants speak a form of "pidgin" English which preserves most of the basic grammatical features of English but incorporates a number of changes in syntax and vocabulary arising from the influence of local cultures. The more than 250 ethnic groups have their own languages as well. The largest of these groups are the Hausa and Fulani on the north, the Yoruba in the southwest, and the Igbo in the southeast. About half the total population, mostly in the north, are Muslim; about one-third of the population, almost all in the south, are Christian. Just over half of the adult population are literate, mostly in English. The economy of Nigeria is mostly agricultural. More than half the work force is engaged in farming (much of it subsistence farming), and a variety of crops are produced, including sorghum, millet, cassava, soybeans, groundnuts, cotton, maize, yams, rice, palm products, rice, and cacao. Goats, sheep, and cattle are raised as well. Periodic droughts frequently reduce agricultural production to the point that food must be imported. Hardwoods such as mahogany and ebony are produced in the forest regions, and there is some industry in the urban regions, though most manufactured products are imported. Nigeria is rich in mineral resources, producing iron, magnesium, niobium, tin, lead, and zinc. The major mineral resource, however, is petroleum: Nigeria is Africa's largest producer. Most of the petroleum reserves (estimated at about twenty billion barrels) are controlled by the government.

The people in what is now southern Nigeria had extensive contact with Europeans as long ago as the end of the fifteenth century, and the region has a rich history that goes back hundreds of years before that. The first centralized state in the region was Kanem-Bornu, probably founded in the eighth century A.D. Important states such as Oyo and Benin had arisen in the area by the fourteenth century, establishing a rich artistic tradition, especially in the production of bronze artifacts. By the seventeenth and eighteenth centuries, the area was one of the centers of a brutal slave trade in which millions of Nigerians were forcibly removed by European traders and brought to the Americas. Arab slave traders had also operated in the region earlier. The slave trade was abolished in the early nineteenth century, but European traders continued to visit the region, exchanging manufactured goods for local agricultural products.

The area occupied by modern Nigeria became one of the most important regions of British colonial power in Africa. Ceded to British control in the Berlin Conference of 1884-1885, the area was the object of extensive missionary activity in the late nineteenth century. British colonial rule was solidified through a massive program of "pacification" that lasted from 1900 to 1920, and the region was officially amalgamated as a single colony in 1914. The pacification program included the intentional destruction of important cultural sites and artifacts, including the great oracle of the Aro (an Igbo people). It also included the military conquest of peoples who resisted British rule. Villages were often subject to so-called punitive expeditions that amounted to massacres of the local population. For example, British-led troops slaughtered much of the population of the village of Ahiara in late 1905, an event echoed in the destruction of the fictional village of Abame in *Things Fall Apart*. The slaughter was precipitated by the killing of one J. F. Stewart, an Englishman traveling by bicycle in the area. This same killing was also the pretext for the massive Bende-Onitsha expedition into the interior of Nigeria, an expedition that included the destruction of an important oracle at Awka and that opened the way for more thorough British penetration of the region.

The British established an elaborate system of "indirect rule" that relied largely on African agents of the colonial government and on co-operative local rulers (often installed as puppets by the British) for its everyday operation, though all important decisions were made by the British governor. British rule led to a great deal of development, such as the building of roads and railways, but the system of indirect rule was an open invitation to corruption and abuse. Moreover, it often came into conflict with long-established local traditions. For example, the culture of the Igbo was based on discussion and decentralized, collective rule by groups of elders, no one of whom could be identified as the local ruler. When the British—bent on dealing with a single person as the leading power in a village—sought to establish such rulers, conflicts necessarily arose. Indeed, well-established social customs and traditions among the Igbo and other peoples in the region were so foreign to the customs and traditions of modern Britain that the British typically concluded that the indigenous peoples were mere savages without any legitimate culture or social structure. This belief was used to justify the various atrocities committed by the British during the period of pacification and to legitimate the continuation of British rule in the ensuing decades.

Nigeria finally gained independence from British rule on October 1, 1960. The new nation was divided into northern, western, and eastern administrative regions along the lines of the natural geographic division of the country. Nigeria became a republic in 1963, with Nnamdi Azikiwe as its first president. The early years of independence were marked by considerable political conflict and unrest, leading eventually to the January 1966 coup. A group of Igbo military officers took control of the government, placing Major General Johnson T. U. Aguiyi-Ironsi in charge of the new military regime. In July 1966, Ironsi was ousted and killed in another coup, this time led by Hausa officers. The new regime, headed by Lieutenant Colonel Yakubu Gowon, attempted to move toward civilian government, but internal troubles (especially the massacre of a number of Igbo living in the Hausa-dominated north) led to continuing instability. The dissatisfaction of the Igbo with their position in Nigeria led to the secession of the Eastern Region, led by Lieutenant Colonel Chukwuemeka Odumegwu Ojukwu. Ojukwu proclaimed the region the Republic of Biafra on May 30, 1967. A bloody civil war ensued, leading eventually to Biafra's surrender in January, 1970, and to the restoration of Nigeria's previous boundaries. In addition to massive casualties from the actual fighting, it is estimated that more than a million Igbo starved to death as a result of the war.

A worldwide boom in oil prices in the early 1970s led to an era of rising prosperity in Nigeria, marked by a massive government program of construction and industrialization, including the founding of the new capital of Abuja. On the other hand, the rapid influx of wealth was unevenly distributed and led to considerable corruption. By 1975, Gowon had still not restored civilian rule, and his regime was toppled in a coup led by General Murtala Muhammed and a group of officers who pledged to return the country to civilian rule as soon as possible. Muhammed was assassinated in an unsuccessful coup attempt a year later and replaced by General Olusegun Obasanjo. By the late 1970s the government had established increasingly close ties with the United States, and a new civilian government was installed, headed by President Alhaji Shehu Shagari and modeled on the American system. The new federal system was plagued by corruption and social disturbances. Shagari was reelected in 1983, but was overthrown in a violent military coup only a few months later. Another coup in 1985 instituted a military regime that held power until 1993, when a joint civilian-military government was installed and elections held. However, on November 17, 1993, General Sani Abacha seized control of the government in a bloodless coup and declared the elections void. Moshood K. O. Abiola, the apparent winner of the election, was jailed a year later when he declared himself president of Nigeria. At this writing Abacha is still in power, amid international outcries against the oppressive policies of his regime. He recently announced plans to hold new elections and to return Nigeria to civilian rule in 1998.

Biographical Background

Chinua Achebe is probably Africa's best known novelist, both in Africa and worldwide. He was born in 1930 in Ogidi, in eastern Nigeria and was originally christened Albert Chinualumogu Achebe. His father was a Christian evangelist and teacher, and his devoutly Christian parents had an intense sense of their difference from the non-Christians around them. Many of Achebe's neighbors and family members still adhered to traditional Igbo cultural and religious practices. Achebe was thus exposed at a very early age to the hybridity that informs postcolonial literature. Indeed, in his autobiographical essay "Named for Victoria, Queen of England," Achebe describes the principal experience of his childhood as one of being "at the crossroads of cultures":

> On one arm of the cross, we sang hymns and read the Bible night and day. On the other, my father's brother and his family, blinded by heathenism, offered food to idols. That was how it was supposed to be anyhow. But I knew without knowing why that it was too simple a way to describe what was going on. (Achebe 1975, 119-20)

Achebe recalls that his parents looked down upon the "heathens" in their community who did not espouse Christianity, but he eventually came to wonder if "it isn't they who should have been looking down on us for our apostasy" (p. 115). In any case, the hybrid nature of Achebe's personal cultural background—which mirrors the hybrid experience of twentieth-century Igbo society as a whole—is a powerful informing factor in his work. As he grew older he began to read the various books that were in his parents' home, most of them either Christian religious tracts or works of European literature that reinforced his vague sense of European cultural superiority to Africa. Achebe was educated in a system designed and administered by the British colonial rulers of Nigeria, first at the local mission school, then at secondary school in the Government College in Umuahia, and finally at University College, Ibadan, where he received his B.A. in 1953.

Achebe's studies of Western literature in college convinced him of the need to develop more literature written from an African perspective and contributed greatly to his decision to become a writer. After graduation from University College, Achebe worked briefly as a producer for the Nigerian Broadcasting Corporation. While still working for the NBC he traveled to London where he studied broadcasting at the British Broadcasting Corporation. He also began writing his first novel during this period. This initial work eventually became two different novels. The first, *Things Fall Apart*, was published in 1958 and established Achebe as one of the important founding figures of the modern African novel in English. Achebe's second novel, *No Longer at Ease* (1994a), was published in 1960, the year of Nigerian independence. A sort of sequel to *Things Fall Apart* (the protagonist of the second book is the grandson of the protagonist of the first), *No Longer at Ease* describes the tensions in a 1950s Nigerian society moving toward independence from British rule.

Achebe continued to work with the Nigerian Broadcasting Corporation, becoming Director of External Broadcasting in 1961. In 1964 he published *Arrow of God*, his second novel about the early interaction between the cultures of the Igbo and the British. Set in the 1920s (slightly later than *Things Fall Apart*), *Arrow of God* describes a colonial Nigeria in which British political rule has been firmly established but in which many Igbo have still had relatively little contact with European culture. The villagers of this book continue to adhere to relatively traditional Igbo religious and cultural practices, but their lives are strongly informed by a sense that British control of Nigeria is firm and that they must learn to deal with the consequences of this alien rule.

In 1966 Achebe published *A Man of the People* (1989b), his first novel to be set in postcolonial Nigeria. A political satire that exposes the widespread corruption that plagued the new nation, *A Man of the People* marks a turn in Achebe's career from an attempt to recreate the past to a critical engagement with the present. At this point, the social and political instability that led to the Nigerian civil war caused Achebe and his family to flee from Lagos back to the Igbo territory in the east. The ensuing conflict caused a great disruption in Achebe's career. Achebe himself attempted to generate international support for the Biafran cause, serving as a sort of roving ambassador around the world. Concerned with the immediate disaster in Biafra and occupied with his work as an Igbo spokesman, Achebe found himself unable to sustain the effort required to write a novel and instead concentrated on writing shorter pieces such as essays and poems. *Beware, Soul Brother* (1972), a book of poems, was first published in 1971, and in 1972 Achebe was awarded the first Commonwealth Poetry Prize. His book of short stories, *Girls at War and Other Stories* (1972), was published in 1972 as well.

Achebe would not publish another novel until 1987, when *Anthills of the Savannah* (1988a) appeared, though a revised version of *Arrow of God* was issued in 1974 (Achebe 1989a). *Anthills of the Savannah* is Achebe's most formally intricate work, employing a complex nonlinear narrative form reminiscent of Western modernist novels but drawing upon African oral forms as well. Partially a meditation on the power and function of storytelling in society, the book is another satire of postcolonial politics, describing a military dictatorship in a fictional African nation (Kangan) that obviously resembles Nigeria. Clearly influenced by the events of the Nigerian civil war, the novel is a powerful indictment of the violence and corruption that have been part of the postcolonial histories of so many African nations. Together, Achebe's five novels constitute an extended fictional history of Nigeria from the moment of the first British colonial intrusion at the end of the nineteenth century to the abuses of power that continue to plague Nigerian politics at the end of the twentieth.

In the twenty-year period between the appearance of his fourth and fifth novels, Achebe spent a considerable amount of time teaching at universities in the United States. He also remained involved in Nigerian politics, becoming the deputy national president of the People's Redemption Party in 1983 after turning down an offer to become the party's presidential candidate in the elections of that year. His international reputation as a master of the craft of fiction continued to grow. His numerous awards included being named an honorary fellow of the Modern Language Association of America in 1975 and a fellow of the British Royal Society of Literature in 1981. He is the only Nigerian to have twice received the Nigerian National Merit Award, his nation's highest honor for intellectual achievement. He has also been awarded more than twenty honorary degrees from universities in Africa, Europe, and America. Achebe's lectures and essays, many of which are published in the collections *Morning Yet on Creation Day* (1975) and *Hopes and Impediments* (1988c), have established him as a major spokesman for modern African culture and as an important leader in the effort to establish an African culture that escapes the domination of Western paradigms. As of this writing, Achebe and his wife live in Annandale-on-Hudson, New York, where they both teach at Bard College.

There is almost certainly more published criticism on Achebe's work than on that of any other African writer. A bibliography of works relevant to Achebe and his works published in Nigeria in 1990 listed 1,453 entries, 287 of which were written by Achebe himself. There are numerous full-length critical readings of Achebe's work (especially the novels), including those by David Carroll (1990), Simon Gikandi (1991), C. L. Innes (1990), G. D. Killam (1977), Benedict Chiaka Njoku (1984), Umelo Ojinmah (1991), and Arthur Ravenscroft (1969). Another important book-length study of Achebe is Robert Wren's *Achebe's World* (1980), which documents the historical background of Achebe's work. Some of the numerous critical essays on Achebe's work are collected in the volumes edited by Innes and Bernth Lindfors (1978) and by Kirsten Holst Petersen and Anna Rutherford (1990). Most general studies of the African novel include extensive treatment of Achebe's work. Critical studies such as Obiechina's *Culture, Tradition and Society in the West African Novel* (1975), JanMohamed's *Manichean Aesthetics* (1983), and Gikandi's *Reading the African Novel* (1987) feature discussions of Achebe's novels. Achebe's work is frequently taught in British and American university courses on literature, and the Modern Language Association has published a volume of essays detailing various approaches to teaching *Things Fall Apart* (Lindfors, ed. 1991).

From *The African Novel in English: An Introduction* (1998), pp. 65-83. Copyright © 1998 by Heinemann Educational, Ltd. Reprinted with permission of Pearson Education, Ltd.

Notes

1. See Irele for a discussion of the inadequacy of Western formalist criticism for the African novel (Irele 1990, xiii).

2. A similar motif occurs in Ferdinand Oyono's *Houseboy* (1990), in which the missionary Father Vandermayer attempts to deliver his sermons in the Ndjem language, but with such poor pronunciation that virtually all of his words "had obscene meanings," resulting in sermons "full of obscenities" (pp. 9, 35).

3. For a good introduction to the tragic aspects of Achebe's work, see Irele (1978). On more specific parallels between *Things Fall Apart* and the Greek concept of tragic drama, see Killam (1977, 13-34) and Landrum (1970).

4. One might compare here Fredric Jameson's controversial suggestion that the protagonists of postcolonial literature can generally be viewed as "national allegories" whose personal experiences parallel the histories of the development of their nations (Jameson 1986). See Ahmad for a detailed critique of Jameson's argument (Ahmad 1992, 95-122).

5. For a succinct discussion of Okonkwo's offenses and subsequent punishments, see Obiechina 1975 (214-15).

6. Achebe's presentation of traditional Igbo society as entirely male-centered may not be entirely realistic. See, for example, Ifi Amadiume (1987) for a discussion of the ways that society placed far more weight on feminine values than Achebe indicates.

7. One might include the treatment of women in this list, though Achebe does not clearly identify the strictly patriarchal nature of the Igbo society depicted in *Things Fall Apart* as a shortcoming.

Works Cited

Achebe, Chinua. 1964. *Arrow of God*. London: Heinemann.

_____. 1972. *Beware, Soul Brother*. Rev. ed. London: Heinemann.

_____. 1972. *Girls at War and Other Stories*. London: Heinemann.

_____. 1975. *Morning Yet on Creation Day*. London: Heinemann.

_____. 1988a. *Anthills of the Savannah*. 1987. New York: Anchor-Doubleday.

_____. 1988c. *Hopes and Impediments: Selected Essays, 1965-87*. London: Heinemann.

_____. 1989a. *Arrow of God*. Rev. ed. 1974. New York: Anchor-DoubleDay.

_____. 1989b. *A Man of the People*. 1966. New York: Anchor-Doubleday.

_____. 1990. "An Interview with Chinua Achebe." Interview by Charles Rowell. *Callaloo* 13.1: 86-101.

_____. 1991. "Teaching *Things Fall Apart*." In *Approaches to Teaching Achebe's "Things Fall Apart."* Ed. Bernth Lindfors. New York: Modern Language Association. 20-24.

_____. 1994a. *No Longer at Ease*. 1960. New York: Anchor-Doubleday.

_____. 1994b. *Things Fall Apart*. 1958. New York: Anchor-Doubleday.

Ahmad, Aijaz. 1992. *In Theory: Classes, Nations, Literatures*. London: Verso.

Amadiume, Ifi. 1987. *Male Daughters, Female Husbands: Gender and Sex in an African Society*. London: Zed.

Bernal, Martin. 1987. *Black Athena*. Vol. 1, *The Fabrication of Ancient Greece, 1785-1985*. New Brunswick, N.J.: Rutgers University Press.

Carroll, David. 1990. *Chinua Achebe: Novelist, Poet, Critic*. 2nd ed. London: Macmillan.

Cary, Joyce. 1989. *Mister Johnson*. 1939. New York: New Directions.

Cobham, Rhonda. 1991. "Making Men and History: Achebe and the Politics of Revisionism." In *Approaches to Teaching Achebe's "Things Fall Apart."* Ed. Bernth Lindfors. New York: Modern Language Association. 91-100.

Conrad, Joseph. 1988. *Heart of Darkness*. 1902. 3rd ed. Ed. Robert Kimbrough. Norton Critical Edition. New York: Norton.

Diop, Cheikh Anta. 1974. *The African Origin of Civilization: Myth or Reality*. New York: Lawrence Hill.

Emenyonu, Ernest N. 1990. "Chinua Achebe's *Things Fall Apart*: A Classic Study in Diplomatic Tactlessness." In *Chinua Achebe: A Celebration*. Ed. Kirsten Holst Petersen and Anna Rutherford. Oxford: Heinemann. 83-88.

Fanon, Frantz. 1968. *The Wretched of the Earth*. Trans. Constance Farrington. New York: Grove Press.

Gikandi, Simon. 1987. *Reading the African Novel*. London: James Currey.

_____. 1991. *Reading Chinua Achebe: Language and Ideology in Fiction*. London: Heinemann.

Innes, C. L. 1990. *Chinua Achebe*. Cambridge: Cambridge University Press.

Innes, C. L., and Bernth Lindfors, eds. 1978. *Critical Perspectives on Chinua Achebe*. Washington, D.C.: Three Continents Press.

Irele, Abiola. 1978. "The Tragic Conflict in the Novels of Chinua Achebe." In *Critical Perspectives on Chinua Achebe*. Ed. C. L. Innes and Bernth Lindfors. Washington, D.C.: Three Continents Press. 10-21.

_____. 1990. *The African Experience in Literature and Ideology*. Bloomington: Indiana University Press.

Iyasere, Solomon O. 1978. "Narrative Techniques in *Things Fall Apart*." In *Critical Perspectives on Chinua Achebe*. Ed. C. L. Innes and Bernth Lindfors. Washington, D.C.: Three Continents Press. 92-110.

Jameson, Fredric. 1986. "Third-World Literature in the Era of Multinational Capitalism." *Social Text* 15: 65-88.

JanMohamed, Abdul R. 1983. *Manichean Aesthetics: The Politics of Literature in Colonial Africa*. Amherst: University of Massachusetts Press.

_____. 1984. "Sophisticated Primitivism: The Syncretism of Oral and Literate Modes in Achebe's *Things Fall Apart*." *Ariel* 15.4: 19-39.

Jeyifo, Biodun. 1991. "For Chinua Achebe: The Resilience and the Predicament of Obierika." In *Chinua Achebe: A Celebration*. Oxford: Heinemann. 51-70.

Killam, G. D. 1977. *The Writings of Chinua Achebe*. London: Heinemann.

Landrum, Roger L. 1970. "Chinua Achebe and the Aristotelian Concept of Tragedy." *Black Academy Review* 1: 22-30.

Lindfors, Bernth, ed. 1991. *Approaches to Teaching Achebe's "Things Fall Apart."* New York: Modern Language Association.

Moses, Michael Valdez. 1995. *The Novel and the Globalization of Culture.* New York: Oxford University Press.

Njoku, Benedict Chiaka. 1984. *The Four Novels of Chinua Achebe.* New York: Peter Lang.

Obiechina, Emmanuel. 1975. *Culture, Tradition and Society in the West African Novel.* Cambridge: Cambridge University Press.

_____. 1993. "Narrative Proverbs in the African Novel." *Research in African Literatures* 24.4: 123-40.

Ojinmah, Umelo. 1991. *Chinua Achebe: New Perspectives.* Ibadan: Spectrum.

Oyono, Ferdinand. 1956b. *Une vie de boy.* Paris: Julliard. Trans. John Reed, as *Houseboy.* London: Heinemann, 1967.

Palmer, Eustace. 1972. *An Introduction to the African Novel.* New York: Africana.

Petersen, Kirsten Holst, and Anna Rutherford, eds. 1990. *Chinua Achebe: A Celebration.* Oxford: Heinemann.

Quayson, Ato. 1994. "Realism, Criticism, and the Disguises of Both: A Reading of Chinua Achebe's *Things Fall Apart* with an Evaluation of the Criticism Relating to It." *Research in African Literatures* 25.4: 117-36.

Ravenscroft, Arthur. 1969. *Chinua Achebe.* Ed. Ian Scott-Kilvert. London: Longman.

Stratton, Florence. 1994. *Contemporary African Literature and the Politics of Gender.* London: Routledge.

Taiwo, Oladele. 1976. *Culture and the Nigerian Novel.* New York: St. Martin's.

Turner, Margaret E. 1990. "Achebe, Hegel, and the New Colonialism." In *Chinua Achebe: A Celebration.* Ed. Kirsten Holst Petersen and Anna Rutherford. Oxford: Heinemann. 31-40.

Walsh, William. 1970. *A Manifold Voice: Studies in Commonwealth Literature.* New York: Barnes and Noble.

Weinstock, Donald, and Cathy Ramadan. 1978. "Symbolic Structure in *Things Fall Apart.*" In *Critical Perspectives on Chinua Achebe.* Ed. C. L. Innes and Bernth Lindfors. Washington, D.C.: Three Continents Press. 126-34.

Wren, Robert M. 1980. *Achebe's World: The Historical and Cultural Context of the Novels of Chinua Achebe.* Washington, D.C.: Three Continents Press.

Further Reading

Achebe, Chinua. 1984. *The Trouble with Nigeria.* London: Heinemann.

Asiegbu, Johnson U. J. 1984. *Nigeria and Its British Invaders, 1851-1920: A Thematic Documentary History.* New York: NOK International.

Ben-Amos, Paula. 1980. *The Art of Benin.* New York: Thames and Hudson.

Crowder, Michael. 1977. *The Story of Nigeria*. 4th ed. London: Faber.

_____. 1979. *Nigeria: An Introduction to Its History*. London: Longman.

Diamond, Larry Jay. 1988. *Class, Ethnicity, and Democracy in Nigeria: The Failure of the First Republic*. Basingstoke, England: Macmillan.

Ekwe-Ekwe, Herbert. 1990. *The Biafra War: Nigeria and the Aftermath*. Lewiston, N.Y.: Mellen.

Isichei, Elizabeth. 1976. *A History of the Igbo People*. London: Macmillan.

_____. 1983. *A History of Nigeria*. London: Longman.

Millar, Heather. 1996. *The Kingdom of Benin in West Africa*. New York: Benchmark.

Ogbalu, F. Chidozie, and E. Nolue Emenanjo. 1975. *Igbo Language and Culture*. Ibadan: Oxford University Press.

Olaniyan, Richard, ed. 1985. *Nigerian History and Culture*. Harlow, Essex: Longman.

Uchendu, V. C. 1965. *The Igbo of Southeast Nigeria*. New York: Holt, Rinehart, and Winston.

The Centre Holds:
A Study of Chinua Achebe's *Things Fall Apart*_____

David Cook

On rereading *Things Fall Apart* I have been struck by the fact that the impression the book as a whole leaves on the mind is different from that gained by breaking off mid-way and considering one's immediate reactions. The book looms large in our memories as a well-proportioned structure, weighty and deliberate, economical in style, impressive in conception. A close-up view shifts the emphasis. Under detailed scrutiny the economy may scale down to spareness, while the large scope may seem to result in ruggedness, even roughness of texture. The plainness which the author was evidently seeking then seems for the moment not far from aridity.

Literary analysis is meaningful only in the service of a new synthesis. Close study of a passage from *Things Fall Apart* out of context is particularly likely to lead to pedantic fault-finding and to have little relation to the full impact the novel makes upon us, since, as I wish to argue in this chapter, the achievement of this work is essentially an epic achievement in which the whole is greater than the parts; and in which the parts cannot be appreciated properly when separated from the whole. Naive praise of *Things Fall Apart* can sometimes lead to an exaggerated reaction which underestimates the significant role that this novel plays in the chronological sequence of African writing in English. It has become an early landmark not only because of its point in time (though such a book could hardly have been written later) but because it is a worthy archetype.

It has not been uncommon to discuss *Things Fall Apart* in relation to Greek concepts of tragedy. In reference to this work and to *Arrow of God* Abiola Irele declares that[1] 'In two of his novels, at least, Achebe succeeds in striking a profoundly tragic note' and identifies Okonkwo's 'inflexibility' as his tragic flaw. Gerald Moore speaks of[2] 'the austere tragic dignity of *Things Fall Apart*' and refers to its 'classic treatment'. John Povey remarks that[3] 'Okonkwo matches other tragic heroes who in their extremes are simultaneously the most heroic and also the most unreasonable of men. . . . His heroism is based upon his unyielding sense of rectitude.' And G. D. Killam takes up this theme,[4] in saying that Okonkwo's story 'is presented in terms which resemble those of Aristotelian tragedy—the working out in the life of a hero of industry, courage and eminence, of an insistent fatality . . . which transcends his ability to fully understand or resist a fore-ordained sequence of events.'

A. G. Thomson ventures on some analogies with heroic poetry in general[5] but does not find this a very promising parallel: 'The ceremonies whose repetition is proper to the heroic poetry of people to whom heroic poetry is natural is a little oppressive in this novel, which invites comparison with other novels rather than with saga or epic.' And he soon withdraws from the discussion: 'Neither, perhaps, is there much point in speaking of modes, and in setting some general concept of the novel or chronicle against a concept of heroic poetry.' Thomson assumes that the epic and novel modes are mutually exclusive, and so wisely decides that there is little point in pursuing their relationship in this negative vein. But it is strange that, having observed a heroic manner to be apt for 'a people to whom heroic poetry is natural', he fails to conceive that this might indeed be a positive aspect of a novel by an Igbo about traditional Igbo society.

If *Things Fall Apart* is to be regarded as epic, then Okonkwo is essentially heroic. Both propositions are tenable. The work is epic in that it celebrates the achievement of a heroic personage in earlier times; and through him embodies a people's conception of their past. The story as a whole is heroic in that it concerns action which has recourse to bold, daring, extreme measures in attempting great things. The strength of an epic is in the structure of events it presents in order to depict in imaginative form the history of a society. In achieving this it may become both grand and somewhat impersonal, sacrificing warmth and detail of characterisation, but this is rather part of the definition of the 'kind' in which Achebe is writing (to adopt a Renaissance term) than a derogatory assessment.

Okonkwo is a hero in that he shows exceptional bravery, firmness, even greatness of soul. A hero is by definition an exceptional figure and so he does not simply embody the average virtues of his society in a fairly typical form; he is very far from being an Everyman.

Okonkwo, indeed, flouts the norms of his society in significant respects and in doing so brings many of his own ills upon his head. But this flouting is not, in terms of the design of the book, merely incidental or accidental; these deviations are highly significant and are made into major issues, so that in the process the norms are all the more clearly defined. He is twice punished for crimes against Ani, the earth goddess: if the last occasion leading to his banishment is an accident beyond his control, this is certainly not true of his infringement of the Week of Peace, on which occasion we are told that[6] 'Okonkwo was not the man to stop beating somebody half-way through, not even for fear of a goddess,' though his first two wives plead with him volubly. Three days short of the New Yam Festival he shoots at his second wife; and he is reprimanded by Chielo, the priestess of the Oracle, for resisting the demand that his daughter shall be brought into the presence of Agbala. Most telling of all, perhaps, is Obierika's final reproof for his role in the killing of Ikemefuna: 'What you have done will not please the Earth.' Okonkwo's aberrations serve to emphasise the social and moral framework.

Okonkwo is unlike the prototype epic heroes of Homer and Virgil in one very important respect which has to do with circumstances rather than character. He is not a founding figure in the fabled history of his people, but the very reverse. He makes a final, grandiloquent assertion of the values of his society before the established pattern of that society is changed beyond all recognition: he sings the swan-song of a tradition which is about to be transformed. He is heroic in standing for certain essential qualities in this long-established social pattern that made it strong, significant and enduring. Every society is unique in the precise balance of values and assumptions that maintain it. Some of the positives of one group may not necessarily be positives in codes of behaviour elsewhere. As Ajofia, speaking for the *egwugwu* of Umuofia, declares:

> We cannot leave the matter in his [Mr Smith's] hands because he does not understand our customs, just as we do not understand his. We say he is foolish because he does not know our ways, and perhaps he says we are foolish because we do not know his.

I do not myself believe that *Things Fall Apart* is concerned to pass judgment on social systems, nor to assert dogmatically that one is better or worse than another. What it does, in a lordly, objective, incontrovertible manner, is to demonstrate that every society depends on a fairly rigid set of conventions which can only be lived as a whole and can therefore only be evaluated as a whole—ideally from the inside. For foreigners to arrive extolling their own familiar social values and habits more or less uncritically and indiscriminately as 'civilised', and dismissing in contrast a different way of life demanding different conformities as 'primitive' was patently arrogant, prejudiced, uninformed, unintelligent. This does not mean that Achebe is bent on bettering their example by creating a mirror image of their bigotry. He prefers to reveal the darker side of both traditions as well as the better side and leave us to draw our own conclusions. He does not romanticise Igbo society nor vilify Christian European behaviour as a whole. There is little point in oversimplifying highly developed systems of human intercourse and labelling those of one's choice 'good' and the rest 'bad'. 'Facile rejection and facile acceptance,' says Ezekiel Mphahlele,[7] 'cannot stand "ironic contemplation".' Achebe is neither arrogant nor simplistic in *Things Fall Apart*: he takes a very long perspective.

As Professor Stock, among other critics, has pointedly observed,[8] for all his non-conformity, Okonkwo accepts the traditional values of his society: when he is banished, for instance, he does not kick against the judgement, but accepts it without question. And indeed he sets about overcoming the problems he has himself created in his life-pattern by methods proper to the very same tradition that has defined his misdemeanours.

What Okonkwo is really opposed to is history, or the inevitability of change resulting from converging forces which cannot now be diverted. These forces include not only the colonialists' self-righteous determination to rule and to impose conformity with their own conventions, backed by the power of guns, but also the counter-force of the oppressed within the traditional society; and the universal tendency of all human beings to want what they see; and yet again the inherent generosity, hospitality and misplaced pity that the Igbo expressed to wandering strangers. It is the whole complex of historical facts that Okonkwo stands against. The goodness or the badness of what is intruding and taking over is not for the moment the essential issue. Achebe is objective in *Things Fall Apart* not because he is indifferent—far from it; but because he is looking beneath the surface of things at the play of forces in a historical context. His refutation of pompous alien critics of Igbo society is incidental: they are the more effectively crushed because this is treated as a fairly elementary issue. Achebe's full subject is much larger and of more lasting significance. An epoch is reviewed in terms of the last-ditch stand of a great champion of that epoch.

His stand can be seen as futile since he is opposing the inevitable. It can also be seen as desperately heroic (a better word than 'noble' since Okonkwo is in fact not noble, nor, incidentally, particularly intelligent). This is a fine, hopeless, ultimate assertion that something that is about to disappear existed, was absolutely itself, and embodied certain great positives which can hardly be recreated exactly in a different context. In part we share the grand, objective viewpoint of the novel as a whole. But the purpose of a powerful objective writer is very often to leave us asking key questions for ourselves, and this surely is true of the author of *Things Fall Apart*. In terms of this work, modern African society can meaningfully review one set of its roots and origins, without sentimental idealising, but attributing proper value where it is due. And we are then bound, surely, to go on to ask how far these values can be properly and appropriately retained, or restored and reasserted in the different context of our own times.

In considering Okonkwo as a heroic figure in an epic framework, it is helpful to compare him to other protagonists whom Achebe has created. The differences between Okonkwo and Obi are numerous, but what interests me for the moment is to observe that when we set them side by side, Obi, in his complex set of dilemmas, is unmistakably a small man in contrast to Okonkwo. Ezeulu in *Arrow of God* is in an intermediate position, but his setting offers him large opportunities, and he is in kind, at least potentially, more similar to Okonkwo than to Obi; and yet this further comparison makes it all the more obvious that the hero of *Things Fall Apart* towers above his successors.

With some irony, Okonkwo's return to Umuofia is referred to as 'the warrior's return';[9] but at this moment the irony is not so much directed against the protagonist himself as against the society which no longer values, or even recognises, a warrior's qualities. Nothing demonstrates more clearly how things have degenerated in his absence in Mbanta than the virtual irrelevance of Okonkwo's stature, and of his very concepts, when he steps in over-confidently to rally the wavering spirit of his people.

Okonkwo has always been known as Roaring Flame. We are told at the very opening of the book that he 'was clearly cut out for great things'. He is a figure with a destiny, who in the proper course of events is ordained to set his mark on the history of his clan. He has the appearance of a hero: 'He was tall and huge, and his bushy eyebrows and wide nose gave him a very severe look.' A symbolic, ritual figure must look the part. Even in appearance, of course, these heroic qualities are not necessarily attractive in the mellower sense—they are grand and austere. Bravery, the quality which is to be assumed in any hero, is admirable but not in itself specially likeable. It is not for his humane endowments that the fighter is adulated. From the outset the tone employed in describing Okonkwo's pre-eminence is amusingly ambiguous. Immediately after the introductory set-piece description of his imposing appearance, the very next thing we learn is of his mighty snoring, which is upon the same scale:

> He breathed heavily, and it was said that, when he slept, his wives and children in their out-houses could hear him breathe.

On the other hand, Unoka, Okonkwo's father, who is despised by his son, has many amiable traits which are fully consistent with tradition: he is a companionable drinker; he loves the flute; he has a talent for good fellowship. We are specifically told that Okonkwo is not convivial—indeed his scorn of his father is increased by the latter's possession of these sociable qualities. At festivities Okonkwo goes through the motions, as a dutiful child of Umuofia, but he does so mechanically, without enthusiasm:

> But somehow Okonkwo could never become as enthusiastic over feasts as other people . . . he was always uncomfortable sitting around for days waiting for a feast or getting over it. He would be much happier working on his farm.

First he looks down upon his father because of his mildness, and then he comes later to spurn his own eldest son, Nwoye, for the very same characteristic. Though grandfather and grandson are in many respects very different, Unoka and Nwoye have in common a hatred for war, the event above all others in which Okonkwo shines. It is a familiar fact about *Things Fall Apart* that in rejecting his father for disgracing him and failing to give him a start in life, Okonkwo comes to hate and fear 'gentleness' to a psychopathic degree:

> Perhaps down in his heart Okonkwo was not a cruel man. But his whole life was dominated by fear, the fear of failure and of weakness.

John Povey is right, then, when he says,[10] 'In spite of our general sympathy Okonkwo is not a lovable man.' He refuses to show the affection that he actually feels. This neurotic repression of his softer emotions is comprehensible, and could have engendered a good deal of sympathy for him as a man tortured by this conditioned self-concealment. But the book gives the reader little encouragement in such reactions. He even throttles into silence the mutual affection between himself and his daughter:[11] 'Okonkwo was specially fond of Ezinma. . . . But his fondness only showed on very rare occasions.' For the most part he treats her sternly, and, with characteristically stubborn rejection of all the warmer contacts within his reach, he broods perversely on his wish that she were a boy.

We see Okonkwo, then, as brusque, impatient, self-sufficient. His lack of humility is demonstrated by the haughty way in which he perpetually finds fault with others, which occasionally leads his fellow elders to reprimand him and demand that he apologise to his victim. If we feel for Okonkwo, it is in his public capacities, not as a private individual. The very first paragraph of the novel sings his praises as a man of action in a context, in this society, which provides one of the great positive opportunities for a man to show his prowess—wrestling. As a successful member of his group Okonkwo—to employ a Western praise-term—is very much a self-made man, and he has much of the thick-skinned self-assurance which that phrase implies.

We should note that our attitude to a successful fighter in the inter-tribal contests of Okonkwo's heyday is determined by the scale upon which these wars were fought in traditional circumstances. Twelve men were killed on the enemy side in a great victory, and two from among the conquerors. Numbers do not, of course, affect the gravity of violent death in itself, one way or the other; nevertheless our attitude is affected by the fact that an action such as this does not run beyond our imagination; it does not dwarf the idea of Man himself; he is not ironically belittled as in the widespread carnage and destruction of modern warfare.

However, much of Okonkwo's self-assertive activity occurs in contexts in which we are not asked to admire him. 'Okonkwo's way of conforming,' says Abiola Irele,[12] 'besides being an inverted sort of nonconformity, is a perversion. The meaning that he attaches to manliness amounts to fierceness, *violence*.' He insists, as we have noted already, on participating in the killing of Ikemefuna, contrary to determined advice; he beats Ojiugo in Peace Week, thereby scandalising the community; he tries to kill his second wife and fails only because he is a bad shot—a scene which is ludicrous but far from amusing. His ferocity alienates his eldest son and drives him into the arms of the Christians. 'It is not Christianity and the world of the whiteman that has broken up Okonkwo's family,' says John Reed.[13] 'It has merely given the disruptive passions within that family their chance.' Looking back from the vantage point of hindsight, his contemptuous dismissal of those who have not succeeded in life is ironic:[14] 'He had no patience with unsuccessful men.' In the last resort how successful is Okonkwo himself? His wilfulness actually earns him the dislike of his clansmen:

> people said he had no respect for the gods of the clan. His enemies said his good fortune had gone to his head. They called him the little bird *nza* who so far forgot himself after a heavy meal that he challenged his *chi*.

Nevertheless, he is punctilious in the niceties of tradition even to his own disadvantage: he will not return to Umuofia before the very day on which the full seven years expire. And when he leaves Mbanta, in spite of his own dislike of public festivities, he surpasses expectation in the feast that he throws as a farewell gesture:

> we expected a big feast. But it turned out to be even bigger than we expected.

Indeed, when one considers how much there is potentially to weight our feelings against Okonkwo, it speaks much for Achebe's achievement in his chosen mode that his protagonist retains for us such indubitable heroic stature. It is of vital importance in this connection that the climax of the whole action is a crucial moment of violent drama in which, however ambiguous its implications, we are essentially in sympathy with Okonkwo; the story is shaped to induce our support at this moment for his gesture of defiant opposition to the arrogant presumption of white rule and the calculated degradation of a great tradition. He stands alone in this last expression of stubborn independence. His is an exalted defeat for which his whole career has prepared him.

Things Fall Apart presents us with a fairly full picture of the Igbo society which Okonkwo takes it upon himself to champion. As we have said, there is no romanticising and yet, once it has been shown to us in depth, the idea that this human complex is merely barbarous when compared to others is clearly the result of social attitudes which are themselves unsophisticated. We are shown a coherent and at the same time contradictory pattern of human existence, in these respects very much like most others. It has achieved a system of controls which assure internal order and allow in the main a humane conduct of daily affairs, based on well recognised positive values. Umuofia prides itself on fighting only for a just cause—not out of blood-thirstiness or rash endeavour; and its neighbours are said to acknowledge the truth of this claim. This policy is not a rationalisation of weakness but takes its stand from a position of strength. Their oracle restrains them from engaging in a 'fight of blame'. It is the pressure of society which forces Okonkwo to withdraw when he humiliates an unsuccessful clansman at a meeting. Uchendu blames the Abame group for killing the first white man to appear in their midst: 'Never kill a man who says nothing.' This is not simply a question of self-interest; it is rational response to a new situation. By the time that Okonkwo acts at the end of *Things Fall Apart*, the white group have not only made their negative position disastrously plain, but this attitude is now seen to be irrevocable and permanent.

Within Igbo society there is no ultimate complacency with regard to social mores. Obierika questions himself searchingly as to the rationale of Okonkwo's ritual banishment, and finds no satisfaction, as he admits himself.

> Obierika was a man who thought about things. When the will of the goddess had been done, he sat down in his *obi* and mourned his friend's calamity. Why should a man suffer so grievously for an offence he had committed inadvertently? But although he thought for a long time he found no answer.

A mature perspective is struck between different life-patterns. Uchendu declares,

> There is no story that is not true. . . . The world has no end, and what is good among one people is an abomination with others.

Complex ironies are involved in the missionaries' rejoicing at Nwoye leaving his parents in the name of the true church. This is orthodox enough Christianity—'Come thou out from among the unbelievers'— but at one and the same time it is counter to the most positive principles not only of the Igbo and of almost all African societies, but also to good middle-class British Victorian morality which found blood to be a good deal thicker than water. Time and again it is the values of traditional society, with its non-materialistic base and its absence of vested interests in any commercial sense, that are stressed—virtues to which most Europeans would surely be bound at least to pay lip-service:

> We do not pray to have money but to have more kinsmen. We are better than animals because we have kinsmen.

These positive values are frankly set against the inhuman practices and irrational taboos that are part and parcel of the conventions and assumptions of the Igbo, epitomised very specifically in the treatment of the osu and the abandonment of twins. Both these items of conduct are mandatory within the Igbo system; nevertheless they have haunted Nwoye's mind long before he finds his own escape route into the new church, as an over-sensitive refugee from his own environment. Nwoye, as Professor Stock well observes,[15] 'was the kind of youth to whom personal feeling meant more than public spirit, which was one reason that he was a nonentity in Umuofia'. Outcasts, misfits and malcontents formed fertile ground for the new breed of spiritual sowers.

Yet there is no question whatever of holding up Christianity as an untarnished alternative. It embraces anomalies which are even more fundamentally paradoxical than Igbo tradition. Not only does the new religion sing hallelujahs when it succeeds in wrenching child converts from 'pagan' parents, but it supports and in turn is supported by the oppressive rule; each basks in the approval of the other:[16] 'Mr Brown's mission grew from strength to strength, and because of its link with the new administration it earned a new social prestige.' It is good avowed respected members of the flock who perpetrate the worst abuses:

> They were beaten in the prison by the *kotma* and made to work every morning clearing the government compound and fetching wood for the white Commissioner and the court messengers. Some of these prisoners were men of title who should be above such mean occupation.

The six elders are captured by a calculated piece of dishonourable treachery; and are thereafter treated altogether inhumanly by men who profess both the virtues of Christianity and of white administration, not always distinguishing between the two.

And so the total effect is one of balance. In the argument between Mr Brown and Akunna, we see little to choose between the two religions in the light of objective analysis: needless to say Mr Brown himself does not entertain such a heretical view, but the honest reader who accepts the validity of the novel finds such a reaction inescapable.

Thus, while it is plain that both systems can be and are in some respects corrupted and oppressive, and while the new white rule is totally blind, on the other hand, to the many excellences of the established system, the main emphasis is not on the stupidity or bigotry of the new order, but on the fact that with it, for better or for worse, lay the inevitable stream of history at the time in question:

> The elders consulted their Oracle and it told them that the strange man would break their clan and spread destruction among them.

This Okonkwo does not or will not believe. He has a blind, superb faith in the possibility of maintaining the past unchanged into the future: 'God will not permit it.'

But the oracle speaks for the gods more fittingly than Okonkwo, who is steadfastly swimming against the strengthening tide, refusing to acknowledge that he is already losing ground in the face of forces which are beyond his control, regardless of whether or not it is desirable to oppose them. Okonkwo's clansmen see their dilemma as more complex and they accept Mr Brown's counsel: 'If Umuofia failed to send her children to the school, strangers would come from other places to rule them.' They are caught in a situation which seems to offer no meaningful choice: they have to play out a game wherein they have no chance either to determine or to challenge the rules. Obierika attributes their position to the wiliness of the Europeans:

> The white man is very clever. He came quietly and peaceably with his religion. We were amused at his foolishness and allowed him to stay. Now he has won our brothers, and our clan can no longer act like one. He has put a knife on the things that held us together and we have fallen apart.

This is true in more than one sense, and yet it overestimates the foresight of the invaders. The whites did not have a concerted plan in this way to take advantage of the factors which Obierika's speech identifies. They were self-infatuated empiricists with a consuming sense of mission who were lucky to have guns and history on their side, forces too great for Okonkwo to have stood against even if he had succeeded in rallying his people. But this is the last moment that heroic protest will be possible, not only against the alien power but against all extra-human forces that seem to support it; and Okonkwo seizes that moment.

Since the appearance of *A Man of the People* the sceptics who could not believe Achebe's claim that his style in the 'trilogy' was deliberately chosen, but presumed that this was the only style he could master, have been silenced. The contrast with *A Man of the People* may encourage us to exaggerate the similarity between the three earlier novels. But while such similarities can be overstated, the three works have a likeness of purpose and a likeness of manner which confirm their identity as a group.

The style, in its 'epic', heroic, objective manner, rests its strength on firm overall structure. The plan of the three books—especially *Things Fall Apart*—is grand, powerful, fully successful in outline. The 'fable' (to use what still seems to be the best translation of an Aristotelian term) is altogether adequate. The spare style of the first novel with its bare vocabulary, its fairly simple structures, and its restraint in imagery apart from the special kind of colouring provided by proverbs, has (like most other styles) its advantages and disadvantages. It is direct, uncloyed, classically stark. Achebe has succeeded in his stated attempt to escape from an essentially British manner in phrasing.

On the other hand, a style which Anne Tibble has joined Gerald Moore in describing as 'laconic' before adding the additional epithet 'flat',[17] may be found to be lacking in texture. As I said earlier, for all one's constant rediscovery of the scope and scale of *Things Fall Apart*, there is a level at which immediate satisfaction falters. The language is plain to the point of losing at later readings intense minute-to-minute interest. The occasional imaginative phrase, which is not directly descriptive or proverbial, emphasises rather than relieves this manner, reminds us of the deliberate rarity of such usages: kites 'hovered over the burning field in silent valediction';[18] 'It was a tremendous sight, full of power and beauty'; 'And whenever the moon forsook evening and rose at cock-crow the nights were as black as charcoal'. These occasional embellishments are for the most part in keeping with the stylistic manner, and do not break the general tenor.

The power of this style is above all cumulative in its effect, especially because of its utter suitability to the whole literary mode that I have been attempting to define, 'a prose', as Margaret Laurence puts it,[19] 'which is plain and spare and at all times informed with his keen sense of irony'. To say that this work is always more impressive as a whole in the mind, in completed retrospect, than in terms of our immediate reaction in mid-paragraph, is not negative praise. It is arguable that the permanent impression that a serious and memorable book leaves with us is the most important thing of all concerning our critical reactions. *Things Fall Apart* is built in such a way that nothing is likely to dislodge it from its place in our memories or in any consideration of the development of anglophone African writing. Artistic stoicism is clearly more appropriate to this ruggedly constructed masterpiece than any purely external fancifulness or richness would be.

It is interesting to observe in passing that Achebe, in escaping from British stylistic clichés and mannerisms, has employed, aptly enough, what is often theoretically declared to be a normal feature in constructing English prose, but which on closer analysis appears to be something of a rarity among well-known British writers. It is asserted in certain types of textbook and guide that there should be, or indeed that there always is in good writing, a 'key' sentence in every paragraph, either at the beginning announcing the subject which is then developed in the body of that particular paragraph, or at the end to bring together the points that have been raised. In practice one can search through writer after writer without distinguishing such a key sentence in each paragraph as a norm (though examples can be collected). Achebe has adopted in *Things Fall Apart* a style which is tightly trussed up and carefully modulated; and to suit his purpose he has employed a rather more formalised conception of the paragraph than many English writers.

There are strong patterns in the structuring of *Things Fall Apart*. Although the design is simple, being centred upon one character, with in the main a linear time progression and a clear placing of the short passage in Mbanta between the two major sections in Umuofia—the whole expressing a clash between two major social forces, there is a rightness about the scheme which suggests the imprint of a master craftsman and artist who can return to first principles and achieve the most difficult of all artistic effects: significant simplicity. From first to last the work gives the impression of having been soundly planned and of being under firm control. The organisation of the chapters defines meaningful spans of the novel: the ending of the first chapter with Okonkwo becoming Ikemefuna's guardian is one of many pointers to the book's planned proportions: and Ikemefuna is the subject of the final paragraphs of both Chapters 2 and 4, just as his name is the last word of Chapter 7, in which he has been killed.

One piece of description of traditional society—the coming of the locusts—turns out to be imaginatively and ironically significant:[20]

> I forgot to tell you another thing which the Oracle said. It said that other white men were on their way. They were locusts, it said, and the first man was their harbinger sent to explore the terrain.

An example of particularly careful patterning of an incident on many levels is to be found after the occasion on which Enoch has violated one of the ancestors:

> That night the Mother of the Spirits walked the length and breadth of the clan, weeping for her murdered son. It was a terrible night. Not even the oldest man in Umuofia had ever heard such a strange and fearful sound, and it was never to be heard again. It seemed as if the very soul of the tribe wept for a great evil that was coming—its own death.

Once a proverb is deliberately repeated to link two parts of the novel—a tautening device which Achebe was to develop in *Arrow of God* and *A Man of the People*.

Things Fall Apart is so clearly an important work that it is easy to forget how early it came in its author's career. In assessing its strengths we may also become aware that certain opportunities have been lost. In this novel Achebe seizes upon a special creative opportunity which lay before him, such as is seldom offered even to the perceptive artist more than once. In later works he learnt to depend on a more complex development of techniques. The intimate display of the whole life of the Igbo is an integral part of the subject of *Things Fall Apart*, yet this does not have to be recounted in disconnected incidents, such as we sometimes find, with little part to play in the development of plot or characterisation or other aspects of the novel. Gerald Moore is right when he says,[21] 'The boredom of daily routines in an isolated forest village must be felt, but not suffered, by the reader, in order that he may feel also the excitement of the festival and the thrilling fear of the unheralded event.' However, the scenes needed to establish our awareness of the way of life that is threatened might more constantly have served other purposes at the same time, for instance the incident in which the elders give judgement in the case of the runaway wife, the long wrestling scene in which Okonkwo is not involved, or the description of the ceremonies in overture to marriage.

Even the tale that Ekwefi tells in Chapter 11 appears to have been selected at random. A traditional fable is essentially a story which can be applied to actual circumstances in a current situation, and so the embedding of such a narrative in *Things Fall Apart* would seem to offer an admirable opportunity to link one aspect of the novel to another by implication at various levels. But I have been unable to perceive any relevance in Ekwefi's tale to the novel at large, and I am not aware that anyone has done so.

When one turns a deliberately critical eye on the book one can see possible cross-references in the subject-matter which seem to cry out for some patterned recognition. For example, upon studied consideration one is struck by the fact that Okonkwo is exiled for his gun going off accidentally and killing someone, whereas earlier he misses his wife when he deliberately shoots at her with the same weapon with intent to kill. Eldred Jones does not convince me,[22] however, that this conjunction has been significantly planned. It may be suggested that since a reader can see a possible ironic linkage here, the author can be said to have deliberately scattered these contradictory events throughout the book with the aim of making the reader search out a connection. This strikes me as too arbitrary a method with too random an effect to be thought of as meaningful structuring.

There are limitations also in the characterisation. Okonkwo is the only individual in *Things Fall Apart* who is presented to us in any detail. Other characters are introduced convincingly enough but are developed only as far as the bare needs of the plot demand—that is to say sketchily at most. Even Ekwefi and Ezinma are slight portraits, and Eldred Jones has rightly complained of the virtual disappearance of the latter from the scene before the climax.[23] Okonkwo is the only character whom we can consider in the round though the novel aspires at this level to be a realistic work.

In many of the respects in which we discover such restrictions in *Things Fall Apart*, *Arrow of God* is a more mature, a less chancy work of art. It is a fine, polished novel, which satisfies us more at each new reading. And yet it still misses something of the happy, rugged strength of *Things Fall Apart* which derives from the self-confident handling of the strong basic structural idea. Nowhere is this clearer than in the ending, which is placed so exactly and surely and is handled with such fine restraint, confirming as we close the book the indelible impression that it will leave upon us.

The well-known final ironic paragraph at the D.C.'s expense is a neat rounding out in key with the controlled distancing of the whole novel. That the D.C. perceives this action as a small, intriguing vignette in the autobiography which is to glorify his image in the eyes of what can only be a petty and uninformed circle of provincial English readers, finally epitomises his own smallness, the narrowness of his vision and the pathetic inadequacy of his ambitions, for all the inflated image he has of himself and his role. But at this stage in the work the D.C. is a fairly easy target within the wide perspective of Achebe's canvas; the author's deeper concern is with the more powerful structural irony which takes shape in the last two pages and provides the serious conclusion to the novel at its most profound and permanent level.

Okonkwo has broken the final taboos of his own society in committing suicide:[24]

> It is an abomination for a man to take his own life. It is an offence against the Earth, and a man who commits it will not be buried by his clansmen. His body is evil, and only strangers may touch it.

How has Okonkwo been brought to deny in his death all that he has lived for? The answer is clear enough. He has reached the point of absolute disillusionment. In the betrayal by his clansmen his life disintegrates; and so the values he has striven to maintain no longer have any meaning. His death is a physical expression of his knowledge that things have irrevocably fallen apart. He, and through him his clan, have been denied three times, but the shame is heaped upon Okonkwo himself: his people will not bury him. In the depth of his chagrin Obierika musters his spirit to put the blame upon the white man to his face, and there is truth in the accusation, just as there is truth in the assertion that Okonkwo has himself committed an abomination:

> That man was one of the greatest men in Umuofia. *You* drove him to kill himself; and now he will be buried like a dog.

This speech expresses the paradox. The aliens are responsible for Okonkwo's death and yet he is to be buried like a dog. And why? The clansmen will not so far break the laws of tradition as to cut down

Okonkwo's body and bury it. Yet they have not lifted a finger to support Okonkwo when he alone made a stand in the name of that very tradition. 'We shall make sacrifices to cleanse the desecrated land.' Yet was not Okonkwo's act in killing the messenger itself a deliberate sacrifice with precisely the aim of cleansing the desecrated land? Obierika's words to the D.C. confirm this—yet at that moment those who are now so nice about social proprieties as to leave the body of their champion in strangers' hands had hung back and left Okonkwo naked. Which is the real desecration—Okonkwo's stoic death, or the meek acceptance of humiliation at the hands of the white man?

After this the irony of the last paragraph takes on a new dimension. It is not just that the D.C. plans to reduce the heroic death pangs of a way of life to a patronising paragraph: it is that the clansmen have allowed themselves to be diminished in this way without resistance. The only figure who escapes this final irony is the dead Okonkwo.

From *African Literature: A Critical View* (1977), pp. 65-81. Copyright © 1977 by Longman Group, Ltd. Reprinted with permission of Longman Group, Ltd.

Notes

1. Abiola Irele, 'Tragic Conflict in Achebe's Novels', *Black Orpheus*; reprinted in *Introduction to African Literature*, ed. Ulli Beier, Longman, London, 1967, p. 167.

2. Gerald Moore, *Seven African Writers*, Oxford University Press, London, 1962, p. 60.

3. John Povey, 'The Novels of Chinua Achebe', *Introduction to Nigerian Literature*, ed. Bruce King, University of Lagos/Evans, 1971, p. 101.

4. G. D. Killam, *The Novels of Chinua Achebe*, Heinemann Educational Books, London, 1969, p. 17.

5. A. W. Thomson, 'The Political Occasion: A Note on the Poetry of John Pepper Clark', *The Journal of Commonwealth Literature*, vii, I, 1972, pp. 84-5.

6. Chinua Achebe, *Things Fall Apart*, Heinemann Educational Books, London, 1958, p. 27; the following two quotations are from pp. 60-1 ('What you have done . . .'), and 1-72.

7. Ezekiel Mphahlele, *The African Image*, Faber, London, 1962, p. 202.

8. A. G. Stock, 'Yeats and Achebe', *The Journal of Commonwealth Literature*, v, 1968, 107.

9. *Things Fall Apart*, p. 165; the following five quotations are from pp. 7 ('was clearly cut out . . .'), 3 ('He was tall . . .'), 3, 34, and 12.

10. John Povey, *op. cit.*, p. 100.

11. *Things Fall Apart*, p. 41.

12. Abiola Irele, *op. cit.*, p. 169.

13. John Reed, 'Between Two Worlds', *Makerere Journal* 7, 1963, p. 13.

14. *Things Fall Apart*, p. 4; the following six quotations are from pp. 28, 152, 126 ('Never kill a man . . .'), 113, 127, and 151.

15. A. G. Stock, *op. cit.*, p. 108.

16. *Things Fall Apart*, p. 164; the following five quotations are from pp. 158, 125, 128 ('God will not permit it . . .'), 164 ('If Umuofia failed . . .'), and 160.

17. Moore, *Seven African Writers*, p. 59; Anne Tibble, *African-English Literature* (Peter Owen, London, 1965, p. 107.

18. *Things Fall Apart*, p. 29; the following two quotations are from pp. 50 ('It was a tremendous . . .'), and 86 ('And whenever the moon . . .').

19. Margaret Laurence, *Long Drums and Cannons*, Macmillan, London, 1968, p. 107.

20. *Things Fall Apart*, p. 125; the following quotation is from p. 168.

21. Gerald Moore, *The Chosen Tongue*, Longman, London, 1969, p. 152.

22. Eldred Jones, 'Academic Problems and Critical Techniques', *African Literature and the Universities*, ed. Gerald Moore, Ibadan University Press, 1965, p. 94.

23. *Ibid*.

24. *Things Fall Apart*, p. 186; the following two quotations are both from p. 187.

Principle and Practice:
The Logic of Cultural Violence
in Achebe's *Things Fall Apart*_____

David Hoegberg

The phrase "cultural violence" need not refer only to violence between people of different cultures. It can also refer to violence that is encouraged by the beliefs and traditions of a given culture and practiced upon its own members. "Cultural violence" used in this sense would include ritual sacrifices, punishments for crimes, and other kinds of communally sanctioned violence. Often, the communal sanction given to acts of violence springs from unexamined assumptions and contradictions within the culture and shared by a majority of its members. This insight, I will argue, is a major theme of Chinua Achebe's 1958 novel, *Things Fall Apart*, one of the most influential fictional statements on violence in a colonial setting. Although Achebe powerfully criticizes the violence of British colonial practices, the British do not enter the picture until after Achebe has explored the internal workings of Igbo culture. The main character, Okonkwo, is frequently violent, but Achebe's statements about the relations of culture to violence are better seen in the actions and beliefs of the group as a whole. Since the majority of Igbo in the novel tend to be less violent than Okonkwo, those forms of violence they do condone and enact are especially revealing of the widespread cultural forces that foster violence. I will argue that two of these cultural forces are particularly important to Achebe. One is the community's tendency to forget, selectively and temporarily, certain defining principles of its culture, so that contradictions arise between specific practices and general beliefs. The other is what Simon Gikandi has called "the Achilles heel in the Igbo epistemology," that is, "its blindness [to], or refusal to contemplate, its own ethnocentrism" (1991, 38). Even violence internal to the culture is often conceptualized in terms of ethnocentric distinctions between insiders and outsiders, borders and border crossings.

In one scene early in the novel, Achebe shows the Igbos' capacity for self-consciousness regarding violence within their culture when he reveals that some violent traditions have been changed. After Okonkwo pays his fine for breaking the Week of Peace, one of the oldest men in the village reflects on the way things used to be done. Ezeudu says, "in the past a man who broke the peace was dragged on the ground through the village until he died. But after a while this custom was stopped because it spoiled the peace which it was meant to preserve" (1959, 33). This brief passage leads us to several important issues at stake in the novel. We are told that the custom of killing offenders changed not because of a gradual and unconscious evolution, not because of personal favoritism toward an offender, but because the practice violated a principle the people wanted to uphold: "because it spoiled the peace which it was meant to preserve." This tells us that the change was conscious and was based on an analysis of the congruence between principle and practice. Since the very existence of the Week of Peace expresses the principle that violence is an affront to the earth, the punishment for violations needs to express the same general principle or there is contradiction. In this case, violence resulted from an unexamined contradiction that was later revealed and rooted out. At a certain point, it occurred to enough people that it made no sense to enforce a rule of non-violence with violence. What are the conditions of possibility for such a cultural change? First, a majority of people must have the freedom and the desire to analyze their traditions for moral and logical consistency. Second, they must see the general principles involved as more valuable than specific rituals or traditions. A culture that already has some violent traditions will tend to keep them as long as its highest priority is the preservation of tradition for its own sake. Finally, people must believe that changing inconsistent traditions makes them stronger as a people, that cultural change is not the same as cultural decay. In the case of the Week of Peace punishment, the change in the tradition is really toward a more perfect expression of the principle behind the tradition.

This example shows that in the not-too-distant past the conditions for questioning and constructive change of violent traditions were present in Igbo society. We might even say that there was a *tradition* of analyzing and adjusting certain traditions within the culture. If the Igbo, as depicted in the novel, fail to make changes in other areas where there are contradictions between principle and practice, then, it cannot be because such change is impossible. Through this brief example, Achebe establishes that violence is not an inherent feature of Igbo society or a necessary consequence of its religious beliefs. If change is always possible, then we must look at other cases of violence in the novel in terms of what forces inhibit or encourage analysis and change.

One of the most important examples of culturally sanctioned violence is the killing of Ikemefuna. Most critics agree that it is a mistake for Okonkwo to participate in this killing because of his special relationship to Ikemefuna (Taylor 1983, 20-21), but many fail to ask why the oracle and elders sanction this violence in the first place (Udumukwu 1991, 333; Obiechina 1991, 35). Some critics attempt to justify the killing as part of accepted practice among the Igbo (Rhoads 1993, 68; Cobham 1991, 95), and argue that condemnations of the killing inappropriately apply Western standards of humanism (Opata 1987, 75-76; Hawkins 1991, 83). Few seem to have noticed that the novel itself teaches us how to critique this incident on the basis of principle. The crime for which the people of Mbaino are punished is the killing of a woman from Umuofia. If there is a general principle operating here and not simply a policy of selfish revenge, it would be that villagers should not kill aliens or visitors in their midst. For Umuofia to punish this crime by taking a boy from Mbaino into their midst and killing him is to violate the very principle they would appear to be enforcing, thereby spoiling the peace they meant to preserve (Wright 1990, 79; Innes 1990, 29).

This objection to Ikemefuna's killing would apply no matter what person from Mbaino was taken as a hostage. When we learn that the hostage is the son of one of the murderers, a second principle comes into play. In one of his "ethnographic" generalizations about the Igbo culture (Gikandi 1991, 46), the narrator explains Okonkwo's rise to prominence by saying: "Fortunately, among these people a man was judged according to his worth and not according to the worth of his father" (Achebe 1959, 11). The ethnographic mode here claims to describe a general principle held by all the people, a central tenet or defining feature of their culture. This tenet seems related to the ability to question and change traditions mentioned above, for it asserts that the members of each generation are entitled to a fresh evaluation of their own merits. Neither worth nor worthlessness should be passed on automatically from father to son; rather, the process of "passing on" is to be interrupted by analysis, just as in the case of the Week of Peace punishment the passing on of a violent custom was interrupted by an analysis of its merits and drawbacks. Okonkwo personally benefits from the fact that this principle is widespread among his people, for it allows him to start with a "clean slate" without being held back by his father's failures. The narrator goes on to connect the principle explicitly with Okonkwo's relation to Ikemefuna. "Age was respected among his people, but achievement was revered. As the elders said, if a child washed his hands he could eat with kings. Okonkwo had clearly washed his hands and so he ate with kings and elders. And *that was how* he came to look after the doomed lad who was sacrificed to the village of Umuofia by their neighbors to avoid war and bloodshed" (1959, 12; italics added). *Because* Okonkwo is not judged according to his father's worth, he becomes so respected in the clan that he is chosen to carry the threat of war to Mbaino and then chosen to keep Ikemefuna in his household. A great irony begins to emerge, however, when we read in the next chapter that Ikemefuna is selected as a hostage precisely because "his father had taken a hand in killing a daughter of Umuofia" (1959, 18). The boy himself is innocent of any wrongdoing but he is not selected at random from the young men of the village. He is judged according to the worth of his father, in direct contradiction of the principle in which we are told "these people" believe. Their attempt to bring about justice seems, according to their own most basic beliefs, to have created a new injustice. The original intent may have been to punish Ikemefuna's father by taking his precious son away from him, but the separation clearly punishes the son as well. At first Ikemefuna is afraid and tries to run away, then he refuses to eat and is ill for three weeks (1959, 29-30). Ikemefuna must feel like a slave or captive at this point, yet he is not guilty except insofar as he is tainted by his father's guilt. Is there any way to explain this contradiction in Igbo practice between the principle that worth is not tied to the father and the treatment of Ikemefuna? Is it intention or unwitting irony that the son who is being punished for his father's crime is placed under the care of a man who is conspicuous for *not* being judged by his father?

Answers to these questions are complicated by the fact that the elders of the clan seem to forget about Ikemefuna altogether for three years. During this time, Ikemefuna overcomes his sadness and fear and begins to enjoy life in Okonkwo's family. His natural liveliness makes him popular with Okonkwo's other children, especially Nwoye (Achebe 1959, 30). Okonkwo himself grows so fond of Ikemefuna that he allows him special privileges, such as carrying his stool to village meetings, and in return Ikemefuna expresses his affection by calling Okonkwo "father" (1959, 30). For three years, then, the story of Ikemefuna is a study in human adaptability. As a stranger in a village where he has no blood ties and where customs, songs, and stories are slightly different (1959, 36), Ikemefuna is able to adjust to the new conditions quite successfully. Likewise, Okonkwo and the other villagers adjust to his alien presence, giving no outward indication (until the oracle's decision) of latent animosity towards Ikemefuna for his father's crime. In transferring his affections and obedience to a new "father," Ikemefuna is like the religious converts later in the novel who take on a new god. His conversion may be forced, but is no less genuine for that.

The success of Ikemefuna's integration into the community makes his execution all the more puzzling. What exactly is the oracle's motive? Ikemefuna's father's punishment cannot be increased by the killing since his son is equally lost to him whether dead or alive, so it does not further the cause of peace by deterring violence. If Ikemefuna had acted like a misfit in Umuofia, the decision could be seen as an admission that the attempt to incorporate him into the clan had failed, but Achebe does not allow this interpretation, either. There is no event or disaster preceding the decision to suggest that the Umuofians feared they were being punished by the gods for delaying the sacrifice. And after three years, emotions are cooled so that even revenge is not a likely motive. Indeed, Achebe's point seems to be that there is no clear and conscious motivation for the killing. Here is a case that cries out for the sort of analysis that led to the change in punishments for the Week of Peace, yet no one seems to notice that the killing violates two basic principles of Igbo culture: the prohibition against killing strangers, and the belief that sons should not be judged by their fathers' worth. These unexamined contradictions give birth to the culturally sanctioned violence against Ikemefuna. Achebe provides readers with enough evidence to critique the killing according to the internal standards of the community itself.

If the conditions for change are present in Igbo tradition, why are they not active in Ikemefuna's case? I would suggest that the very success of Ikemefuna's conversion or assimilation is a key factor in the meaning of this incident. Over the course of three years, Ikemefuna's status in Umuofia becomes more and more ambiguous. Is he an alien or a son of Okonkwo, a sacrificial victim awaiting execution or just another boy of the village? By the time he is killed, Ikemefuna has become a symbol of blurred boundaries between self and other. The oracle's decision suggests that the community is willing to tolerate such ambiguous status only up to a point and only for so long. Once the limit of tolerance is reached, the matter is settled by identifying Ikemefuna once and for all as an alien, a hostage, rather than an adopted son. Whatever its conscious motivation, the killing of Ikemefuna is *in effect* a denunciation of the adaptation process, a reminder that in the oracle's and the elders' minds, Ikemefuna can never be accepted no matter how well-liked or well-assimilated he may be. When Ezeudu says to Okonkwo, "That boy *calls* you father" (Achebe 1959, 55; italics added), his phrase highlights both the extent of Ikemefuna's conversion and its futility in the "official" view of the elders. Pretending that Okonkwo is his father has become second nature to the boy, Ezeudu seems to say, but this is finally only pretense and it can go on no longer. When seen as a story about adaptation and rejection, the story of Ikemefuna is thematically parallel to the later parts of the novel involving the alien presence of Christians and British officers. The oracle declares that the alien boy should not be assimilated and must be attacked, taking the same sort of hard-line stance Okonkwo later takes regarding the alien presence of the whites and their religion.

The full irony of the oracle's attempt to enforce a communal boundary appears only when we look at its consequences. As is well known, Ikemefuna's killing is so emotionally devastating to Nwoye that he becomes alienated from both his father and his culture (Innes 1990, 29). When this happens he is a prime candidate for conversion to Christianity, whose preaching, says the narrator, "seemed to answer a vague and persistent question that haunted his young soul—the question of the twins crying in the bush and the question of Ikemefuna who was killed" (Achebe 1959, 137). By showing the causes of Nwoye's interest in Christianity, Achebe shows that the attempt to strengthen boundaries between "us" and "others" actually weakens those very boundaries. The attempt to squelch Ikemefuna's conversion hastens Nwoye's conversion.

Another case of inherited guilt accompanied by a fear of permeable boundaries can be seen in the community's treatment of its *osu*, or outcasts. The narrator tells us that an *osu* is "a person dedicated to a god, a thing set apart—a taboo for ever, and his children after him" (Achebe 1959, 146). That *osu* is an hereditary category means that, like the punishment of Ikemefuna, its existence violates the general principle that sons should not be judged according to the worth of their fathers. Furthermore, although *osu* are natives of the village, every effort is made to treat them as permanent strangers or outsiders. The *osu* "could neither marry nor be married by the freeborn. He was in fact an outcast, living in a special area of the village, close to the Great Shrine. Wherever he went he carried with him the mark of his forbidden caste—long, tangled and dirty hair" (1959, 146). These rules about marriage, residence, and appearance mean that *osu* can never be fully assimilated, either biologically or socially, into village life; clear boundaries are set up indicating the communal fear of ambiguous status. Although Ikemefuna is not placed in the category of *osu* when he arrives, these details shed light on his case, for he is killed at the very moment when he threatens to lose the marks of his otherness, something the *osu* are required by law to preserve. "He had become wholly absorbed into his new family," says the narrator at the beginning of chapter seven, "he was like an elder brother to Nwoye" (1959, 51). Since it is later in the same chapter that the intent to kill Ikemefuna is announced, we are invited to conclude that his successful merging with the community may be precisely what sparks the oracle's decision.

In the context of a discussion of cultural boundaries and their permeability, the fact that Ikemefuna's story is also a version of the Biblical story of Abraham and Isaac becomes very interesting. Many critics have noticed this allusion but few have discussed its significance as a cross-cultural literary gesture (Cobham 1991, 95; Bascom 1988, 71). The Biblical parallel, the novel's title, and other Western allusions in the novel show that it was part of Achebe's plan to create an intertextual work, one that would to some extent blur the boundary between African and Western literature. The allusion to Abraham and Isaac occurs at the very moment when Achebe's characters are trying to reassert a cultural boundary. The act of rejecting the assimilated alien, Ikemefuna, takes literary form as a textual assimilation of an alien (non-Igbo) religious text. The parallel helps to clarify Achebe's own position when we see that he is *doing* in the very act of telling the story what the characters in the story fail to do socially, that is, accepting the alien as something that can add strength and value (Ikemefuna's name means "let my strength not become lost"). Just as important, however, is the fact that the Biblical text is changed as it is digested. The god asks Okonkwo to relinquish not his own son but an adopted son from another village. This difference complicates the meaning of obedience in the story, for in this context to obey is both a gift to the god and a continuation of a conflict between rival villages; in other words, both an act of love and an act of hate. Furthermore, the violation of cultural principles involved calls the oracle's judgment into question in a way that does not apply to the Biblical text. In what sense can the oracle be said to "speak for" the group or to carry absolute authority when its words are in direct opposition to other revered elements in the culture? For Achebe, blind obedience to the god, whether by Okonkwo or the other elders, is not necessarily the wisest course, as it is for Abraham. Remember that Obierika, the "man who thought about things" (Achebe 1959, 117), is the one elder who stays away from the killing even though he has no fatherly tie to the boy (1959, 64). The two stories side by side show the different ways in which divine authority can be textualized as either absolute or limited depending on how a narrative is structured. The biblical text presents God's judgment as unquestionably right and Abraham's faith as laudable, whereas in Achebe's story such faith is neither demanded nor particularly useful (see Jeyifo 1990, 57-61). Achebe's use of an alien text, then, provides an implicit criticism of the Igbo rejection of the alien without holding the Western example up as better; in short, it is Achebe's act of inclusion with critical scrutiny, not Abraham's act of obedience, that is most important here.

Further illumination of the logic of cultural violence is provided by the Igbo traditions regarding the *ogbanje*, children who torment their parents by dying and returning only to die again. In the Igbo belief system, *ogbanje* (the word means "repeater" [Uchendu 1965, 102]) such as Okonkwo's daughter, Ezinma, are seen as travelers between the spirit world and the world of the living. Ekwefi's series of dead children is described as the "evil rounds of birth and death" (Achebe 1959,

76) of a single soul or identity. When Ezinma reaches the age of six, her parents believe that "perhaps she had decided to stay" (1959, 76), yet her recurring bouts of illness raise the fear that she will depart again. Since the *ogbanje* is imagined as a traveler, it is subject to the same cultural anxieties about border crossing that we have seen in the other examples and, as in the other examples, these anxieties are expressed through ritual interventions. In the case of *ogbanje*, however, there are two possible ritual responses, each performed by a medicine man and each relying upon different principles and methods. The first attempts to use violence to intimidate the *ogbanje* spirit into stopping its cycle of reincarnations. This is the method Okonkwo and Ekwefi try after the death of their third child, Onwumbiko. The medicine man mutilates the body of the child with a razor and drags it away to the Evil Forest. "After such treatment it would think twice before coming again, unless it was one of the stubborn ones who returned, carrying the stamp of their mutilation—a missing finger or perhaps a dark line where the medicine man's razor had cut them" (1959, 75). The principle or theory underlying this approach is that violence is a strong deterrent to future harm. The *ogbanje* is classified as an enemy and physically attacked. Notice, however, that the cultural sanction for this violence also comes with a disclaimer. Mutilation ought to scare the *ogbanje* away for good *unless* it is "one of the stubborn ones" who respond to violence not by staying away but by strengthening their resolve. As Achebe describes it, in other words, the belief system that condones the violent approach includes an awareness that violence may not produce the desired result and may even backfire.

Okonkwo and Ekwefi engage the second ritual option, the search for the buried *iyi-uwa*, after Ezinma has almost died from a serious illness at the age of nine. More elaborate than the mutilation ritual, this option receives a lengthy description from Achebe indicating its importance to the overall design of the novel. A medicine man asks Ezinma where she buried her *iyi-uwa* and encourages her to lead him to the exact spot. All of the family and some of the neighbors participate as spectators of the search, quietly and cheerfully following Ezinma as she takes them on a long journey into the bush and back home to Okonkwo's compound (Achebe 1959, 77-79). The journeying of the ritual recapitulates the *ogbanje*'s habitual wandering while reducing its power to hurt because the family and neighbors—the very people who would be most grieved if Ezinma were to die—actually go along on the journey. The ritual thus produces travel without departure. It also casts Ezinma in the role of leader of the group, making her own decisions about direction and destination despite the presence of her elders. As Achebe says, her "feeling of importance was manifest in her sprightly walk" as she playfully runs, stops, doubles back, while "the crowd followed her silently" (1959, 78). Cultivating this "feeling of importance" may in fact be the main function of the ritual, for Ezinma's "sprightly walk" is the sign of a link between a person's physical symptoms and how s/he feels about her/his relationship to (or position in) the community. If the Igbo believe in such a link (even if none "actually" exists), it would explain how a ritual like this is *supposed* to work to stop the *ogbanje*'s cycle of illness and death. Making a child feel important, welcome, and valued (the theory goes) would produce a sprightliness, a vigor, and therefore a tendency toward healthiness. Conversely, a child treated with suspicion and fear that s/he might be an *ogbanje* or, worse, one of the "really evil children," would tend to feel unwelcome and depressed. The medicine man's demeanor also serves the ritual's goal of cultivating social bonds. Throughout the scene his voice is described as "cool," "confident," and "quiet" (1959, 77, 79). When Okonkwo fumes at Ezinma with threats such as "if you bring us all this way for nothing I shall beat sense into you" (1959, 78), Okagbue, the medicine man, restores calm: "I have told you to let her alone. I know how to deal with them" (1959, 78). Okonkwo's repeated outbursts threaten to turn this ritual into a version of the mutilation ritual, but Okagbue holds his ground and will allow no intimidation or violence. Characteristically, Okonkwo does not see that the spirit and method here are entirely different and fails to understand the power of gentleness.

The two main rituals that constitute the Igbo response to *ogbanje*—the mutilation of the dead child and the search for the *iyi-uwa*—offer violent and non-violent approaches to the same problem. Both rituals are designed to settle the *ogbanje* child's ambiguous status by resolving its continual crossing of boundaries between worlds into either permanent absence or permanent residence. Suspicion and fear of the traveler motivate the violent approach and intimidation is its method. The non-violent approach, by contrast, uses kindness to disarm the child's power to torment and requires tolerance and flexibility from the group. In my reading of the *iyi-uwa* scene, it is not the finding of the buried object that matters most but the relationship between child and community that is set up in and through the journey. The large number of "spectators" who participate and the medicine man's gentle manner help to stress the ritual's function of communal inclusion. The ritual is designed not to scare the child away but to break its "bond with the world of *ogbanje*" (Achebe 1959, 77) by forging new and unbreakable ties to the world of the village, especially the extended family and neighbors. Notice, however, that Achebe does not suggest that the non-violent method is any more or less effective at controlling disease than the violent one, for both methods sometimes fail (1959, 75, 77) and Ezinma gets sick even after her *iyi-uwa* is found. The main point for my purposes lies in the cultural beliefs about principle and method expressed in the two different practices. That the *Igbo* have no one consistent approach towards the *ogbanje* is a measure of the complexity and variety its traditions can accommodate. The very existence of the second option demonstrates that the community constructs and endorses alternatives to violence and, more specifically, non-violent ways of dealing with those perceived as strangers or dangers in their midst.

Suspicion of hybrid cases and border crossings, of course, extends to the British as well. One of the clearest examples of this is Mr. Smith, the missionary. Unlike Mr. Brown, whose "policy of compromise and accommodation" (Achebe 1959, 169) had brought many converts into the Christian churches and schools, Mr. Smith "saw things as black and white" (1959, 169). He is intolerant of converts who lack a complete understanding of Christian doctrine or who retain some of their Igbo religious beliefs along with the Christian. Achebe demonstrates Smith's intolerance by describing one of his earliest acts among the Igbo:

> Within a few weeks of his arrival in Umuofia Mr. Smith suspended a young woman from the church for pouring new wine into old bottles. This woman had allowed her husband to mutilate her dead child. . . . Four times this child had run its evil round. And so it was mutilated to discourage it from returning.
>
> Mr. Smith was filled with wrath when he heard of this. He disbelieved the story which even some of the most faithful confirmed, the story of really evil children who were not deterred by mutilation, but came back with all the scars. (Achebe 1959, 169-70)

The woman's husband uses intimidation to try to banish the spirit of the *ogbanje* from their household. Mr. Smith's response is to be "filled with wrath" and to suspend the woman from the household of the church. As a convert, the woman is a border-crosser like the *ogbanje* and her tolerance of the mutilation ritual tells Smith that she has not left the Igbo world completely. The metaphor of new wine in old bottles shows how suspicious Smith is of people who live in two worlds at once. Apparently, however, the irony of his response is completely lost on Mr. Smith himself. He does not see that he is acting on the same *principle* as the woman's husband—that intimidation deters future injury—and that he is therefore in essence performing a version of the ritual he claims to disapprove. Why is Smith so blind to the implications of his own actions? I would argue that it is because he has not learned to analyze human behavior in terms of the principles it expresses. Smith objects to the use of the mutilation ritual not because he rejects intimidation as a tactic (which he clearly does not) but because it is an Igbo practice and not a Christian one. He is thinking in terms of loyalty or disloyalty to specific cultures and not in terms of underlying principles, and this leads him to fall into the trap of self-contradictory action. Interestingly, some of the "most faithful" of his own congregation try to warn him of this. When these faithful Christians tell him "the story of really evil children who were not deterred by mutilation, but came back with all the scars," he simply disbelieves it without hearing the implied warning it carries. The point of the story is that those who use intimidation may see their actions backfire, and this applies as much to Smith's "wrath" as it does to the woman's husband. Smith does not have to believe in the literal existence of *ogbanje* to get this message from the story, but he does have to be willing to submit himself and his culture to scrutiny.

Achebe encourages in his readers the sort of analysis that leads to positive cultural change by pinpointing contradictions between principle and practice that alienate members of a community and lead to violence. Using traditions of violence as examples, he also makes the more general point that the moral principles expressed in cultural practices are more important than the specific practices themselves. The stories of Ikemefuna, Nwoye, and Ezinma, along with several smaller episodes, are thematically linked by notions of conversion, assimilation, and the crossing of boundaries. In a subtle but persistent way, Achebe shows that victims of violence and oppression are often conceptualized as hybrids or ambiguous cases, suggesting that one of the main underlying motives for violence among the Igbo is fear of the instability believed to result from the blurring of familiar categories. The irony is that this fear of instability is itself a source of instability.

From *College Literature* 26, no. 1 (1999): 69-79. Copyright © 1999 by *College Literature*. Reprinted with permission of *College Literature*.

Works Cited

Achebe, Chinua. 1959. *Things fall apart*. New York: Fawcett Crest.

Bascom, Tim. 1988. The black African and the "white man's God" in *Things fall apart*: Cultural repression or liberation? *Commonwealth Essays and Studies* 11:1: 70-76.

Cobham, Rhonda. 1991. Making men and history: Achebe and the politics of revisionism. In *Approaches to teaching "Things fall apart,"* ed. Bernth Lindfors. New York: Modern Language Association.

Gikandi, Simon. 1991. *Reading Chinua Achebe: Language and ideology in fiction*. Portsmouth: Heinemann.

Hawkins, Hunt. 1991. *Things fall apart* and the literature of empire. In *Approaches to teaching "Things fall apart,"* ed. Bernth Lindfors. New York: Modern Language Association.

Innes, C. L. 1990. *Chinua Achebe*. Cambridge: Cambridge University Press.

Iyasere, Solomon O. 1992. Okonkwo's participation in the killing of his "son" in Chinua Achebe's *Things fall apart*: A study of ignoble decisiveness. *College Language Association Journal* 35:3: 303-15.

Jeyifo, Biodun. 1990. For Chinua Achebe: The resilience and the predicament of Obierika. In *Chinua Achebe: A celebration*, ed. Kirsten Holst Petersen and Anna Rutherford. Portsmouth: Heinemann.

Obiechina, Emmanuel. 1991. Following the author in *Things fall apart*. In *Approaches to teaching "Things fall apart,"* ed. Bernth Lindfors. New York: Modern Language Association.

Olorounto, Samuel B. 1986. The notion of conflict in Chinua Achebe's novels. *Obsidian II* 1:3: 17-36.

Opata, Damian. 1987. Eternal sacred order versus conventional wisdom: A consideration of moral culpability in the killing of Ikemefuna in *Things fall apart*. *Research in African Literatures* 18:1: 71-79.

_____. 1991. The structure of order and disorder in *Things fall apart*. *Neohelicon* 18:1: 73-87.

Rhoads, Diana Akers. 1993. Culture in Chinua Achebe's *Things fall apart*. *African Studies Review* 36:2: 61-72.

Taylor, Willene P. 1983. The search for values theme in Chinua Achebe's novel *Things fall apart*: A crisis of the soul. *Griot* 2:2: 17-26.

Uchendu, Victor C. 1965. *The Igbo of southeast Nigeria*. New York: Harcourt Brace.

Udumukwu, Onyemaechi. 1991. The antinomy of anti-colonial discourse: A revisionist Marxist study of Achebe's *Things fall apart*. *Neohelicon* 18:2: 317-36.

Wright, Derek. 1990. Things standing together: A retrospect on *Things fall apart*. In *Chinua Achebe: A celebration*, ed. Kirsten Holst Petersen and Anna Rutherford. Portsmouth: Heinemann.

The Possibilities and Pitfalls of Ethnographic Readings:
Narrative Complexity in *Things Fall Apart*_____

Carey Snyder

> The District Commissioner changed instantaneously. The resolute admin-
> istrator in him gave way to the student of primitive customs. . . . As he
> walked back to the court he thought about [the book he planned to write].
> Every day brought him some new material. The story of this man who had
> killed a messenger and hanged himself would make interesting reading.
> One could write almost a whole chapter on him. Perhaps not a whole chap-
> ter but a reasonable paragraph, at any rate. There was so much else to in-
> clude, and one must be firm in cutting out details. He had already chosen
> the title of the book, after much thought: *The Pacification of the Primitive
> Tribes of the Lower Niger.*

These famous closing lines of Chinua Achebe's *Things Fall Apart*
(1958, hereafter *TFA*) represent a dramatic shift of perspective, whereby
the protagonist's life story, which has been the subject of the previous
twenty-four chapters, is unceremoniously condensed into a brief anecdote in a foreign text: we are thrust from what is figured as an intimate,
insider's view of Igbo life to a jarringly alien one. The outsider's proposed ethnography of the region's purportedly primitive tribes exemplifies a tradition of colonial discourse that Achebe powerfully counters in *TFA*.[1] Okonkwo's tragic death—prefiguring for the reader the
demise of the clan's traditional ways—serves the government anthropologist merely as raw material to appropriate and possibly turn to a
profit.[2] Not only is the prominent Okonkwo stripped of his individual
identity as he is transformed into a nameless African in a Western text,
but the particularities of the sophisticated Igbo culture, which the novel
has taken pains to elaborate, are also erased as they are lumped together in the essentialist category of *primitive tribes*. Moreover, though
the Commissioner has shown himself to be a poor reader of native cus-

toms and beliefs, lacking both the intellectual curiosity and the humility that are requisite to understanding another culture, he nonetheless passes as an African authority in the West. Achebe's narrative works to redress the reductive and distorted representation of traditional African cultures emblematized by the Commissioner's text.

The reference to the colonial text within the novel may be taken as an embedded reference to the extra-textual politics of representation in which the novel participates. Achebe reports that it was his anger at what he took to be the caricatures of Nigerians in Joyce Cary's novel *Mr. Johnson* that initially inspired him to write a counter-narrative, sympathetic to the indigenous perspective (Flowers 1989, 4). By the author's account, the novel is meant at once to "write back" to the Western canon,[3] correcting erroneous representations of Africa and Africans, and to restore to his people an awareness of the dignity and humanity of precolonial Africa—reminding them "what they lost" through colonization (Achebe 1973, 8). Published two years before Nigeria gained independence from Great Britain, *TFA* aims to wrest from the colonial metropole control over the representation of African lives, staking a claim to the right to self-representation.

While raising issues of authority and authorship, at the same time, the District Commissioner's indisputably alien perspective at the novel's end functions to reinforce the impression of the foregoing narrative's ostensible authenticity: as Neil ten Kortenaar perceptively argues, Achebe's "appeal to an obviously false authority deploys irony to establish Achebe's own credentials as a historian of Igboland" (2003, 124). Against the egregiously misinformed interpretation of an outsider, the rest of the novel is fashioned as a view "from the inside," as the author himself has described it (Flowers 1989, 4). With such remarks, Achebe has contributed to the aura of authenticity that surrounds his book, positioning himself as a kind of native anthropologist, who represents from within the life of the fictionalized Eastern Nigerian village, Umuofia (based on the author's native Ogidi).

Selling millions of copies and taught not only in literature classrooms, but in anthropology, comparative religion, and African Studies courses as well, *TFA* is widely appreciated for its richly detailed, "inside-perspective" of a traditional West African culture.[4] Indeed, the novel has frequently been deemed "ethnographic" for its vivid representation of the customs, ceremonies, and beliefs of the Igbo people. An early review captures this sense of confidence in the author's credentials as an ethnographic reporter: "No European ethnologist could so intimately present this medley of mores of the Ibo tribe, so detail the intricate formalities of the clan."[5] In 1980, critic David Carroll presents what by then is a received view, when he writes, "With great skill Achebe . . . combines the role of novelist and anthropologist, synthesizing a new kind of fiction. This is where his essential genius lies" (1980, 183). In 1991, the MLA's *Approaches to Teaching Achebe's Things Fall Apart*, based on a survey of several hundred teachers of African literature in the U.S., Africa, and Europe, lists among the principal reasons for teaching this novel the perception that it offers "an unusual opportunity to discover the foreign from within": "Readers everywhere may enter Achebe's Igbo worldview and see past and present African experiences from an indigenous perspective" (Lindfors 1991, 15, 2).[6] Finally, in another pedagogical volume, *Understanding Things Fall Apart*, Kalu Ogbaa informs teachers and students that Achebe's novel may be regarded as "an authentic information source on the nineteenth-century Igbo and their neighbors" (1999, xvii).

As a literary critic (in the American academy) and not an anthropologist, I have no intention of questioning the accuracy of Achebe's cultural portrait of the Igbo, which seems deserving of its reputation as authoritative.[7] What I do want to question is this persistent rhetoric of *authenticity*, *intimacy*, and (to coin a clumsy word) *insiderness* which pervades discussions of Achebe's text. Further, I want to challenge the pervasive ethnographic or anthropological mode of reading Achebe's novel, which I take as paradigmatic of a common approach to African literature, and to ethnic literatures more generally, at least in the West.[8]

As M. Keith Booker points out, "anthropological readings . . . have sometimes prevented African novels from receiving serious critical attention as literature rather than simply as documentation of cultural practices."[9] The naïve ethnographic or anthropological reading treats a novel like *TFA* as though it transparently represents the world of another culture, ignoring the aesthetic dimensions of the representation. Ato Quayson suggests that the tendency to read Achebe's novels as though they unproblematically represent historic and cultural reality is not limited to critics unfamiliar with the African context: West African critic Emmanuel Obiechina "duplicates this tendency from an insider's perspective," reading *TFA* "as reflective or mimetic of traditional beliefs and practices in an almost unmediated way" (Quayson 2003, 225).[10] (While I agree with the thrust of Quayson's critique, I will quarrel with his reification of the categories of insider and outsider shortly.) It is not merely that such readings give short shrift to the literary dimensions of this fiction, but in reading fiction like ethnography, some critics operate from the false assumption that ethnographic texts themselves are transparent.[11] In another context, Elizabeth Fernea defines the "ethnographic novel" as one "written by an artist from within the culture," which presents an "authentic" representation of that culture (1989, 154, 153). Leaving aside the objection that "auto-ethnographic" might be a more fitting term here, Fernea's definition highlights a common assumption of such readings: the writer's "insider" status rather circularly verifies the "authenticity" of the representation.

This article seeks to complicate the construction of postcolonial writers like Achebe as cultural insiders. My analysis demonstrates that neither the author nor the narrative voice of *TFA* can be aligned simply with a monological African (or even West African, Nigerian, or nineteenth-century Igbo) perspective, despite the persistent critical tendency to do so. Raised by Christian evangelists in a small village in Eastern Nigeria, Achebe has written eloquently about his childhood alienation from his family's ancestral traditions. I show that Achebe's perspective at the "cultural crossroads" (his phrase) is manifest in the narrative voice of *TFA*, which moves along a continuum of proximity and distance in relation to the culture it sympathetically describes. In this way, Achebe's position vis-à-vis the Igbo does exemplify many of the dilemmas of ethnographic observation—if we understand the relationship between the observer and the observed to be more complicated, and sometimes fraught, than most anthropological readings of the novel assume. To uncover the complexities in the narrative voice, I argue, we need to read the novel not naïvely as providing a clear window onto an alien culture—in contrast with the presumably distorted vision of colonial writers like Joyce Cary—but *meta-ethnographically*, in a way that attends to the complexity inherent in any ethnographic situation.[12] Such a reading restores Achebe's text to the realm of the literary, by encouraging subtle attention to the narrative's achievements *as fiction*, rather than as cultural documentation.

A Voice from the Inside

Lauding Achebe's judicious and multifaceted representation of the Igbo in *TFA*, David Carroll writes, "It was an achievement of detachment, irony and fairness, demonstrating in the writing those qualities he admires in his own people" (1980, 29). But in what sense are the turn-of-the-century Igbo represented in the novel the author's "own people"? The formulation simplifies the writer's subject position, while ignoring the heterogeneity of the Igbo, as of all cultures. Achebe's divided identity as a colonial subject is emblematized by his christened name, Albert Chinualumogu, a tribute on the one hand to Queen Victoria's consort, Prince Albert, and on the other, to the writer's African heritage; at University, he dropped the former and cropped the latter name, refashioning his identity in a way that could be read as simultaneously indigenizing (by effacing the colonial marker) and modernizing (in his words, making the name "more businesslike") (Achebe 1975, 118). Achebe explains that he was born at the "crossroads of cultures": "On one arm of the cross, we sang hymns and read the Bible night and day. On the other, my father's brother and his family, blinded by heathenism, offered food to idols" (1975, 120). He attended a missionary school, not surprisingly, since his father was one of the first converts in the area (Ezenwa-Ohaeto 1997, 3), and, as a Christian, learned to look down on "heathens" and their pagan customs: Christians were regarded as "the people of the church," while heathens were "the people of nothing" (Achebe 1975, 115). Achebe has suggested that writing *TFA* was "an act of atonement" for this early repudiation of ancestral traditions, offered up by a "prodigal son" (120). At the same time, he recalls being fascinated by the traditional customs and rituals taking place in the village, and even "partaking of heathen festival meals" unbeknownst to his parents. Thus Achebe's relationship to traditional Igbo ways is rooted in ambivalence.

Like many African writers of his generation, Achebe received a colonial education—meaning one calibrated to an English frame of reference—at both the prestigious secondary school he attended at Umahia and at the University of Ibadan, where he became well acquainted with the English literary canon. In an oft-quoted passage, Achebe reflects on the psychological ramifications of studying colonial fiction, for a young, black African man:

> When I had been younger, I had read these adventure books about the good white man, you know, wandering into the jungle or into danger, and the savages were after him. And I would instinctively be on the side of the white man. You see what fiction can do, it can put you on the wrong side if you are not developed enough. In the university I suddenly saw that these books had to be read in a different light. Reading *Heart of Darkness*, for instance, . . . I realized that I was one of those savages jumping up and down on the beach. Once that kind of enlightenment comes to you, you realize that someone has to write a different story. (Qtd. in Flowers 1989, 343)

This sudden shift in readerly identification is a kind of parable of the fracturing of identity under colonization: Achebe is split between identifying with the white adventurer and with the savage, and though he consciously decides to take up the "savage's" cause, to tell "a different story," his experience suggests that ultimately it is not as simple as choosing sides. Achebe remains a divided subject: "living between two worlds," he affirms, "is one of the central themes of my life and work" (Qtd. in Flowers 1989, 333).

The pervasive rhetoric of insiderness associated with this writer obscures the more apt trope of the artist situated at cultural crossroads. Achebe has referred to his position straddling cultures as one of the "major advantages" he has enjoyed as a writer (Okpewho 2003, 72): as Simon Gikandi notes, the Nigerian novelist learned to regard "the chasm between himself and the Igbo traditions" as a generative artistic space (1996, 15). Gikandi's word "chasm" denotes Achebe's alienation from indigenous customs. Yet I would stress that it is distance (a "chasm") in tension with *proximity* to traditional ways that is the enabling condition for Achebe's art. In this way, he resembles the figure of the modern fieldworker in the tradition of Bronislaw Malinowski, whose methodology of participant-observation involves shuttling back and forth between perspectives—adopting the native's point of view as a participant, and then pulling back, as an observer, to place customs and beliefs in context (Clifford 1988, 34). Exploring these affinities in greater detail will shed light on the intricacies of Achebe's narrative technique.

A Participant-Observer

Mindful of the tendency to read Achebe's works in an ethnographic mode, one interviewer asked the author whether he regarded his novels as "a competent source of cultural information . . . about Igbo society"; Achebe concurred, explaining that he aimed to present "a total world and a total life as it is lived in that world," and adding, "If somebody else thinks, as some do, that this is sociology or anthropology, that's their own lookout" (Flowers 1989, 64). That Achebe is far from dis-

couraging ethnographic readings of his fiction follows from his pedagogical view of art: to Achebe, the novelist is a teacher, and educating
Africans and foreigners about a heritage that has been demeaned and
eroded through colonization is a viable way of fulfilling an important
social mission.[13]

The phrase Achebe uses to describe the purview of his novels ("a total world and a total life") resonates with the language of cultural holism employed by anthropologists like Malinowski to describe their
object of study—typically, a tribal village prior to extensive contact
with foreigners.[14] In another interview, Achebe states that while some
African writers may object that Africans are "not tribal anymore," "My
world—the one that interests me more than any other—is the world of
the village" (Flowers 1989, 77). In its scope and orientation, *TFA* resembles the traditional village study of an anthropologist, except
Achebe's "field" is both home and strange (or, rather, *estranged*). In
aiming to capture what he perceives as a vanishing way of life (he
speaks of observing "the remains" of village traditions in his youth
[1975, 18]), Achebe also resembles the figure of the modern fieldworker, bent on what James Clifford has called a project of "ethnographic salvage."[15] In Achebe's case, the travel that is also a condition
of conventional fieldwork is figurative: the village he "visits" and re-
creates in his historical fiction is one of the past, from which he is separated by time, education, and experience.

The fieldwork methods associated with British Social Anthropology and pioneered in the first decades of the twentieth century required
the fieldworker to develop a close rapport with the natives and to take
part in native customs and rituals, as well as to observe them. Referring
to the fieldworker's oscillation between empathic identification and
objective analysis, Clifford writes that participant-observation entails
"a delicate management of distance and proximity" (1997, 72). The
narrative voice of Achebe's first novels has been described in terms
that resonate with these: Okpewho asserts that the "most striking quality" of *TFA* is "its empathic account of the Igbo society," a perspective

inexplicably mitigated, in his characterization, by the "objective distance" of the narrative voice (25). Similarly Carroll lauds the opening of the sequel to *TFA*, *Arrow of God*, as "an extraordinary achievement of sympathy and detachment" (1980, 183). These critics fail to recognize—or at least to explore the ramifications of—the near paradox of this description, which makes the narrative voice of *TFA* more interesting than many acknowledge. Like the traditional anthropologist, this African novelist navigates between poles of empathy and objectivity, attitudes that are potentially at odds with one another. Achebe's account of his relationship to Igbo traditions illustrates this tension:

> I was brought up in a village where the old ways were still active and alive, so I could see the remains of our tradition actually operating. At the same time I brought a certain amount of detachment to it too, because my father was a Christian missionary, and we were not fully part of the "heathen" life of the village. (Achebe 1973, 18)

Achebe is at once the insider, speaking of "our tradition," and the outside observer, regarding village ways with a certain "detachment."

Rather than compromising his authority as a representative of Igbo culture, though, *distance* emerges in Achebe's account as the necessary condition for representation:

> I think it was easier for me to observe. Many of my contemporaries who went to school with me and came from heathen families ask me today: "How did you manage to know all these things?" You see, for them these old ways were just part of life. I could look at them from a certain distance, and I was struck by them. (Achebe 1973, 18)

Achebe implies that his "heathen contemporaries" can't see the cultural forest for the trees: too close to their own customs, they fail to see them clearly. Malinowski also insinuates that cultural insiders suffer a kind of conceptual myopia in relation to their own culture: in his words, "The natives obey the forces and commands of the tribal code, but they do not comprehend them" (1984, 11). Whereas Malinowski infantilizes the natives in this statement, implying they are incapable of comprehending abstraction, Achebe expresses a similar sentiment without condescension: his unique perspective, he implies, is a factor of an inherited position. In Achebe's assessment, the distance imposed between him and the old ways "by the accident" of his birth is an asset: "The distance becomes not a separation but a bringing together like the necessary backward step which a judicious viewer may take in order to see a canvas steadily and fully" (1975, 120).[16] The aesthetic analogy transforms Achebe into that "judicious viewer," able to comprehend the canvas of Igbo culture more fully than the participants whose proximity prevents them from making sense of the details. Achebe may overstate the fortuitousness of his position: the simile also reminds us that Achebe is an artist, as well as an intellectual, and, as such, is by (self-)training and inclination a self-conscious observer.

While Achebe freely acknowledges his partial disconnection from traditional ways, at the same time, he promotes an image of himself as an intimate observer, who has "largely picked up" his knowledge of indigenous culture through conversation and personal observation—that is, through firsthand experiences (Achebe qtd. by Wren, 16-17). This characterization is somewhat misleading: as Gikandi cautions, "however appealing" the temptation to read Achebe as "an authentic voice" of his people might be, "it must be resisted because it is not possible for the writer to appeal to an original notion of Igbo culture. . . . Igbo reality, insofar as it is available to Achebe, comes to him (and hence to the reader) mediated by the novelist's sources, both Igbo and colonial" (1991, 31). We know, for example, that Achebe studied West African religion with Geoffrey Parrinder at University (Ezenwa-Ohaeto 1997, 42-44), and that he read the works of P. Amaury Talbot, the administrator-anthropologist, and of G. T. Basden, the missionary-anthropologist on whom the character Mr. Brown is based; Robert Wren suggests that Achebe's fiction is informed by this reading (1980,

17-18). In effacing the textual sources that inform his understanding of native life, Achebe again resembles the self-mythologizing field-worker of the early twentieth-century, who purportedly comes to know a culture through close identification and empirical observation, not through scholarly research (see Clifford 1997).

Finally, as an African novelist writing in English, Achebe, like the traditional anthropologist, confronts the challenge of rendering indigenous experience in a foreign tongue. The non-native reader of *TFA* is reminded of the act of translation that lies behind the entire work each time she stumbles over an untranslated Igbo word. In the Preface to *Argonauts of the Western Pacific*, Malinowski stipulates that ethnographers should incorporate native phrases into their texts as a means of establishing authority, by demonstrating their supposed mastery of the indigenous language (1984, 23). With shifted emphasis, Kortenaar observes of the Igbo words that pepper Achebe's narrative, "These foreign traces in an English text refer metonymically to a whole world that cannot be adequately translated, a world that Achebe implicitly shares with the characters he writes about. The non-Igbo reader, by implication, can only achieve a mediated knowledge of that world" (Kortenaar 2003, 127). I would suggest that, like all cultural knowledge, Achebe's is also *mediated* in ways I have mentioned, though certainly he possesses what might be called a "fluency" in Igbo culture, and thus—even as his "world" is not identical to theirs—shares a great deal with the characters he represents. In my reading, rather than functioning to reinforce an "us" vs. "you" divide for the non-Igbo reader, the native phrases woven into the largely English text of *TFA* serve to linguistically render the borderland from which Achebe writes.[17]

In an essay exploring the concept of anthropology as *cultural translation*, Talal Asad asserts that the skilled translator, whether of languages in a limited sense or of cultures more generally, "seeks to reproduce the structure of an alien discourse within the translator's own language" (1986, 156). For Achebe, the situation approximates the reverse: he has argued that "The African writer . . . should aim at fashioning an English which is at once universal and able to carry his peculiar experience" (1975, 100). As several critics have argued, Achebe *indigenizes* the English language, reproducing attributes of African oral tradition in a written text.[18] Reversing Asad's formula for traditional translation, one could say that Achebe "seeks to reproduce the structure of *native* discourse within an *alien* language"; yet for a writer who has described himself as "perfectly bilingual" (119) and who has written eloquently about his alienation from ancestral traditions, the native/alien binary does not quite hold.

Hence, though I have suggested that Achebe's position vis-à-vis the Igbo has much in common with that of a traditional anthropologist— similarities the insider/outsider dichotomy would obscure—important differences mark his position as well. Unlike Malinowski among the Trobriand Islanders, Achebe is not a stranger pitching his tent among natives; he is a native son, albeit a prodigal one. The stakes are also very different for Achebe than for the traditional anthropologist: he attempts to "salvage" a "vanishing" culture not out of disinterested intellectual curiosity or the necessity of establishing professional credentials (via the disciplinary rite-of-passage, fieldwork), but rather, as a cultural nationalist interested in recuperating a culture fragmented and maligned by colonization.

In many ways, then, a more apt analogy for this African novelist at cultural crossroads is the *native anthropologist*, who complicates the inside/outside binary that governs characterizations of conventional fieldwork. Like the postcolonial writer, the native anthropologist is liable to be read uncritically as offering an "authentic perspective," a reading that has recently met with criticism from within the discipline. Kirin Narayan, a fieldworker and scholar who uncomfortably bears the label in question, rejects the native/non-native binary, suggesting that, instead, we should "view each anthropologist in terms of shifting identifications amid a field of interpenetrating communities and power relations" (1993, 671). Considering such factors as "education, gender, sexual orientation, class, race, or sheer duration of contact," she points out that the "loci along which we are aligned with or set apart from those whom we study are multiple and in flux." In this way, her work urges a rethinking of the relationship between cultural observers and those they observe, casting serious doubt on "the extent to which anyone is an authentic insider" (671). Raised in Bombay by a German-American mother and Indian father, educated in a university in the United States, and conducting fieldwork in diverse regions in India, Narayan's own situation amply demonstrates the multiple and shifting identifications she describes.

Achebe's relationship to the Igbo parallels the complex positioning of the native anthropologist vis-à-vis her native informants, which scholars such as Narayan and Clifford suggest overlaps in significant ways with that of a traditional anthropologist. As if with Achebe in mind, Clifford writes, "Going 'out' to the field now sometimes means going 'back,' the ethnography becoming a 'notebook of a return to the native land'" (1997, 80). Like Narayan, Clifford stresses that "'native' researchers are complexly and multiply located vis-à-vis their worksites and interlocutors," experiencing "different degrees of affiliation and distance" (77). He also challenges the inside/outside binary, pointing toward a continuum model, where cultural observers move fluidly between poles of sympathetic identification and critical explication in relation to those they study: for "even when the ethnographer is positioned as an insider, a 'native' in her or his community, some taking of distance and translating differences will be part of the research, analysis, and writing" (86). Clifford suggests that for the "native researcher" as well as the traditional anthropologist, distance and translation are preconditions of ethnographic representation. As the next section argues, the narrative voice of *TFA* manifests the varying "degrees of affiliation and distance," which typify the dynamic relationship of all cultural observers to the field, but which is intensified in the case of the native anthropologist.

Things Fall Apart: A Dialectic of Proximity and Distance

Part I of Achebe's first novel plunges the non-native reader into the world of the Igbo, with detailed descriptions of the people's customs, beliefs, and ceremonies. Seamlessly woven into the narrative fabric are accounts of the Feast of the New Yam, the negotiation of bride price, the ceremony of the *egwugwu* (ancestral spirits), the *nso-ani* (sacrilege) of committing violence during the Week of Peace, and so on; these details, together with the numerous proverbs embodying clan wisdom that punctuate the narrative,[19] function collectively to create a rich, vivid portrait of a traditional Nigerian culture. The narrator's intimate acquaintance with Igbo culture is signaled by the ability to closely document such beliefs and practices, to use the native tongue, and to omnisciently enter into Igbo characters' minds.

Not surprisingly, then, critics have interpreted the narrative voice as emanating "from the inside." In Carroll's estimation, "The voice is that of a wise and sympathetic elder of the tribe" (1980, 31). Innes also stresses the speaker's identification with the natives' point of view: "the narrative voice is primarily a recreation of the persona which is heard in tales, history, proverbs and poetry belonging to an oral tradition; it represents a collective voice through which the artist speaks *for* his society, not as an individual apart from it—he is the chorus rather than the hero" (1990, 32). Recently, Angela F. Miri has echoed these readings, asserting that *TFA*'s "storyteller undoubtedly represents the Igbo voice or the *vox populi*" (2004, 102). Whether the voice is individuated (a tribal elder) or collective (a communal chorus), critics persist in casting Achebe and the narrator in the role of native informant for the Western reader.

Yet assertions like Innes's that the narrator "speaks *for* his society, not as an individual apart from it" will not withstand close reading: the narrator frequently stands apart, becoming (in my terms) an observer, rather than an implied participant. We are told, for example, that "Darkness held a vague terror *for these people*, even the bravest among them. Children were warned not to whistle at night for fear of evil spirits" (Achebe 1996, 7; my emphasis). These remarks clearly install distance between the narrator—who presumably is not afraid of the dark, and likely does not believe in evil spirits—and "these people," who are cowed by their fear of the night. Here the narrator is aligned more closely with non-native readers than with the Igbo perspective, and, in this mediating role, is more ethnographic observer than native informant. The move is akin to what James Buzard has called the "self-interrupting style" of ethnographic narratives, whereby the ethnographer insists that however closely s/he may identify with the natives, s/he is not really one of them (2005, 34).

For the most part, pinning down the narrative perspective is not a case of discerning whether the narrator is inside or outside native culture, but, rather, of detecting the fluid movement between these vantage points. The slipperiness of the narrative voice is evident in a passage that begins, "Umuofia was feared by all its neighbours. It was powerful in war and in magic, and its priests and medicine-men were feared in all the surrounding country" (Achebe 1996, 8). That Umuofia is "powerful in magic" is presented in a declarative sentence that renders without question or judgment the native point of view. The narrator continues, "on one point there was general agreement—the active principle in that medicine had been an old woman with one leg. In fact, the medicine itself was called *agadi-nwayi*, or old woman" (8-9). This story of the origin of native belief is flagged as consistent with the clan world view: they agree that the old woman with one leg is the source of their reputation in magic. At the same time, the anecdote is consonant with anthropological accounts of primitive cultures that regard disability as a source of metaphysical power. Thus the narrator subtly provides an alternate frame of reference—a way of understanding Umuofia's reputation that accords with Western disbelief in magic. Rather than operating from a fixed viewpoint, the narrator moves freely between divergent perspectives.

Another passage that illustrates the narrative's liminal perspective—jockeying between inside and outside perspectives in ethno-graphic fashion—is the description of the Oracle, Agbala, in Chapter Three:

> No one had ever beheld Agbala, except his priestess. . . . It was said that when such a spirit appeared, the man saw it vaguely in the darkness, but never heard its voice. Some people even said that they had heard the spirits flying and flapping their wings against the roof of the cave. (Achebe 1996, 12)

The passage is respectful of the Oracle's sacredness to the Igbo: the narrator does not overtly proclaim disbelief. Yet the existence of Agbala is left in question: no one has seen it, except in dubious conditions ("vaguely in the darkness") and no one has "heard its voice." Indeed, what can be heard in the cave—the "flapping of wings"—above all conjures the image of bats, the probable denizens of a dark, dank place. Hence, again, the narrator subtly provides an alternative frame of reference, accommodating skepticism alongside Igbo belief.

The very few critics who avoid the reductive insider reading of *TFA* tend to equate the intermittent distance of the narrative to which I have been alluding with an anthropological perspective. For instance, Gikandi observes that the narrator at times "adopts distance and represents the Igbo as if they were an anthropological 'other'" (1996, 46). Similarly, Kortenaar notes that Achebe occasionally "lapses into the knowing tone of the anthropologist" (2003, 132), as in the glossary, when he defines several Igbo terms with "thoroughgoing disbelief."[20] While usefully complicating naïve ethnographic readings that fail to problematize the narrator's insiderness, these critics operate from an equally fallacious assumption that an anthropological perspective is inherently alienated. In doing so, they fail to realize that the anthropological perspective itself mediates between near and far, inside and outside, distance and proximity. They conflate distance and disbelief with the alien perspective of an anthropologist, rather than recognizing that the anthropological voice mediates between ostensible native and foreign perspectives—alternately *suspending* disbelief, to closely identify with a native perspective, and explicating belief, from an external vantage point.

This is more than a question of semantics. By reading the narration's often overlooked complexity as *ethnographic*, I hope not only to underscore the novel's artistry, but also to usefully complicate our understanding of ethnographic relationships themselves. When Achebe's best critics reverse the more common "naïve ethnographic reading" that I've been discussing by equating the novel's anthropological perspective with "a view from *outside*," they unwittingly replicate the kind of dichotomous thinking Achebe himself so assiduously avoids in his nuanced narrative. On a stylistic level, the slippery narrative voice manifests the ongoing process of positioning and repositioning oneself at cultural crossroads.

Acknowledging inconsistencies in perspective that most Achebe critics ignore, Gikandi argues that the ambivalent narrative voice signals contradictions inherent within Igbo culture, contradictions highlighted by the character of Nwoye, who functions as an internal critic of such practices as the disposing of twins and the killing of Ikemefuna. For Gikandi, it is erroneous to read the narrator as either a representative insider or a unified, collective voice because a stable field of social values doesn't exist in the novel: precolonial Umuofia is represented as "a society with various voices and conflicting interests" (1996, 45). While taking Gikandi's point, I would stress that the fluctuations of the narrative voice also express the shifting affiliations of the author, who, like the native anthropologist, is pulled between the values and traditions of sometimes conflicting cultural frameworks.

Another notable exception to the reductive insider reading is that of Abdul JanMohamed, who interprets the novel's balancing act between sympathy and objective distance—or, in his terms, between "sacred" and "secular" perspectives—as narrative "double consciousness." JanMohamed conceives of this dualism as the author's creative solution to a dilemma he describes in this way: Achebe is "challenged with the unenviable task of ensuring that his characters do not seem foolish because they believe in the absence of [the] border [between the sacred and the secular], while he is obliged to acknowledge it for the same reason"; "double consciousness," then, is the simultaneous "awareness of the border and its deep repression" (1984, 32-33). Rather than serving to pander to a Western audience who will regard native belief with possible disdain (by regarding the characters as "foolish"), I have argued that the narrative tension between belief and skepticism registers the author's own shifting frame of reference, one akin to that of an ethnographic observer, continually navigating between indigenous and foreign viewpoints. Moreover, in its maneuverings among different Igbo as well as Western perspectives, the narrative consciousness that emerges is more than double; it has multiple, shifting permutations, as a final example will show.

Illustrating the narrative's ever-shifting vantage point is Chapter Ten's description of the trial, presided over by nine *egwugwu* (masked ancestral spirits) and their leader, the "Evil Forest."[21] To begin with, conjuring the momentousness of the ceremony, the *egwugwu* are deemed "the most powerful and the most secret cult in the clan" (Achebe 1996, 63); their voices are represented as "guttural and awesome" (62). The description continues, throwing the reader into the center of the action: "The *egwugwu* house was now a pandemonium of quavering voices: *Aru oyim de de de de dei!* Filled the air as the spirits of the ancestors, just emerged from the earth, greeted themselves in their esoteric language" (62-63). From the vantage point of the believer, the voices are presented as those of the ancestral spirits. The Igbo greeting remains untranslated, such that the narrator serves as the custodian of knowledge unshared with the reader. Yet the word "esoteric" signals that members of the clan also remain in the dark as to the significance of the utterance: "No woman ever asked questions" about the exclusively male cult (63). From a position of privileged omniscience, then, the narrator moves not only between an inside and an outside perspective, but also between the semi-opaque boundaries that divide the male and female spheres. This narrative flexibility resembles the shifting field relationships of the native anthropologist, as described by Narayan, with points of affiliation and disaffiliation that are "multiple and in flux" (Narayan 671).

It is only after building up a sense of the ceremony's significance from a point of view identified with the initiate that the narrator steps back from the event to give another perspective:

> Okonkwo's wives, and perhaps other women as well might have noticed that the second *egwugwu* had the springy walk of Okonkwo. And they might also have noticed that Okonkwo was not among the titled men and elders who sat behind the row of *egwugwu*. But if they thought these things they kept them within themselves. The *egwugwu* with the springy walk was one of the dead fathers of the clan. (Achebe 1996, 64)

The passage begins by subtly casting doubt on the native belief in ancestral spirits—*unmasking* the *egwugwu*, as it were—by intimating that one of them has "the springy walk of Okonkwo," and thus is a man, not a spirit. The narrative voice draws the female characters into complicity with its skeptical perspective, by tentatively attributing to them a glimmering awareness of Okonkwo's telltale walk; they "might have noticed" what the narrator knows for certain: there is a human being beneath the ceremonial disguise. If Wren is correct when he asserts that the Igbo perceive the *egwugwu* not as "mortals masked but [as] transcendent—even transubstantiate—beings, living presences of the dead fathers of the nine villages of Umuofia" (Achebe 1996, 35), then calling attention to Okonkwo's disguise represents a major breach with the insider's view. An episode toward the end of the novel lends support for this reading: when Enoch publicly unmasks an *egwugwu*, "reduc[ing] its immortal prestige in the eyes of the uninitiated," he is represented as "killing . . . an ancestral spirit," thereby throwing Umuofia into a state of "confusion," and effectively presaging the "death" of the "soul of the tribe" (131-32). The language literalizes the belief that the *egwugwu* embody the spirits of the clan, as does the closing sentence of the passage quoted above, which rejoins the perspective of the devout believer, by affirming that the *egwugwu* in question actually "was one of the dead fathers of the clan." Thus the narrator inhabits shifting and sometimes contradictory perspectives, along a continuum that stretches from the most credulous believer to the skeptic or cultural outsider.

Through these maneuverings, the narrative voice replicates the dynamic positioning of the native anthropologist—at once part of Igbo culture and apart from it, a participant and a judicious observer, at turns closely identifying with various Igbo perspectives and "taking the distance" that is the precondition for ethnographic representation.

Conclusion

It is tempting to read *TFA* as a voice from the inside for a number of reasons. The novel itself encourages this reading, with its detailed documentation of cultural practices, its fluid incorporation of native words and phrases, and its juxtaposition of the principal narrative perspective with the reductive and distorted view of outsiders like the District Commissioner. By construing his narrative as combating the misinformed representations of colonial writers, Achebe has contributed to the impression of the book's documentary realism.

Additionally, like other postcolonial literature, *TFA* has entered the Western canon as a kind of sequel to British Modernism, one that is perceived as providing a corrective to the ideological blind-spots of writers from the earlier historical period. Frequently partnered with Joseph Conrad's *Heart of Darkness* in introductory-level courses and British literature surveys (including my own), *TFA* appears on the syllabus to show the "other side" of the colonial encounter. Too often this impulse leads critics and teachers to regard postcolonial writers as rendering the experience of colonized and pre-colonial societies in an unproblematic, unmediated way.

Yet this mode of reading oversimplifies the relationship between Achebe and traditional Igbo culture, threatening to fetishize the voice of the former colonial subject, while ignoring the complexity of the narrative voice, which is more dynamic than such readings acknowledge. Dubbing the novel ethnographic or anthropological is equally reductive, when these terms are understood to imply a kind of photographic realism, and when the author's indigenous status is assumed to vouch for an uncomplicated textual authenticity. The opposing, but still misguided, assumption that the novel's anthropological perspective is inherently *alienated* likewise simplifies the dynamic ethnographic relationship, which the novel subtly reproduces at the level of style.

Notwithstanding these cautions, I believe that literature is one of the most valuable tools we possess for imagining life in other cultures. Thus we should not stop reading ethnographically, but rather, by appreciating the complexity of the ethnographic project, especially when undertaken by a "native son," we can better appreciate the corresponding complexities of narratives that emerge from cultural crossroads.

Notes

1. In *Morning Yet on Creation Day*, Achebe terms this voice the "sedate prose of the district-officer-government anthropologist" of the early twentieth-century (1975, 5).

2. In the sequel to *TFA*, *Arrow of God*, we learn that the Commissioner *has* profited from colonial anthropology, since his book has "become a colonial classic, a manual of empire-building," as Nahem Yousaf notes (2003, 39).

3. The phrase is not Achebe's, but rather an allusion to the well-known and seminal work of postcolonial criticism, *The Empire Writes Back* (1989).

4. According to Isidore Okpewho, as of 2003, the novel had been translated into nearly sixty languages and sold close to nine million copies. Charles Larson states that following Nigerian independence, *TFA* became required reading at the secondary level in Nigeria (Okpewho 2003, 27), but my focus in this essay is primarily the novel's critical reception in the U.S.

5. Hassoldt Davis, *Saturday Review*, 1959 (qtd. in Larson 15-16).

6. Other respondents to the survey stated that they wanted to "give students a sense of African history and the effects of colonialism on Africa, as well as to dispel stereotypes about Africa," and many stressed that the novel provides an accessible, evocative introduction to African literature or to postcolonial literature more generally (Lindfors 1991, 15).

7. I employ "authoritative" as a relative, not an absolute, term, by which I mean "well informed." The authority I would ascribe to *TFA*—as to any well-founded historical and/or ethnographic representation—is that of what James Clifford calls a "partial construction" and what Donna Harraway calls "situated knowledge."

8. See, for example Eleni Coundouriotis, who has demonstrated that African novels frequently have been read (by Africans as well as Europeans and North Americans) as bearing ethnographic witness to their authors' cultures, such that their historical specificity is muted or erased (1999, 4-5). Elizabeth Jane Harrison identifies a similar tendency in scholarship on the fiction of Zora Neale Hurston and Mary Hunter Austin whose "literary strategies" have been neglected "in favor of an analysis of the cultural context of their narratives" (1997, 44). Likewise, Henry Louis Gates complains that European and American critics too often appropriate African and African-American literature as "anthropological evidence" about these cultures (1984, 4).

9. Booker, *The African Novel in English* (1998, 65). As early as 1969, G. D. Killam makes an almost equivalent statement: "So much has been written about the anthropological and sociological significance of *Things Fall Apart* and *Arrow of God*—their evocation of traditional nineteenth- and earlier twentieth-century Ibo village life— . . . that the overall excellence of these books as pieces of fiction, as works of art, has been obscured" (Booker 1998, 1).

10. Pointing out that Achebe's fellow Nigerian writer, Wole Soyinka, has labeled Achebe a "chronicler" of the past, Nahem Yousaf similarly objects that Achebe's fiction has been assessed in too limiting terms, "according to its verisimilitude, its facility for reflecting external reality" (2003, 4).

11. Since the publication of James Clifford and George Marcus's *Writing Culture* (1986), there has been general acknowledgement within the field of anthropology that the classic genre associated with fieldwork, the ethnography, is a *text*—that the experience of fieldwork is mediated by language which shapes/constructs that experience.

12. I am using *meta* in the sense connoted by the term *metafiction*, meaning fiction that self-consciously alludes to its own artificiality or literariness, announcing, in effect, "I am fiction." To read *meta-ethnographically*, by extension, means to read in a way that is self-reflexive of ethnographic practice, attentive to the dynamism inherent in the ethnographic voice.

13. See "The Novelist as Teacher" (Achebe 1975, 67-73).

14. Cultural holism in British Social Anthropology has its roots in the discipline's first text book, E. B. Tylor's 1871 *Primitive Culture*, which defined culture as a "complex whole." Primitive villages, believed to be isolated from outside contact, organically integrated, and relatively simple in their organization, were regarded as ideal "laboratories" for studying culture (see for example Mead 2001, 6). However, the idea of the pristine native village has been critiqued in recent years as a romantic construct: for example, Arjun Appadurai writes, "Natives, people confined to and by the places to

which they belong, groups unsullied by contact with a larger world, have probably never existed" (1988, 39). See also Clifford (1997).

15. Cf. Coundouriotis, who argues that "unlike the 'salvage ethnography' of European ethnographers who sought, as Clifford has explained, to preserve what was already lost, Achebe's autoethnography aims at affirming the contemporaneity of native cultures with those of the West" (1999, 38).

16. Ruth Benedict also employs an aesthetic metaphor in discussing the anthropologist's unique perspective: for Benedict, a kind of "gestalt" vision enables the cultural observer to make sense of a foreign culture, such that "hundreds of details fall into over-all patterns" (1946, 12). "Pattern" becomes an operative trope for Benedict, evident in the title of her 1934 anthropological classic, *Patterns of Culture*. For an analysis of the relationship between Benedict's concept of culture and the approach to art of literary studies' New Critics (both seeking organic unity and a complex whole in their objects of study), see Manganaro (2002, 151-74).

17. The allusion is to Gloria Anzaldúa's innovative and powerful textualization of bi-lingual, bi-cultural experience in *Borderland/La Frontiera*, which poetically theorizes the experience of literally and symbolically inhabiting the borderland between Mexico and Texas, from a Chicana perspective.

18. See JanMohamed (1984), Kortenaar (2003), Booker (1998).

19. By conjuring the effect of language in translation, the novel's proverbs evoke the semblance of cultural authenticity, yet ironically, it has been well established that these proverbs at best loosely approximate Igbo sayings, and in some cases are Achebe's pure invention. See Shelton (1969, 86-87).

20. See footnote 21.

21. Even the definition of *egwugwu* in the book's glossary reveals a shifting relationship to Igbo culture: prior to the 1996 edition, the term was glossed as "a masquerader who impersonates one of the ancestral spirits of the village" (Achebe 1996, 149)—a definition that reflects "thoroughgoing disbelief," as Kortenaar notes (2003, 130). The most recent edition of the text revises this definition to "the masked spirit, representing the ancestral spirits of the village" (liii)—wording that presumably more closely aligns with the Igbo perspective.

Works Cited

Achebe, Chinua. 1996. *Things Fall Apart*. 1958. Reprint. Oxford: Heinemann.
_____. 1973. "The Role of the Writer in a New Nation" (1964). In *African Writers on African Writing*, ed. G. D. Killam. Evanston: Northwestern University Press.
_____. 1975. *Morning Yet on Creation Day*. Garden City, New York: Anchor Press.
Appadurai, Arjun. 1988. "Putting Hierarchy in Its Place." *Cultural Anthropology*, 3.1: 36-49.
Asad, Talal. 1986. "The Concept of Cultural Translation in British Social Anthro-

pology." In *Writing Culture: The Poetics and Politics of Ethnography*, ed. James Clifford and George E. Marcus. Berkeley: University of California Press.

Benedict, Ruth. 1946. *The Chrysanthemum and the Sword; Patterns of Japanese Culture*. Boston: Houghton Mifflin.

Booker, M. Keith. 1998. *The African Novel in English: An Introduction*. Portsmouth, NH: Heinemann.

Buzard, James. 2005. *Disorienting Fiction: the Autoethnographic Work of Victorian Fiction*. Princeton: Princeton University Press.

Carroll, David. 1980. *Chinua Achebe*. London: Macmillan Press Ltd.

Clifford, James. 1988. *The Predicament of Culture: Twentieth-Century Ethnography, Literature, and Art*. Cambridge: Harvard University Press.

_____. 1997. *Routes: Travel and Translation in the Late Twentieth Century*. Cambridge: Harvard University Press.

Clifford, James, and George Marcus, ed. 1986. *Writing Culture: The Poetics and Politics of Ethnography*. Berkeley: University of California Press.

Coundouriotis, Eleni. 1999. *Claiming History: Colonialism, Ethnography, and the Novel*. New York: Columbia University Press.

Ezenwa-Ohaeto. 1997. *Chinua Achebe: A Biography*. Oxford: James Currey Press.

Fernea, Elizabeth. 1989. "The Case of *Sitt Marie Rose*: An Ethnographic Novel from the Modern Middle East." In *Literature and Anthropology*, ed. Philip A. Dennis and Wendell Aycock. Lubbock: Texas Tech University Press.

Flowers, Betty Sue, ed. 1989. *Bill Moyers: A World of Ideas: Conversations with Thoughtful Men and Women about American Life Today and the Ideas Shaping Our Future*. Garden City, New York: Doubleday.

Gates, Henry Louis, Jr., ed. 1984. *Black Literature and Literary Theory*. New York: Methuen.

Gikandi, Simon. 1991. *Reading Chinua Achebe: Language and Ideology in Fiction*. London: James Currey Publishers.

_____. 1996. "Chinua Achebe and the Invention of African Literature." Preface to *Things Fall Apart*. Oxford: Heinemann.

Griffiths, Gareth. 1978. "Language and Action in the Novels of Chinua Achebe." In *Critical Perspectives on Chinua Achebe*, ed. C. L. Innes and Bernth Lindfors. Washington, DC: Three Continents Press.

Harrison, Elizabeth Jane. 1997. "Zora Neale Hurston and Mary Hunter Austin's Ethnographic Fiction: New Modernist Narratives." In *Unmanning Modernism: Gendered Re-Readings*, ed. Elizabeth Jane Harrison and Shirley Peterson. Knoxville: University of Tennessee Press.

Huggan, Graham. 1994. "Anthropologists and Other Frauds." *Comparative Literature*, 46.2 (Spring): 113-28.

Innes, C. L. 1990. *Chinua Achebe*. Cambridge: Cambridge University Press.

JanMohamed, Abdul. 1984. "Sophisticated Primitivism: The Syncretism of Oral and Literate Modes in Achebe's *Things Fall Apart*." *Ariel*, 15: 4, 19-39.

Kalu, Anthonia C. 2002. "Achebe and Duality in Igbo Thought." In *Modern Critical Interpretations: Chinua Achebe's Things Fall Apart*, ed. Harold Bloom. Philadelphia: Chelsea House Press.

Killam, G. D. 1977. *The Novels of Chinua Achebe*. 1969. Reprint. London: Heinemann.

Kortenaar, Neil ten. 2003. "How the Center Is Made to Hold in *Things Fall Apart*." In *Chinua Achebe's Things Fall Apart: A Casebook*, ed. Isidore Okpewho. New York: Oxford University Press.

Larson, Charles. 1971. *The Emergence of African Fiction*. Bloomington: Indiana University Press.

Lindfors, Bernth, ed. 1991. *Approaches to Teaching Achebe's Things Fall Apart*. New York: MLA.

_____. 1997. *Conversations with Chinua Achebe*. Jackson: University Press of Mississippi.

Malinowski, Bronislaw. 1984. *Argonauts of the Western Pacific*. 1922. Reprint. Prospect Heights, Illinois: Waveland.

Manganaro, Marc. 2002. *Culture, 1922: The Emergence of a Concept*. Princeton: Princeton University Press.

Mead, Margaret. 2001. *Coming of Age in Samoa*. 1928. Reprint. New York: HarperCollins.

Miri, Angela F. 2004. "The Survival of Oral Speech Patterns in Modern African Literature: The Example of Chinua Achebe's Fiction." In *Emerging Perspectives on Chinua Achebe*, Volume II: *Iskinka, the Artistic Purpose: Chinua Achebe and the Theory of African Literature*, ed. Ernest N. Emenyonu and Iniobong I. Uko. Trenton, NJ: African World Press.

Narayan, Kirin. 1993. "How Native Is a 'Native' Anthropologist?" *American Anthropologist, New Series*, 95.3 (September): 671-86.

Ogbaa, Kalu. 1999. *Understanding Things Fall Apart: A Student Casebook to Issues, Sources, and Historical Documents*. Westport, CT: Greenwood Press.

Okpewho, Isidore, ed. 2003. *Chinua Achebe's Things Fall Apart: A Casebook*. Oxford: Oxford University Press.

Quayson, Ato. 2003. "Realism, Criticism, and the Disguises of Both: A Reading of Chinua Achebe's *Things Fall Apart* with an Evaluation of the Criticism Relating to It." In *Chinua Achebe's Things Fall Apart: A Casebook*, ed. Isidore Okpewho. Oxford: Oxford University Press.

Rhoads, Diana Akers. 1993. "Culture in Chinua Achebe's *Things Fall Apart*." *African Studies Review*, 36.2 (September): 61-72.

Rowell, Charles H. 2003. "An Interview with Chinua Achebe." In *Chinua Achebe's Things Fall Apart: A Casebook*, ed. Isidore Okpewho. Oxford: Oxford University Press.

Shelton, Austin J. 1969. "The 'Palm-Oil' of Language: Proverbs in Chinua Achebe's Novels." *Modern Language Quarterly*, 30: 86-111.

Stocking, George W., Jr. 1983. "The Ethnographer's Magic: Fieldwork in British Anthropology from Tylor to Malinowski." In *Observers Observed: Essays on Ethnographic Fieldwork*. Milwaukee: University of Wisconsin Press.

Wren, Robert. 1980. *Achebe's World: The Historical and Cultural Context of the Novels of Chinua Achebe*. Washington, DC: Three Continents Press.

Yousaf, Nahem. 2003. *Chinua Achebe*. Devon: Northcote House Publishers Ltd.

Rhythm and Narrative Method in Achebe's *Things Fall Apart*_____

B. Eugene McCarthy

Before the publication of Chinua Achebe's *Things Fall Apart* in 1958 public awareness in the West of fiction from Africa was confined chiefly to white writers such as Doris Lessing, Alan Paton, or Nadine Gordimer. Thus Achebe's first novel, written in English, though he is himself a Nigerian of the Igbo people, was a notable event. More noteworthy was the fact that it was a very good novel and has become over the years probably the most widely read and talked about African novel, overshadowing the efforts of other West African novelists as well as those of East and South Africa. Its reputation began high and has remained so, stimulating critical analysis in hundreds of articles, many books, and dissertations. Its story describes, whatever one may expect from its Yeatsian title, the life of a traditional Igbo rural village and the rise of one of its gifted leaders, Okonkwo, before colonization, and then observes the consequences for the village and the hero as they confront the beginnings of the colonial process. Achebe's subsequent three novels, more or less related but not sequential, *No Longer at Ease* (1960), *Arrow of God* (1964), and *Man of the People* (1966), though all respected, have not matched its success. Achebe's fiction established firmly that there is an African prose literature—poetry had probably been well known since Senghor in the 1940s—even when written in English. Not that there has not been debate over and criticism of *Things Fall Apart*, and from Achebe's standpoint a good deal of misunderstanding through refusal of readers to take its African character seriously; but as a recent study confirms he continues to be "the most widely read of contemporary African writers."[1] His first novel has been "as big a factor in the formation of a young West African's picture of his past, and of his relation to it, as any of the still rather distorted teachings of the pulpit and the primary school,"[2] and of course he has influenced his fellow writers just as significantly in finding their own subject matter and voice.

When beginning Chinua Achebe's novel *Things Fall Apart*, readers are often struck by the simple mode of narration and equally simple prose style, which critics have seen as Achebe's desire to achieve an "English . . . colored to reflect the African verbal style [with] stresses and emphases that would be eccentric and unexpected in British or American speech."[3] He reshapes English in order to imitate the "linguistic patterns of his mother tongue," Igbo.[4] I would like, as a further means of understanding this special quality of Achebe's prose, to propose a way of reading and of understanding the novel through the concept of rhythm, within the oral tradition.

In the opening passage of the novel, the narrator's repetition of words and phrases, both verbatim and synonymous, and his mode of emphasis and patterning suggest a deliberateness and complexity well beyond the surface simplicity:

> Okonkwo *was* well known *throughout the nine villages and even beyond.* His fame *rested on solid personal achievements. As a young man of eighteen* he *had brought* honour *to his village by* throwing Amalinze the Cat. Amalinze *was the great wrestler who for* seven years *was unbeaten, from Umuofia to Mbaino. He was called* the Cat *because his back would never touch the earth. It was* this man *that* Okonkwo threw *in a fight which the old men agreed was one of the* fiercest *since the founder of their town engaged a spirit of the* wild *for* seven days and seven nights.
>
> *The drums beat and the flutes sang and the spectators held their breath.* Amalinze *was a* wily *craftsman, but* Okonkwo *was as* slippery *as a fish in* water. Every nerve and every muscle stood out *on their arms, on their backs and their thighs, and one almost heard them* stretching to breaking point. *In the end* Okonkwo threw the Cat.[5]

The narrator's repetitions in this passage are a technique of the traditional oral storyteller, sitting talking to a group of listeners (though he is not a *griot*, or oral historian).[6] For example, the subject "A" repeats four times, the modifier "a" repeats but varies to add meanings; other words, such as those about the intensity of the fight, likewise are repeated to emphasize their importance and to vary meanings. Walter Ong refines our understanding of oral thought and expression in prose by pointing out that the oral narrator's "thought must come into being in heavily rhythmic, balanced patterns, in repetitions and antitheses, in alliterations and assonances, in epithetic and other formulary expressions. . . ." Such primary devices for memory ("for rhythm aids recall") and communication simplify the story so that the listeners can grasp characters and events graphically and surely. More specifically, oral expression is "additive rather than subordinative," "aggregative rather than analytical," "redundant or 'copious,'" that is, "backlooping" by means of "redundancy, repetition of the just-said."[7] The additive and redundant elements are apparent in the above passage, when Achebe's narrator repeats a phrase, for example, "Amalinze the Cat," then carries it forward with new information. Once a name or event is introduced he proceeds by moving forward, then reaching back to repeat and expand, moving onward again, accumulating detail and elaborating: "well known" advances to "fame" and to "honour," just as "It was this man that Okonkwo threw" repeats what has gone before and underlines its importance. Karl H. Bottcher calls the narrator's method "afterthoughts,"[8] but Ong's "backlooping" conveys better the active methodology of the narrator.

The style is not "aggregative" for key epithets are not attached to characters, no doubt because the novel is written, not spoken. A more important departure from strict oral procedure is the narrator's distance from his characters and his reluctance to intrude his views, for as Ong tells us, empathy and participation are elements of orality, objectivity a consequence of writing.[9] For the most part the narrator reveals only what was done or said by others: "a fight which the *old men agreed* was one of the fiercest . . . ," "*it was said* that, when he slept . . . ," "he *seemed* to walk on springs, *as if* . . . ." We understand an apparent intrusion such as the following as reflecting not the narrator's bias but the way the people thought: "When Unoka died he had taken no title at all and he was heavily in debt. Any wonder then that his son Okonkwo was ashamed of him? Fortunately, among these people a man was judged according to his worth and not according to the worth of his father" (6).

The patterning and repetition in Achebe's novel are characteristics of the self-conscious artistry of oral narrative performance, where plot moves by repetition and predictability. Harold Scheub argues the "centrality of repetition in oral narratives as a means of establishing rhythm."[10] Such rhythmic textures establish the narrative method as imitative of the African oral rather than the English "literary" tradition. Indeed rhythm is a quality at the heart of African culture. Léopold Sédar Senghor has written: "Rhythm is the architecture of being, the inner dynamic that gives it form, the pure expression of the life force." The dramatic interest of a work is not sustained, he writes, by "avoiding repetition as in European narrative . . . , [but] is born of repetition: repetition of a fact, of a gesture, of words that form a *leitmotiv*. There is always the introduction of a new element, variation of the repetition, unity in diversity."[11] In the text where he quotes this statement, Jahnheinz Jahn illustrates prose rhythms with a passage from Nigerian writer Amos Tutuola's *Palm-Wine Drinkard*: "the rhythmical kind of narrative in which the repetition intensifies the dramatic quality of the action, makes Tutuola's story oral literature."[12]

As Robert Kellogg tells us, there are many sorts of rhythm, "phonic, metrical, grammatical, metaphoric, imagistic, thematic";[13] and modern studies have argued that prose as well as verse has its rhythms, usually found first in syntax.[14] The repetitions of syntactic patterns of word and phrase underscore emphases (sometimes vocal) and stresses of meaning. Thus Roger Fowler describes in passages from David Storey the syntactic repetitions by which "syntax becomes rhythmical" and finds "sentence- and phrase-rhythms" there like "'thickening, deepening, then darkening'": "When syntax is repetitious, highlighting by reiteration a small number of patterns," he argues, "a palpable rhythm is established through the regularity of voice tunes."[15] Such repetition is the most obvious stylistic feature we notice in the passage from Achebe's novel. Syntactically, these repetitions stress key words, often polysyllables in contrast to the predominating one or two syllable words, chiefly subject nouns, object nouns, pronouns and modifiers of these nouns, and verbs, with occasional stress on time or place. Though emphasis may be difficult to assess uniformly—e.g., "through the NINE villages," or "through the NINE VILLAGES," or even possibly "through the nine VILLAGES"—there are some evident emphases on subjects, objects, or verbs; for example, "In the end Okonkwo threw the Cat" stresses all three. Parallelism enhances the repetitions and strengthens the rhythms: the parallel subject-verb sentence opening: "Okonkwo was" with "fame rested," or "Amalinze was" with "he was" with "It was." In the third (unquoted) paragraph, the parallel repetitions become insistent, as the verbs become increasingly active: "he was tall," "he breathed," "he slept," "he walked," "he seemed to walk," "He was going," "he did pounce," "he had," and finally, "He had no patience. . . ." Alliteration too accents these repetitions: "called" and "Cat"; "fight," "fiercest," and "founder"; "Spirit," "seven," and "seven." One may even discern a distinct metrical rhythm in some lines, such as, "The drums beat and the flutes sang and the spectators held their breath," which could be marked, short, long, long; short, short, long, long, and so on. The third paragraph summarizes with a strongly trochaic, blues-like line: "That was many years ago, twenty years or more," but the near domination of metric regularity changes to "and during this time, Okonkwo's fame . . . ." If there is such a thing as a dominant meter in prose (English is considered to be naturally iambic),[16] Achebe's prose would seem to be largely anapestic: "It was this/ man that Okon/ kwo threw/ in a fight/ which the old/ men agreed/ was one/ of the fierc/ est since the found/ er of their town/ engaged a spir/ it of the wild/ for sev/ en days/ and sev/ en nights," ending with a series of four iambs. Note another anapestic line: "Every nerve/ and every mus/ cle stood out/ on their arms/ on their backs/ and their thighs." The point here is not to scan the lines but to show the rhythmical quality of the prose, more markedly rhythmical than traditional English prose, closer to an oral African quality.

I will explore now further levels of rhythm in the novel, moving from the stylistic to the structural, and then to the thematic, for not only the style but the entire narrative method can be considered rhythmical. Critics have mentioned the structuring of events in the novel in terms of rhythm. According to David Carroll, "the narrator then moves from this larger rhythm of the generations to the rhythm of the seasons, to Okonkwo and his sons repairing the walls; . . . yet the compassionate narrative voice seems to establish another rhythm, contrapuntal to Okonkwo's success."[17] S. O. Iyasere says, "Against the joyfully harmonic rhythm of this event [the locusts], the withdrawn, controlled formalism of the judgment of the *egwugwu* stands in sharp relief. By juxtaposing these events, Achebe orchestrates the modulating rhythms of Umuofia."[18] The structural tightness of the novel has been demonstrated by critics such as Robert Wren on the novel as a whole,[19] and Karl Bottcher on the narrator's voice and other stylistic techniques.[20] The narrative procedure that we see in the opening passages, involving a regular introduction of new materials, a little at a time, awaiting further amplification, is similar to African polymetric rhythms in which various meters are heard simultaneously, though not introduced at one time.[21] This is not a rhythm of percussive stress or beat, but an accentuation by word, phrase or theme. As our awareness is sharpened to the introduction of new materials—the "additive" element of orality—we become aware of the multiple rhythms at work: words that emulate the "redundant" aspect of orality by early or late repetition (e.g. "breathe," "seven"), themes that are briefly expanded or developed later (e.g. fierceness, wrestling), and those such as *masculine* and *feminine* that evolve slowly but consistently. We thus become more conscious of the process of development of words, phrases, and themes, and are less likely to overemphasize one and miss another. We will also see that the narrative makes increasingly evident a connection between these rhythmic elements of style and form and the basic rhythm of clan life, with the result that rhythm becomes significant thematically to Okonkwo's response to clan life and to the ultimate breaking of that life. I will sketch the pattern of the thirteen chapters of Part One to show how the narrative is laid before us, like pieces of a complex puzzle that slowly reveal coherence.

In Chapter One we meet Okonkwo as a man of great achievement and greater potential, and we see the heritage of his father the failure, a heritage Okonkwo wishes to flee. But as Okonkwo hastens to achieve his goals he inadvertently becomes involved with the hostage, the boy Ikemefuna whom the narrator refers to as "doomed" and "ill-fated," though we are unsure why at this point. The pacing of Chapter Two is particularly suggestive of the narrative method used thereafter in the novel. Set in three parts the chapter begins with Okonkwo, about to go to bed, hearing "a clear overtone of tragedy in the crier's voice." We drift briefly from that motif to hear lore of the night before we continue the episode of Ikemefuna's arrival in Umuofia into the care of Okonkwo. The second part turns abruptly to the character of Okonkwo, "dominated by fear, the fear of failure and of weakness," specifically of being thought an "agbala," a woman, or a man with no titles, like his father. "And so Okonkwo was ruled by one passion—to hate everything that his father Unoka had loved. One of those things was gentleness and another was idleness" (10). When in the third part the chapter returns to details of Ikemefuna's arrival—as Bottcher says, "the point of departure is resumed almost word by word"[22]—we have in a nutshell the whole novel: Okonkwo's passions, hatred of weakness or womanliness, his success and strengths, his connection with the hostage, and the overtones of tragedy.

The three parts of Chapter Two offer an episodic advancement of the plot, both adding to what has been mentioned and reflecting on the parts to which they are juxtaposed for commentary and contrast, as well as introducing new materials, all in the oral-rhythmic process of addition of new and amplification of old themes. Chapter Three, also of three parts (though the chapters vary generally from one to four parts), begins with Agbala, not the scornful title of "woman" but the Oracle whose priestess people visit "to discover what the future held . . . or to consult the spirits of their departed fathers" (12). Agbala had once told Unoka why he was a failure. Now, to overcome the disadvantages of a useless father, Okonkwo visits not Agbala but, more practically, a wealthy man for a loan of yams to start his own farm. Part Three then reverses the trend of the story thus far, for Okonkwo fails, and establishes the possibility of things going badly to the point of suicide. "The year had gone mad," and all his seed yams have been destroyed. One man hangs himself, but Okonkwo survives because of "his inflexible will."

Having established Okonkwo's direction, the narrator wishes to expand the context of the novel and offer several correctives, for the implications of the incident of Okonkwo's "survival" are not resolved until Chapter Four. "'Looking at a king's mouth,' said an old man, 'one would think he never sucked at his mother's breast.' He was talking about Okonkwo" (19), who had indeed forgotten his maternal life, and preferred "to kill a man's spirit" by calling him "woman." Okonkwo's fear of weakness is here qualified as specifically anti-feminine: "To show affection was a sign of weakness," so he beats his hostage, and in the next part beats one of his wives in violation of the Week of Peace dedicated to the Goddess Ani, an evil act that "'can ruin the whole clan. The earth goddess whom you have insulted may refuse to give us her increase, and we shall all perish'" (22).

The importance of the feminine element in the culture could be overlooked because of the emphasis Okonkwo places on masculine virtues and achievements for which he is justly celebrated. But the novel steadfastly points to the centrality of the feminine.[23] Okonkwo's masculine sensibility terrorizes his son Nwoye whom he wishes to be "a great farmer and a great man" (23), and enhances his affection for the already manly Ikemefuna, who significantly entertains such "womanly" traits as telling (24) and hearing (42) folk tales. Okonkwo's emphasis on "his inflexible will" as the cause of his survival is corrected here when the narrator explicitly states, "the personal dynamism required to counter the forces of these extremes of weather would be far too great for the human frame" (24).

One new element is introduced in this chapter, the concern with customs. Since Okonkwo had violated the custom of the Week of Peace, the discussion is appropriate, but its importance here is in revealing that the clan's customs are not absolute: "the punishment for breaking the Peace of Ani had become very mild in their clan." The men mock those clans who do not alter customs as they see fit: "they lack understanding." If we think too much on change as things-falling-apart, we are apt to miss the ameliorative process of change which is inherent in the clan. Throughout the story several old men and some young men ponder the sanity of customs, such as the particularly agonizing one of killing twins, and we are conscious that eventually it too would be changed. Desire for change, founded in emotional distress, is what brings Nwoye to Christianity for solace.

Chapter Five returns to another feast of the Earth Goddess to elaborate her position. The "source of all fertility[,] Ani played a greater part in the life of the people than any other deity. She was the ultimate judge of morality and conduct" (26). During her feast, for which the local women inscribe themselves and their huts with detailed patterns, and to which visitors come from the motherland (and reportedly spoil the children!), the violence of Okonkwo once more erupts. He rages that a tree has been killed—"As a matter of fact the tree was very much alive"—and then shoots at his wife, the one who (as we later learn) had left her husband out of admiration for Okonkwo's excellence as a wrestler. The implications of this wild act of shooting eventually become clear for though there was no formal violation of the harvest festival, Okonkwo here mishandles a gun as he will later do in fatefully killing a boy.

The remainder of Chapter Five is filled with the wonderful power of the drums, like the rhythmic pulse of the heart of the clan, sounding insistently behind the action—"Just then the distant beating of drums began to reach them" (30), "The drums were still beating, persistent and unchanging" (31), "In the distance the drums continued to beat" (32). They are a pulse countered only by Okonkwo's roaring at his daughter Ezinma whom he wished were a boy. At this point rhythm takes on thematic dimensions as the narrator contrasts Okonkwo's eccentric or asymmetrical behavior with the rhythmic spirit of the clan. The significance of the drum beat is amplified in the following chapter (Six) where the chief entertainment of the clan, wrestling, takes place on the *ilo*, the village circle, a dramatic space where the central physical and cultural acts of the people occur (recall the spiritual "dark, endless *space* in the presence of Agbala," 12). Later (Chapter Ten) judgments are passed there on major legal cases, and finally (Chapter Twenty-three) when the clan is disrupted and the imagery is of coldness and ashes, no acts take place: "the village *ilo* where they had always gathered for a moon-play was empty" (139). Our attention is drawn inexorably to the *ilo* by the drums so that by the time the celebration begins, we watch the people drawn in every sense together by the drums, for the drummers are literally "possessed by the spirit of the drums" (33) and their "frantic rhythm was . . . the very heart-beat of the people" (35-36). Rhythm is central. We are to see this celebration as the focal dramatic act of the dramatic space which is the center of the people— harmonic life—as if we as visitors to the clan must see at least once what rhythm means in its fullest articulation, must be reminded what it was like when, as the novel opened, Okonkwo threw the Cat, and when now, in almost exact repetition for Okonkwo, for his wife, for the clan, "The muscles on their arms and their thighs and on their backs stood out and twitched, . . .

> *Has he thrown a hundred Cats?*
> *He has thrown four hundred Cats.*" (36)

This is the cultural center of the novel—the *ilo* becomes a metaphor for the dramatic space of the novel, the cultural locus upon which

Okonkwo performs, first as wrestler, then as tragic actor. In *Achebe's World* Robert Wren also emphasizes this chapter: the novel's twenty-five chapters "are upon closer analysis divided into four groups of six chapters each, with one pivotal chapter, XIII, where Okonkwo accidentally kills Ezeudu's son and must flee."[24] Wren goes on to note that Part One actually "has two six-chapter units plus the pivotal chapter." The stress then is on Chapter Six, the drum chapter, as a center of this Part (for with Seven we move to the killing of Ikemefuna), so there is an imbalance with Chapter Thirteen: the "alternating chapters show Okonkwo in crisis": VII, IX, XI and XIII.[25]

Hereafter in Chapter Seven as things begin to break down, we can view Okonkwo's eventual tragedy as a violation of this harmony. We notice how he stands obnoxious and restless against the festival of drums: "never . . . enthusiastic over feasts," he picks a quarrel over the "dead" tree, shoots at his wife, jealously sees Obierika's son become wrestling hero instead of his son (34). Playwright and critic Wole Soyinka tells us that a person must constantly attempt to bridge the gulf between the area of earthly existence and the existence of deities, ancestors and the unborn by "sacrifices, the rituals, the ceremonies of appeasement to those cosmic powers which lie guardian to the gulf. . . . Tragedy, in Yoruba traditional drama, is the anguish of this severance, the fragmentation of essence from self."[26] Achebe's narrator underscores the same sense of cosmic responsibility in Chapter Thirteen: "A man's life from birth to death was a series of transition rites which brought him nearer and nearer to his ancestors" (85). Achebe's is not Yoruba fiction, but Soyinka's description gives, I think, an important clue to Okonkwo's tragedy: separation from what the clan adheres to as value, specifically here the rhythmic center of life.

In Chapter Seven the actions run together without division and there is a symbolic heightening of word and action as if we are continuing from the previous chapter with specially meaningful narrative. As Okonkwo told Nwoye and Ikemefuna "masculine stories of violence and bloodshed . . . they sat in darkness," a terrible symbolic image, especially in contrast to Nwoye's love of "stories his mother used to tell," folk tales of mercy and pity at which "he warmed himself" as Vulture did in the tale (38). (Note that Okonkwo almost inadvertently remembers in detail his mother's folk tale, 53.) Then the locusts came, destroyers later identified with "the white man" (97). Okonkwo is warned "to have nothing to do with" killing Ikemefuna, for "He calls you his father." But then—in the suddenly symbolic phrasing of the narrator, "in the narrow line in the heart of the forest," the narrow line between obedience to the Oracle or obedience to humanity and the advice of Obierika, a line which crossed either way would be destructive—"Dazed with fear, Okonkwo drew his matchet and cut him down. He was afraid of being thought weak" (43). And Nwoye, knowing what his father had done, felt "something . . . give way inside him," just as he did before when he "heard the voice of an infant crying in the thick forest," thrown there to die in a pot. "It descended on him again, this feeling, when his father walked in, that night after killing Ikemefuna" (43).

The rhythm of the narrative does not end here with the broken rhythm of Okonkwo's life. The style continues much as before; Wilfred Cartey observes Achebe's repetition of images in Part Two: "When the rain finally came, it was in large, solid drops of frozen water which the people called 'the nuts of the water of heaven'" (92); similarly, Nwoye feels Christianity "like the drops of frozen rain melting on the dry palate of the panting earth" (104).[27] In the first chapter of Part Two, Okonkwo is instructed through a kind of repetition or review of his life from childhood to manhood, for the purpose of renewing his way of seeing. The first truth he is taught is the role of the female; not only has Okonkwo committed a female crime of inadvertently killing a boy when his gun exploded, but his penalty is seven (the number we saw in the opening passage) years exile in his motherland:

Can you tell me, Okonkwo, why it is that one of the commonest names we give our children is Nneka, or 'Mother[A] is Supreme'? *We all know that a man is the head of the family and his wives do his bidding.* A child belongs to its father *and his family and* not to its mother *and her family.* A man belongs to his fatherland *and* not to his motherland. *And yet we say* Nneka. . . .

You do not know the answer? So you see that you are a child. . . . Listen *to me.* . . . *It's true that* a child belongs to its father. *But when a father beats his child, it* seeks sympathy in its mother's hut. A man belongs to his fatherland *when things are good and life is sweet. But when there is sorrow and bitterness he finds* refuge in his motherland. *Your* mother is there to protect you. *She is buried there. And that is why we say that* mother is supreme. (94)

In spite of the additive qualities of the motherland (D) as sympathy, refuge and protection, Okonkwo's course is clear cut: he will eschew the feminine and, unchanged, act towards others as he acted before. Though the rhythms of the clan are by no mean perfect, he refuses to respond to their fulfillment and direction, and refers later to these years as "wasted." "He cannot see the wise balance," Ravenscroft writes, "in the tribal arrangement by which the female principle is felt to be simultaneously weak and sustaining."[28] But the newly introduced element of the white men will alter his course much further. As subtle as the colonists' entrance is the narrator's addition of a feature at a time: at first an unknown, the white men become a joke, then formidable missionaries, then government, then place of judgment, then "religion and trade and government" and prison (123).

For all the disruption wrought by the whites, Christianity is not itself necessarily bad. The customs of the clan, which had been considered by some to be foolish or baneful and would in time be altered as others had, are accelerated to change by Christianity. Nwoye accepts the religion primarily because it answers a felt need. "It was the poetry of the new religion, something felt in the marrow," like the folk tales he loved earlier. "The hymn about brothers who sat in darkness and in fear seemed to answer a vague and persistent question that haunted his young soul [just as he and Ikemefuna had sat in darkness listening to Okonkwo's tales of the past]—the question of the twins crying in the bush and the question of Ikemefuna who was killed" (104). Christianity speaks directly to Nwoye's needs, not in rational or doctrinal terms but in mercy and comfort of spirit. Nor does it seem that his reaction is destructive of any of the prior values of the clan; certainly Ikemefuna was a richly responsive human, lacking neither masculine strength nor feminine mercy, and the only counter to Nwoye's inclinations was Okonkwo's insistence on masculinity. Christianity itself is greatly varied by its practitioners, the missionaries, for whereas Brown (midway between black and white) actually tried to understand African belief and respond with some sensitivity to the people (he is still obtuse: "a frontal attack . . . would not succeed," 128), another, with the nondescript name of Smith, "saw things as black and white. And black was evil" (130). Such dogmatic cruelty had not appeared in the novel until this missionary; and of course he succeeds because he is inflexible and tyrannical, while complex persons of compassion are overcome or bypassed.

> Seven years *was a long time* to be away *from one's* clan. A *man's* place *was not always there, waiting for him. As soon as he* left, *someone else rose and filled it. The* clan *was like a lizard; if it* lost *its tail it soon grew another.*
>
> *Okonkwo* knew *these things. He* knew *that he had* lost *his* place *among the nine masked spirits who administered justice in the* clan. *He* had lost *the chance to lead his warlike* clan *against the new religion, which, he was told, had gained ground. He* had lost *the years in which he might have taken the* highest titles *in the* clan. *But some of these* losses *were not irreparable. He was determined that his* return *should be marked by his people. He* would return *with a flourish, and regain the seven wasted years.*
>
> *Even in his first year of exile he had begun to plan for his return. The first thing he* would do *would be to* rebuild *his compound on a more magnificent scale. He* would build *a bigger barn than he had before and he* would build

huts for two new wives. Then he would show *his wealth by initiating his sons in the 'ozo' society. Only the* really great men *in the* clan *were able to do this. Okonkwo* saw *clearly the* high esteem *in which he* would be held, *and* he saw *himself taking the* highest title *in the land.* (121)

The rhythms are clearly evident with the beat of key words and tenses and voices: "he knew" (twice), "he had lost" (three times), and so on to "he would return," "he would build," "he would show," "he would be held," and "he saw." One of the peculiar effects of this repetition is that "he" is doing all the acting and thinking so that the repetitions advance with very little return to the beginning for elaboration. The "redundancy" lacks the element of "addition." Okonkwo marches forward, dreaming, not reflecting, not in fact building upon the prior words and thoughts. His mind works from knowing in truth to seeing in fantasy, from knowledge of loss to determination to overcome and excel. The repetitions mirror the stress between Okonkwo's linear mentality and the clan's circular, rhythmic mode of repetition. For Okonkwo personally nothing has changed at home: he curses his son Nwoye from the family and wishes Ezinma were a boy, "She understood things so perfectly" (122). Socially, however, outside Okonkwo's mind, there is now the new religion, trade, government; and everyone knew the white man "'has put a knife on the things that held us together and we have fallen apart'" (124-25).

The rhythmic coherence of the novel is sustained through to the end, at least when the narrator is describing the actions of the clan. The words of the District Commissioner, however, or words describing his actions, appear to be syntactically and philosophically different. For instance, in the final chapter we read the complex sentence:

When the District Commissioner arrived at Okonkwo's compound at the head of an armed band of soldiers and court messengers he found a small crowd of men sitting wearily in the obi. *He commanded them to come outside, and they obeyed without a murmur.* (146)

The sentences are "subordinative" and sequential in narration of facts—this happened and then that—not at all in the "additive" rhythmic manner of accumulation of detail by repetition.[29] We are confronted by the difference between his speech and the clan's speech when the Commissioner complains to himself, "One of the most infuriating habits of these people was their love of superfluous words," for redundancy or copiousness is indeed one of the marks of oral speech. Rhythmic language follows as Obierika and his fellows approach Okonkwo's body hanging from a tree:

> There was a small bush behind Okonkwo's compound. The only opening into this bush from the compound was a little round hole in the red-earth wall through which fowls went in and out in their endless search for food. The hole would not let a man through. It was to this bush that Obierika led the Commissioner and his men. They skirted round the compound, keeping close to the wall. The only sound they made was with their feet as they crushed dry leaves.

The passage features assonance of the "o" to depict the "round hole," the now-familiar parallelism, repetition, specificity of detail and images, and continual expansion of the scene by repetition and addition. The verb "to be" dominates the sentences—"There was," "the opening . . . was," "it was"—and the weight of meaning is carried by objects, "bush," "compound," "hole," as if one's actions are relatable chiefly to stable poles of identification in the village rather than to one's personal activities.[30] The monosyllabic detail of the words quoted above gives them a symbolic tone, as if that little hole were the impossible fissure through which Okonkwo had passed by suicide into non-existence. The rhythmic phrasing stands sharply against the closing words of the Commissioner which are again logical and process-oriented, analytical, unsuperfluous, and non-African, with weight on verbs: he "arrived," "found," "commanded . . . and they obeyed." His arrogant dismissal of Okonkwo's story as deserving a bare paragraph in his book is mirrored in the straightforward, one-dimensional prose.

The style of the novel and its structure thus draw attention to the exquisite tension between traditional English prose and the unique African and/or Igbo quality Achebe has created; it is, as Lloyd Brown says, "a total cultural experience, . . . the embodiment of its civilization."[31] Achebe himself is keenly aware of this quality of African style, as he points out in a passage from a Fulani creation myth: "You notice . . . how in the second section . . . we have that phrase *became too proud* coming back again and again like the recurrence of a dominant beat in rhythmic music?"[32] In a discussion of his own prose, he illustrates "how I approach the use of English":

> *'I want one of my sons to join these people and be my eyes there. If there is nothing in it you will come back. But if there is something there you will bring home my share. The world is like a Mask, dancing. If you want to see it well you do not stand in one place. My spirit tells me that those who do not befriend the white man today will be saying* had we known *tomorrow.'*
>
> *Now supposing I had put it another way. Like this for instance:*
> *'I am sending you as my representative among these people—just to be on the safe side in case the new religion develops. One has to move with the times or else one is left behind. I have a hunch that those who fail to come to terms with the white man may well regret their lack of foresight.'*[33]

Though Achebe does not spell out the differences between these passages, he seems fully conscious that the repetition of the "if" clauses creates that quality of rhythm which is missing in the "English" version, the metaphorical phrasing which, we should observe, is used in a colloquial rather than philosophical or proverbial sense. Rhythm, as Achebe seems well aware, thus can range from a stress within a phrase or sentence, to the structuring principle of a paragraph, to the form of an entire work. Through such a reading we may learn about the nature of rhythm and orality, and about the form of the novel, but especially we may better see the unique English Achebe has created and realize its African tone in order "to understand another whose language" one, as a non-African, "does not speak."[34]

Notes

1. C. L. Innes and Bernth Lindfors, eds., *Critical Perspectives on Chinua Achebe* (Washington, D.C.: Three Continents Press, 1978), p. 1.

2. *Ibid.*, p. 5, quoting from *TLS* in 1965.

3. John Povey, "The English Language of the Contemporary African Novel," *Critique* XI, 3 (1969), 93.

4. Ihechukwu Madubuike, "Achebe's Ideas on African Literature," *New Letters* 40, 4 (1974), 87.

5. Chinua Achebe, *Things Fall Apart* (London: Heinemann, 1958), p. 3. All subsequent quotations from the text are from this edition. Note: the word "men" above is written "man" in the text, which seems inconsistent with the referent "founder of their town."

6. Meki Nzewi, "Ancestral Polyphony," *African Arts* 11, 4 (1978), 94: "But Chinua does not see a link between the modern Igbo novelist and the traditional storyteller." According to Professor Chidi Ikonne of Harvard University, the narrator is not a *griot* (from private conversation). Yet Kofi Awoonor, *The Breast of the Earth* (Garden City, N.Y.: Doubleday, 1976), p. 257, adds, there is a "straight-forward simplicity about the language . . . that recalls the raconteur's voice."

7. Walter J. Ong, S.J., *Orality and Literacy* (London: Methuen, 1982), pp. 34, 37-40. Ong says Achebe's *No Longer at Ease* "draws directly on Ibo oral tradition . . . [providing] instances of thought patterns in orally educated characters who move in these oral, mnemonically tooled grooves," p. 35.

8. Karl H. Bottcher, "The Narrative Technique in Achebe's Novels," *New African Literature and the Arts* 13/14 (1972), 7.

9. Ong, pp. 45-46. See Bottcher on narrator's distance, pp. 1-5.

10. Unpublished essay as quoted by Ron Scollon, "Rhythmic Integration of Ordinary Talk," in *Analyzing Discourse: Text and Talk*, ed. Deborah Tannen (Georgetown: Georgetown University Press, 1982), p. 337. See also Emmanuel Obiechina, *Culture, Tradition and Society in the West African Novel* (Cambridge: Cambridge University Press, 1975), p. 174: "The main impulse in [Nigerian novelist Gabriel Okara's] *The Voice* obviously derives from the oral tradition . . . especially his deliberate repetitions, his metaphorical and hyperbolic elaborations and his colloquial rhythm."

11. Quoted in Jahnheinz Jahn, *Muntu* (New York: Grove Press, 1961), pp. 164-66. See original, Senghor, "L'Esthétique Negro-Africaine," *Liberté I, Negritude et Humanisme* (Paris: Editions du Seuil, 1964), pp. 211-12; and his premise: "*Image* et *rythme*, ce sont les deux traits fondamentaux du style négro-africain," p. 209. See also Obiechina: "The most striking feature of Okara's art is the repetition of single words, phrases, sentences, images or symbols, a feature highly developed in traditional narrative," p. 173; and Daniel P. Biebuyck, *Hero and Chief, Epic Literature from the Banyanga* (Zaire Republic) (Berkeley: University of California Press, 1978), p. 79: "Somewhat related to the formulaic system are the innumerable repetitions that add emphasis, effect, clarity and thus give fullness to the description [and] lend sonority, additional rhythm, and emphasis to the statements."

12. *Ibid.*, p. 168.

13. Robert Kellogg, "Literature, Nonliterature, and Oral Tradition," *New Literary History* 8 (Spring, 1977), 532. This issue of *NLH* has a valuable collection of essays on "Oral Cultures and Oral Performances."

14. Roger Fowler, *Linguistics and the Novel* (London: Methuen, 1977), p. 28: "the surface structure of a text (which is a sequence of sentences) has, like the surface structure of a sentence, qualities such as sequence, rhythm, spatial and temporal expressiveness." Raymond Chapman, *The Language of English Literature* (London: Edward Arnold, 1982), pp. 84-85: "We have seen that the traditional metres of English poetry have some connection with the rhythms of ordinary speech. . . . Rhythm of course is not confined to poetry . . . prose can have its distinctive cadences." Richard Ohmann, "Generative Grammars and the Concept of Literary Style," in *Linguistics and Literary Style*, ed. Donald Freeman (New York: Holt, Rinehart and Winston, 1970; previously published 1964), p. 260: "let me state this dogmatically—in prose, at least, rhythm as perceived is largely dependent upon syntax, and even upon content, not upon stress, intonation, and juncture alone."

15. Fowler, pp. 60, 63. See also Michael Riffaterre, "Criteria for Style Analysis," in *Essays on the Language of Literature*, eds. Seymour Chapman and Samuel Levin (Boston: Houghton Mifflin, 1967), pp. 428-29.

16. Raymond Chapman, p. 43: "One of the most common metrical lines in English poetry is the iambic pentameter. . . . It follows very closely the pattern of everyday speech. . . . The iambic pentameter can be given many variations, but it remains close to what sounds 'natural' in English."

17. David Carroll, *Chinua Achebe* (New York: Twayne, 1970), pp. 37, 47.

18. Solomon O. Iyasere, "Narrative Techniques in '*Things Fall Apart*,'" *New Letters* 40, 3 (1974), 76. See also Iyasere, "Oral Tradition in the Criticism of African Literature," *Journal of Modern African Studies* 13, 1 (1975), 111-14.

19. Robert Wren, *Achebe's World* (Washington, D.C.: Three Continents Press, 1980), pp. 23 ff.

20. Bottcher, pp. 1-12.

21. Cf. Jahn, p. 165; and J. H. Kwabena Nketia, *The Music of Africa* (New York: Norton, 1974), p. 136: "the crucial point in polyrhythmic procedures . . . is the spacing or the placement of rhythmic patterns that are related to one another at different points in time so as to produce the anticipated integrated structure." All of Chapter 12 is rele-

vant here. Isidore Okpewho, *The Epic in Africa: Toward a Poetic of Oral Performance* (New York: Columbia University Press, 1979), pp. 61-2, asks, "What is the nature of this musical element in African heroic song?" and responds, "one fundamental aspect, its polyrhythmic nature, is relevant here. . . . Polyrhythms . . . vary as one moves from east to west, with West Africa as the region of greatest complexity."

22. Bottcher, p. 7.

23. For discussions of the feminine, see Ernest Champion, "The Story of a Man and His People," *NALF* 6 (1972), 274; G. D. Killam, *The Novels of Chinua Achebe* (New York: Africana, 1969), pp. 20 ff.; Iyasere, "Narrative . . . ," pp. 79 ff.; Wilfred Cartey, *Whispers from a Continent* (New York: Random House, 1969), Chapter 1, "Mother and Child." Awareness of the masculine/feminine element is now widely manifested by critics.

24. Wren, p. 23.

25. *Ibid.*, p. 24.

26. *Myth, Literature, and the African World* (Cambridge: Cambridge University Press, 1976), pp. 144-45.

27. Cartey, p. 100.

28. Arthur Ravenscroft, *Chinua Achebe* (London: Longmans, Green, 1969), p. 13.

29. Cf. Senghor, p. 214: "Il y a plus, la structure de la phrase négro-africaine est naturellement rythmée. Car, tandis ilue les langues indo-européennes usent d'une syntaxe logique de subordination, les langues négro-africaines recourent, plus volontiers, à une syntaxe intuitive de *coordination et de juxtaposition.*" See also Robert Kauffman, "African Rhythm: A Reassessment," *Ethnomusicology* 24, 3 (1980), 402, 406.

30. In the quotation from p. 123 the repetition of "he" and active verbs—"He knew," "he would do," "he would rebuild"—confirms our sense that Okonkwo is operating outside the cultural rhythms of the clan. Marjorie Winters in "An Objective Approach to Achebe's Style," *Research in African Literatures* 12, 1 (1981), 55-68, describes the length of the narrator's sentences, his spare use of adjectives and adverbs, the "unusual" number of "introductory demonstratives," the clarity achieved by his "redundancy of connective signposts" ('and so'), "as well as other repetitious elements." Her approach differs from mine but her results do not oppose conclusions drawn here.

31. Lloyd Brown, "Cultural Norms and Modes of Perception in Achebe's Fiction," *Critical Perspectives on Nigerian Literature*, ed. Bernth Lindfors (Washington, D.C.: Three Continents Press, 1976), p. 133.

32. Chinua Achebe, "Language and the Destiny of Man," *Morning Yet on Creation Day* (New York: Doubleday, 1975), pp. 56-7.

33. Achebe, "The African Writer and the English Language," *Morning Yet on Creation Day*, pp. 101-02.

34. Achebe, "Where Angels Fear to Tread," *Morning Yet on Creation Day*, p. 79.

Achebe's Sense of an Ending:
History and Tragedy in *Things Fall Apart*_____

Richard Begam

One of the more notable consequences of cultural globalization has been the exchange that has occurred over the last decade or so between what we have come to call postmodernism and postcolonialism.[1] This meeting of First World and Third World has inspired more controversy than consensus, but on one point there seems to have been wide agreement: if we want to understand colonialism, then we must understand how it is represented. As Hayden White has argued, speaking of historiography in general, the "form" is the "content," and this means that the language, vocabulary, and conceptual framework in which the experience of colonialism is produced inevitably determine what can and cannot be said about it.[2] To borrow Homi K. Bhabha's formulation, "nation" and "narration" are not easily separated—the one implies the other.[3]

The present paper explores the intersection between narrative construction and colonial representation by focusing on an aspect of literary form that has received little attention in postcolonial studies—namely, the question of closure or ending. It is puzzling that this subject, which has generated so much commentary in modern and postmodern studies, has gone virtually unexamined in the area of postcolonial literature. Yet it is certainly reasonable to assume that a literature that identifies itself as *post*colonial and defines itself in terms of the aftermath of colonialism, will have a passing interest in the way endings are narratively achieved, in what they mean and how they are fashioned. Of particular interest in this regard is the highly problematic relation that postcolonial literature has to its own past and, more specifically, to the writing of its own history.[4]

We may begin to appreciate some of the difficulties entailed in this relation by considering a number of connected questions. First, where do postcolonial writers locate their past? Is it to be found in the colonial, precolonial, or postcolonial period? Second, can we neatly separate the different historical strands that traverse and intersect these various epochs? Can we confidently assign to them decisive beginnings and conclusive endings? Third, what historical stance should postcolonial writers assume toward their own history, especially if they wish to forge a sense of national identity after colonization? To what extent does "critical history," of the sort described by Nietzsche, become a luxury that the postcolonial writer cannot afford?[5]

In examining these questions, I want to take up the case of Chinua Achebe's *Things Fall Apart* because, as an exercise in historical recuperation, it is necessarily concerned with issues of formal shaping and narrative closure. Of course, at first glance, the novel appears to have a perfectly transparent narrative line: it tells the tragic story of Okonkwo's rise and fall among the Igbo people, concluding with that least ambiguous of all endings, the death of the hero. With only a few exceptions, critics have understood the novel in precisely these terms, seeing its closing pages as entirely unproblematic.[6] Yet any straightforward reading of Achebe's ending must reconcile itself with the fact that the novel describes a situation of profound cultural entropy, a society in which the norms of conduct and institutions of governance are in the process of "falling apart." What is more, while Achebe's novel movingly elegizes the passing away of traditional Igbo culture, the long view it adopts—looking ahead to the future establishment of Nigeria—suggests that Achebe's own position on the modernization of Africa is, at the very least, complicated. Given the subject of Achebe's novel and his own divided response to it, we would expect a fairly open-ended conclusion, one that acknowledges its own closure as tentative, even contingent.

In what follows, I will argue that *Things Fall Apart* resists the idea of a single or simple resolution by providing three distinct endings, three different ways of reading the events that conclude the novel. At the same time, I will relate these endings to three different conceptions of history, especially as it is produced within a postcolonial context.

First, Achebe writes a form of nationalist history. Here the interest is essentially reconstructive and centers on recovering an Igbo past that has been neglected or suppressed by historians who would not or could not write from an African perspective. As Achebe observed in 1964, four years after Nigerian independence: "Historians everywhere are re-writing the stories of the new nations—replacing short, garbled, despised history with a more sympathetic account."[7] Nationalist history tends to emphasize what other histories have either glossed over or flatly denied—namely that "African people did not hear of culture for the first time from Europeans; that their societies were not mindless but frequently had a philosophy of great depth and value and beauty, that they had poetry and, above all, they had dignity."[8] Second, Achebe writes a form of adversarial history. Here the emphasis falls not on the reconstruction of an authentic past that has been lost, but on the deconstruction of a counterfeit past that has been imposed. Adversarial history enables Achebe to write against what he himself has called "colonialist" discourse, against the attitudes and assumptions, the language and rhetoric that characterized British colonial rule in Nigeria. Third, Achebe writes a form of metahistory. This kind of history calls attention to itself as a piece of writing, a narrative construction that depends on principles of selection (what material will be included?), emphasis (what importance will be attached to it?) and shaping (how will it be organized and arranged?).[9]

Yet *Things Fall Apart* is concerned not only with writing history, but also with fashioning tragedy. Achebe himself made this point in an interview with Robert Serumaga, in which he discussed the political implications of tragedy and explicitly referred to his novel as an example of that genre.[10] A good deal of the critical literature has focused on this issue, addressing the question of whether the novel is indeed a tragedy and, if so, what kind of tragedy. Thus, Bruce Macdonald and Margaret Turner maintain that *Things Fall Apart* fails as an Aristotelian tragedy; Alastair Niven asserts that it succeeds as "modern" tragedy; while Afam Ebeogu treats it as an example of Igbo tragedy, and Abiola Irele considers it more generally as an instance of cultural and historical tragedy.[11] It will be my contention that much of the disagreement over generic classification has resulted from a failure to identify Achebe's multi-perspectival approach to the problem—a failure to recognize that he has written three distinct endings. Hence, I also want to argue that the novel offers us a variety of responses to tragedy, as well as history. According to the model I shall develop, nationalist history is associated with classical or Aristotelian tragedy; adversarial history is associated with modern or ironic tragedy; and metahistory is associated with critical discourse. My larger purpose in pursuing this line of analysis is to suggest that *Things Fall Apart* demands what is, in effect, a palimpsestic reading, a kind of historical and generic archaeology, which is designed to uncover, layer by layer, those experiences that have accreted around colonialism and its protracted aftermath.

* * *

The first of the novel's three endings centers on Okonkwo's killing of the messenger, his failed attempt to rouse his people to action, and his subsequent suicide. This ending presents the events of the novel largely from an African perspective, equating Okonkwo's demise with the collapse of Igbo culture. The idea that Okonkwo is a great man whose destiny is linked with that of his people is immediately established in the novel's celebrated opening:

> Okonkwo was well known throughout the nine villages and even beyond. His fame rested on solid personal achievements. As a young man of eighteen he had brought honor to his village by throwing Amalinze the Cat. Amalinze was the great wrestler who for seven years was unbeaten, from Umuofia to Mbaino. He was called the Cat because his back would never touch the earth. It was this man that Okonkwo threw in a fight which the old men agreed was one of the fiercest since the founder of their town engaged a spirit of the wild for seven days and seven nights. (p. 7)

In this passage history recedes into myth, as the narrator presents the seven-year reign of Amalinze and the seven-day struggle of the founder of the village in epic terms (here seven obviously functions as a conventional rather than a naturalistic number[12]). The passage also serves both to connect Okonkwo with the beginnings of Umuofia (through his wrestling exploits he is compared with the village's symbolic progenitor) and to look forward to his own and his people's end (the "spirit of the wild," representing Nature, will be replaced by the more powerful alien force of British imperialism.) In a few deft strokes, Achebe illustrates how Okonkwo has come to personify the destiny of his community, extending from its earliest origins to its final destruction.[13]

The larger effect of Achebe's opening is to establish Okonkwo as a particular kind of tragic protagonist: the great warrior who carries with him the fate of his people. Seen from the standpoint of the first ending, he is, as Michael Valdez Moses has argued, a Homeric hero cast in a distinctly Achillean mold:

> Like Achilles, Okonkwo is "a man of action, a man of war" (p. 7). His "fame" among the Igbo rests "on solid personal achievements" (p. 3), foremost of which are his exploits as the greatest wrestler and most accomplished warrior of the nine villages. He is a man renowned and respected for having brought home from battle five human heads; and on feast days and important public occasions, he drinks his palm wine from the skull of the first warrior he killed.[14]

Okonkwo is, in other words, identified with his community to the extent that it esteems the martial ethos he embodies, and while his village certainly does more than make war, it especially prizes those men who win distinction on the battlefield ("in Umuofia . . . men were bold and warlike" [p. 151]).

This is not to say, however, that Okonkwo epitomizes all the virtues of Igbo culture, or that he is himself without fault. On the contrary,

Achebe himself understands that, within an Aristotelian framework, his hero is necessarily a flawed character, guilty of errors in judgement—guilty, to use the Greek term, of *hamartia*. As Achebe has observed in an interview with Charles Rowell: "[The tragic protagonist is] the man who's larger than life, who exemplifies virtues that are admired by the community, but also a man who for all that is still human. He can have flaws, you see; all that seems to me to be very elegantly underlined in Aristotle's work."[15] Obviously Okonkwo is "larger than life" ("He was tall and huge, and his bushy eyebrows and wide nose gave him a very severe look" [p. 7]) yet his epic proportions carry a figurative as well as a literal significance: they indicate the difficulty he experiences fitting within the boundaries of any social order. So it is that as a "man of action," a great athlete and warrior, he is excessive both in his high-spiritedness, what the Greeks called *thymos* ("whenever he was angry and could not get his words out quickly enough, he would use his fists" [p. 8]), and in his prideful arrogance, what the Greeks called *hybris* ("The oldest man present said sternly [to Okonkwo] that those whose palm-kernels were cracked for them by a benevolent spirit should not forget to be humble" [p. 28]). Indeed, like many of the heroes of classical tragedy, Okonkwo's immoderate behavior consistently places him at cross-purposes not merely with his fellow Umuofians, but with the gods themselves ("Okonkwo was not the man to stop beating somebody half-way through, not even for fear of a goddess" [p. 31]), and it comes as no surprise when, in the second part of the novel, he is sent into temporary exile for offending Ani, the Earth deity. Nevertheless, if we are to appreciate the tragedy of the first ending—something that Achebe clearly intends—then we must recognize that Okonkwo's faults are essentially virtues carried to an extreme, and that while he is obviously not perfect, he nevertheless represents some of the best qualities of his culture.[16] As Obierika remarks near the novel's end, "That man was one of the greatest men in Umuofia" (p. 191).[17]

The crisis of the novel comes in the penultimate chapter when an impudent messenger, sent by the colonial authorities, orders a tribal meeting to disband. Okonkwo the warrior is moved to action:

> In a flash Okonkwo drew his machete. The messenger crouched to avoid the blow. It was useless. Okonkwo's machete descended twice and the man's head lay beside his uniformed body.
>
> The waiting backcloth jumped into tumultuous life and the meeting was stopped. Okonkwo stood looking at the dead man. He knew that Umuofia would not go to war. He knew because they had let the other messengers escape. They had broken into tumult instead of action. He discerned fright in that tumult. He heard voices asking: "Why did he do it?"
>
> He wiped his machete on the sand and went away. (p. 188)

The scene is presented with a devastating simplicity. From the perspective of the first ending, the people of Umuofia have deserted Okonkwo and in the process betrayed themselves, but the wiping of the machete is the only eloquence he permits himself. It is an ordinary and everyday gesture, yet in the present context it acquires special significance: Okonkwo remains true to the martial ethos that his people have abandoned, here represented by the warrior's care of his weapon; at the same time, he symbolically dissolves his connection with his people, wiping away the blood bond that has joined them. This gesture is especially resonant because, as critics have pointed out, in killing the messenger he is shedding the blood of a fellow Igbo.[18]

The suicide that follows is itself a profound violation of Igbo law, which strictly prohibits acts of self-destruction. The question of how we should respond to Okonkwo's final deed has been examined in detail by Kalu Ogbaa and Damian Opata, but with strikingly different results. For Ogbaa the suicide grows out of Okonkwo's failure to act with sufficient piety toward the Igbo gods and traditions, while for Opata it is a consequence of the Igbos' refusal to rally around Okonkwo and join him in resisting the British.[19] As was the case with discussions of the novel's tragedy, the disagreement arises in the first place because the reader has difficulty establishing Achebe's position on a number of issues—difficulty knowing, for example, where he stands on the question of violent resistance to the British. Of course, this interpretive problem largely disappears once we begin to read the novel palimpsestically as a layering of diverse perspectives on history and tragedy. Hence, understood within the terms of the novel's first ending, Okonkwo's suicide is the logical and necessary consequence of an idealistic and absolutist position. Both nationalist history and heroic tragedy demand that he remain unyielding and that the Igbos honor their cultural heritage by refusing assimilation. Even in this final gesture, then, Okonkwo functions as the true representative of his people. For, as he sees it, Igbo culture has willingly succumbed to its own annihilation, committing what is a form of collective suicide by submitting to the British. In taking his own life, Okonkwo has simply preceded his people in their communal destruction. Once again he has led the way.

* * *

The novel's second ending, which I associate with adversarial history, views events from the heavily ironized perspective of the District Commissioner. Igbo culture is now presented not from the inside as vital and autonomous, but from the outside as an object of anthropological curiosity, and its collapse is understood not as an African tragedy but as a European triumph. As the final scene of the novel unfolds, the Igbos take the District Commissioner to the place where the suicide was committed:

> Then they came to the tree from which Okonkwo's body was dangling, and they stopped dead.
> "Perhaps your men can help us bring him down and bury him," said Obierika. "We have sent for strangers from another village to do it for us, but they may be a long time coming."

The District Commissioner changed instantaneously. The resolute administrator in him gave way to the student of primitive customs.

"Why can't you take him down yourselves?" he asked.

"It is against our custom," said one of the men. "It is an abomination for a man to take his own life." (p. 190)

What is particularly noteworthy in this episode is the way the District Commissioner effortlessly shifts from the "resolute administrator" to the "student of primitive customs." Here Achebe demonstrates that, within a colonial context, the Foucauldian power-knowledge nexus is much more than a speculative theory—it is an inescapable and omnipresent reality. Thus, those who wrote historical and anthropological accounts of the Igbos were typically either representatives of the British government or their semi-official guests, and the colonial administration not only helped to enable such research by "opening up" various regions, but also relied upon it in determining local policy.[20] In the case of Igboland, the earliest anthropological studies were written by P. Amaury Talbot, himself a District Commissioner, and G. T. Basden, a missionary whose safety and well-being literally depended on the colonial office. As Robert M. Wren has shown, both Talbot and Basden were, by the standards of the day, sympathetic observers of the Igbos—indeed, the latter was a personal friend of Achebe's father— but this did not prevent them from expressing in their published writings typically European attitudes towards the Africans.[21] By way of illustration we might consider how the scene with the District Commissioner continues:

"Take down the body," the Commissioner ordered his chief messenger, "and bring it and all these people to the court."

"Yes, sah," the messenger said, saluting.

The Commissioner went away, taking three or four of the soldiers with him. In the many years in which he had toiled to bring civilization to different parts of Africa he had learned a number of things. One of them was that

---

a District Commissioner must never attend to such undignified details as cutting a hanged man from the tree. Such attention would give the natives a poor opinion of him. In the book which he planned to write he would stress that point. (p. 191)

Achebe makes much the same point himself, though obviously to very different effect, in his essay "Colonialist Criticism":

> To the colonialist mind it was always of the utmost importance to be able to say: "I know my natives," a claim which implied two things at once: (a) that the native was really quite simple and (b) that understanding him and controlling him went hand in hand—understanding being a pre-condition for control and control constituting adequate proof of understanding.[22]

Yet notice how carefully Achebe has chosen his words: it is important for the colonialist mind not to know the natives but to be able to *say* "I know my natives." What the District Commissioner ultimately achieves is not genuine understanding but the illusion of understanding that comes with the power to control:

> Every day brought him some new material. The story of this man who had killed a messenger and hanged himself would make interesting reading. One could almost write a whole chapter on him. Perhaps not a whole chapter but a reasonable paragraph, at any rate. There was so much else to include, and one must be firm in cutting out details. He had already chosen the title of the book, after much thought: *The Pacification of the Primitive Tribes of the Lower Niger.* (p. 191)

With these words, *Things Fall Apart* completes its passage from the heroic tragedy of the first ending to the biting irony of the second ending. In his well-known essay on *Heart of Darkness*, Achebe argues against European accounts of Africa that have reduced its people to—I quote Achebe quoting Conrad—"rudimentary souls" capable only of "a violent babble of uncouth sounds."[23] In presenting Okonkwo's epic story, epitomized by the first ending, Achebe offers a powerful counter-statement to the "dark continent" idea of Africa. But with the second ending he does something more. By ironically undermining the perspective of the District Commissioner, by exposing the latter's personal ignorance (not a "whole chapter" but a "reasonable paragraph") and political interests (the "pacification" of the Lower Niger), Achebe seeks to confront and finally to discredit the entire discourse of colonialism, those quasi-historical, quasi-anthropological writings that have treated Africa as nothing more than—again I quote Achebe—"a foil to Europe, a place of negations."[24]

At the same time, the second ending begins to redefine our point of view on the tragic events of the novel. Although this ending is clearly meant to undermine the District Commissioner's position, indeed to portray him as a fool, it nevertheless substantially alters the tone and mood of Achebe's resolution. Obviously the novel would read very differently—and its tragedy function very differently—if it concluded with, say, a heroic recitation of Okonkwo's suicide by Obierika. In other words, the final chapter of *Things Fall Apart* serves not as a simple denouement—one that helps us sort out a rather messy climax—but as a significant qualification of what has gone before, a distinctly new ending that complicates our sense of Achebe's approach to both history and tragedy.[25] In this regard, it is important to remember what Achebe himself has observed in interviews and essays: that while the passing away of traditional Igbo culture involved profound loss, it also held out the possibility of substantial gain. Thus, when he was asked about returning to pre-colonial society, the kind of world Okonkwo inhabited before "things fell apart," Achebe responded, "It's not really a question of going back. I think if one goes back, there's something wrong somewhere, or else a misunderstanding."[26] In another interview, he pushed this position further, arguing that colonization was a multi-faceted phenomenon, which had produced benefits as well as burdens: "I am not one of those who would say that Africa has gained nothing at all during the colonial period, I mean this is ridiculous—we gained a lot."[27] Finally and most tellingly, he has insisted that, despite his own ambivalence on the subject, modernization is a necessary and essential part of Africa's future: "The comprehensive goal of a developing nation like Nigeria is, of course, development, or its somewhat better variant, modernization. I don't see much argument about that."[28]

What all of this means is that Achebe's response to colonization is far more nuanced, far more complex, than most critics have recognized or been willing to acknowledge. How such complexity expresses itself, and how it modifies Achebe's sense of tragedy, is further explored in the third ending.

* * *

What I shall identify as the third ending is located in *No Longer at Ease*, the sequel to *Things Fall Apart*. No doubt, the assertion that one text contains the ending of another will immediately strike some readers as dubious. Such a claim begins to gain credibility, however, when we remember that Achebe originally conceived of his two novels as the first and third sections of a single work.[29] In other words, the compositional history of *Things Fall Apart* and *No Longer at Ease* provides some justification for treating the latter as a continuation of the former, an extension that qualifies Okonkwo's story, even redirects its course. Indeed, there is good reason to argue that *No Longer at Ease* is not only a continuation of *Things Fall Apart* but also a rewriting of it, one that essentially recapitulates the action of the earlier novel, though in a markedly different setting. Hence, both novels tell the story of a representative of the Igbo people who takes a stand on a question of principle and is destroyed in the ensuing collision between African and European values. To paraphrase one critic, the fall of Okonkwo's machete is replaced by the fall of the judge's gavel, as we are transported from a heroic to a legalistic world, but the narrative outline remains essentially the same. The very structure of *No Longer at Ease* indicates, then, that Okonkwo's story has not reached its end, that the tragic destiny it implies continues to be lived out.

This does not mean, however, that in writing *Things Fall Apart* and *No Longer at Ease* as independent works Achebe somehow betrayed the internal logic of his own narrative. On the contrary, the decision to treat Okonkwo's and Obi Okonkwo's stories separately contributes to what I have called Achebe's palimpsestic effect, the sense that the same or similar events acquire new meanings in different contexts. It is therefore not surprising that in moving from the first novel to the second, we observe Okonkwo's traditional tragedy transform itself into Obi's modern tragedy, as the heroic gives way to the ironic.

The point of intersection between the two novels, the scene in which I locate the third ending of *Things Fall Apart*, occurs when Okonkwo's grandson, Obi, a university-educated civil servant, finds himself discussing tragedy with a British colonial officer. Obi advances the opinion—of special interest given the first ending of *Things Fall Apart*—that suicide ruins a tragedy:

> Real tragedy is never resolved. It goes on hopelessly forever. Conventional tragedy is too easy. The hero dies and we feel a purging of the emotions. A real tragedy takes place in a corner, in an untidy spot, to quote W. H. Auden. The rest of the world is unaware of it. Like that man in *A Handful of Dust* who reads Dickens to Mr. Todd. There is no release for him. When the story ends he is still reading. There is no purging of the emotions for us because *we are not there*.[30]

Obi draws a distinction in this passage between two kinds of tragedy. In traditional or Aristotelian tragedy, there is a clear resolution, an aesthetic pay-off that comes in the form of *catharsis*; but in modern or ironic tragedy, the tragedy described in Auden's "Musée des Beaux Arts," the fall from a high place is likened to Brueghel's famous painting of Icarus. In the foreground the ploughman ploughs his field; in the background a ship sails on its way. And it is only after careful inspection that we are able to discover the place of tragedy: there in the corner, barely perceptible, we see Icarus's two legs breaking the surface of the water, sole testimony of his personal catastrophe.

While the point of departure for Obi's discussion of tragedy is Graham Greene's *The Heart of the Matter*, his observations have an obvious application to *Things Fall Apart*. Okonkwo's story as viewed from the Igbo perspective presents history in the form of classical or heroic tragedy. Okonkwo's story as viewed from the District Commissioner's perspective presents history in the form of modern or ironic tragedy. One of Obi's remarks is particularly apposite: there is no purging of the emotions in modern tragedy, because "we are not there." These words perfectly describe the situation of the District Commissioner. He "was not there" in the sense that he was never in a position genuinely to understand Okonkwo, to appreciate who he was and what he represented.

It is important to stress, however, that the novel's first ending is not in some way compromised because it is associated with the "conventional," while the novel's second ending is in some way enhanced because it is associated with the "real." Indeed, if Achebe provides us with any controlling point of view, it comes with the third ending, which illustrates the vexed and ambiguous relation in which the postcolonial stands to its own past. For with his remarks on tragedy, Obi is offering a narrative analysis of what is *literally* his own past. In describing a tragedy that ends in suicide, he is describing his grandfather's tragic fall and its significance for Igbo culture after it was lost, after "things fell apart."

What the novel's third ending illustrates, then, is that the boundaries between the "conventional" and the "real," the heroic and the ironic, are not clearly or cleanly drawn. From Obi's perspective—and, for that matter, the reader's—Okonkwo functions both as a literary persona and a living person, an epic hero and an historical anachronism. Yet the novel does not invite us to select one of these alternatives so much as to understand the various, though decidedly distinctive, truths they articulate. In other words, we are not meant to choose from among three possible endings, but to read all of them, as it were, simultaneously and palimpsestically. If we are able to do this, we shall see how Achebe's sense of an ending is intimately bound up with his sense of cultural loss; how the tragedy of the past necessarily depends on the perspective of the present; and how history is inevitably written for both the "they who were there" and the "we who are not there."

* * *

At the beginning of this paper I asked three questions about the relation of postcolonial literature to the writing of history. I would now like to propose, however provisionally, some answers to these questions. First, where do postcolonial writers locate their past? There is certainly no single or definitive response to this question, but a writer like Achebe is acutely aware of how problematic are the issues it raises. For this reason *Things Fall Apart* and *No Longer at Ease* not only situate themselves in periods of historical transition (Nigeria at the turn of the century and in the late 1950s) but also superimpose these periods on each other through a series of intertextual connections, suggesting that postcolonial writers are the products of all the historical periods through which their cultures have lived. Second, can we confidently assign decisive beginnings and conclusive endings to the various epochs of colonial and postcolonial history? It is not immediately apparent how Achebe would answer this question, but his experiment in extended closure reminds us that the narrative shaping that necessarily comes with beginnings and endings is a human creation—a product of what Richard Rorty calls "contingency"—rather than a naturally occurring or divinely given reality.[31] So it is that each of the three endings with which Achebe concludes *Things Fall Apart* grows out of different interests, different assumptions, different intentions, and none of these is, ultimately, true in itself. Finally, what historical stance should postcolonial writers assume toward their own history? This is a particularly difficult problem and one that cannot be fully treated in the space that remains. Still, it is worth observing that Achebe has not only qualified the kind of nationalist history with which his work is so often associated, but also that he has shown a willingness to criticize traditional Igbo culture. While Achebe urgently feels the need to recuperate an African past that has been lost or overlooked, to tell the story that has not been told, he nevertheless recognizes the importance of maintaining a sense of intellectual and historical integrity:

> The question is how does a writer re-create this past? Quite clearly there is a strong temptation to idealize it—to extol its good points and pretend that the bad never existed. . . . [But] The credibility of the world [the writer] is attempting to re-create will be called into question and he will defeat his own purpose if he is suspected of glossing over inconvenient facts. We cannot pretend that our past was one long technicolour idyll. We have to admit that like other people's pasts ours had its good as well as its bad sides.[32]

The last general point I would like to make touches upon methodology. Too often the literature we call postcolonial has been read as little more than an exercise in political thematics. Such an approach is not surprising, given the enormous historical pressure out of which this literature was born, but it has led many critics to ignore crucial issues of form and technique. Yet, as I have sought to show, we can only begin to appreciate how a writer like Achebe envisions his past, both as history and tragedy, if we understand how he narratively shapes his material, how he achieves his sense of an ending. Attention to formal organization is particularly important in the case of Achebe, because he conceives of history neither in teleological nor positivistic terms, but as something human beings create, a series of stories built around beginnings and endings, a narrative construction. This is not to say that Achebe is fundamentally a postmodern writer, but neither is he exclusively a postcolonial writer. Or rather, to put the matter more precisely, he is a postcolonial writer insofar as he is a product of cultural globalization, insofar as he is an African who has grown up and continues to live at "the crossroads of cultures."[33]

Obviously, life at the crossroads is not easy. As a student of classical tragedy—not to mention a sometime rebellious son—he is aware of the perils, as well as the possibilities, that await us at those places of Oedipal intersection: "the crossroads does have a certain dangerous potency; dangerous because a man can perish there wrestling with multiple-headed spirits, but also because he might be lucky and return to his people with the boon of prophetic vision."[34] But if forebears like Okonkwo, and alter egos like Obi, have been vanquished wrestling the demons of multiplicity, Achebe has emerged from these spiritual contests with a deeper and more comprehensive sense of what it means to inhabit the alternate worlds of postcolonialism, worlds that are at once aristocratic and democratic, heroic and ironic, ancient and contemporary. We are all of us the heirs of Achebe's prophetic vision, grappling with the problems and promises of a globalized modernity, working our way through its diverse scenarios, its different endings.

From *Studies in the Novel* 29, no. 3 (Fall 1997): 396-411. Copyright © 1997 by the University of North Texas. Reprinted with permission of the University of North Texas.

Notes

1. For a discussion of "globalization" and "postcolonialism," see Michael Valdez Moses, *The Novel and the Globalization of Culture* (New York: Oxford Univ. Press, 1995). The relation between "postmodernism" and "postcolonialism" has produced an exhaustive, not to say exhausting, bibliography: some of the better known essays are Kwame Anthony Appiah's "The Postcolonial and the Postmodern," in Appiah's book *In My Father's House: Africa in the Philosophy of Culture* (New York: Oxford Univ. Press, 1992); Reginald Berry's "A Deckchair of Words," *Landfall* 40 (1986): 310-23; Diana Brydon's "The Myths that Write Us: Decolonising the Mind," *Commonwealth* 10.1 (1987): 1-14; Simon During's "Postmodernism or post-colonialism today," *Textual Practice* 1.1 (1987): 32-47; Linda Hutcheon's "'Circling the Downspout of Empire': Post-Colonialism and Postmodernism," *Ariel* 20.4 (1989): 149-75; and Helen Tiffin's "Post-Colonialism, Post-Modernism and the Rehabilitation of Post-Colonial History," *Journal of Commonwealth Literature* 23.1 (1988): 169-81.

2. See Hayden White, *The Content of the Form: Narrative Discourse and Historical Representation* (Baltimore: The Johns Hopkins Univ. Press, 1987).

3. Bhabha discusses the connection between "nation" and "narration" in the introductory essay of *Nation and Narration* (London: Routledge, 1990).

4. On narrative closure and postcolonial history, see Homi K. Bhabha, *Nation and Narration*, pp. 1-3 and Robert Young, *White Mythologies* (London: Routledge, 1990), pp. 33-41, 65-67, 137-40, 156; on historiography and postcolonialism, see Stephen Slemon, "Post-Colonial Allegory and the Transformation of History," *The Journal of Commonwealth Literature* 23.1 (1988): 157-68 and Helen Tiffin, "Post-Colonialism, Post-Modernism and the Rehabilitation of Post-Colonial History."

5. In "On the Uses and Disadvantages of History for Life," the second section of *Untimely Meditations* (Cambridge: Cambridge Univ. Press, 1983), Nietzsche argues that there are three different species or kinds of history: the "monumental," which celebrates the past; the "antiquarian," which investigates the past; and the "critical," which condemns the past.

6. Helen Tiffin, Simon Gikandi, and Michael Valdez Moses are among the few critics who have seen the ending of Chinua Achebe's *Things Fall Apart* (New York: Fawcett, 1969) as less than straightforward. In "Post-Colonialism, Post-Modernism and the Rehabilitation of Post-Colonial History," Tiffin maintains that Achebe's novel "resists linear narrative techniques" (p. 174) until the British appear in Umuofia and asserts that the novel as a whole works against "closure" and "British textual containment" (p. 174). While I am not persuaded that the novel may neatly be divided into a linear, European narrative vs. a non-linear, African narrative, I agree with Tiffin's larger argument—namely, that the novel deliberately plays with the narrative conventions of linearity, chronology, and closure. While neither Gikandi nor Moses has focused on the novel's ending, both have suggested how the narrative shift to the District Commissioner's perspective introduces important complications into the novel's closing pages; see Gikandi, *Reading Chinua Achebe*: *Language and Ideology in Fiction* (London: James Currey, 1991), pp. 49-50 and Moses, pp. 132-33.

7. Chinua Achebe, "The Role of the Writer in a New Nation," *African Writers on African Writing*, ed. G. D. Killam (Evanston: Northwestern Univ. Press, 1973), p. 7.

8. *Ibid.*, p. 8.

9. Such a conception of history may initially appear to be more postmodern than postcolonial, but it is closely related to the figure of the *griot*, the African storyteller who combines the functions of historian and poet. Achebe discusses the *griot* in an interview with Charles Rowell: "the role of the writer, the modern writer, is closer to that of the *griot*, the historian and poet, than any other practitioner of the arts"; Charles H. Rowell, "An Interview with Chinua Achebe," *Callaloo* 13.1 (1990): 86.

10. Robert Serumaga, "Interview," *African Writers Talking: A Collection of Interviews*, Dennis Duerden and Cosmo Pieterse, eds. (London: Heinemann, 1972), pp. 16-17.

11. For a discussion of tragedy in *Things Fall Apart*, see Afam Ebeogu, "Igbo Sense of Tragedy: A Thematic Feature of the Achebe School," *The Literary Half-Yearly* 24.1 (1983): 69-86; Abiola Irele, "The Tragic Conflict in Achebe's Novels," *Introduction to African Literature: An Anthology of Critical Writing from "Black Orpheus"*, ed. Ulli

Beier (Evanston, IL: Northwestern University Press, 1970); Roger L. Landrum, "Chinua Achebe and the Aristotelian Concept of Tragedy," *Black Academy Review* 1.1 (1970): 22-30; Bruce F. Macdonald, "Chinua Achebe and the Structure of Colonial Tragedy," *The Literary Half-Yearly* 21.1 (1980): 50-63; Michael Valdez Moses, *The Novel and the Globalization of Culture*; Alastair Niven, "Chinua Achebe and the Possibility of Modern Tragedy," *Kunapipi* 12.2 (1990): 41-50; Chinyere Nwahuananya, "Social Tragedy in Achebe's Rural Novels: A Contrary View," *Commonwealth Novel in English* 4.1 (1991): 1-13; Clement A. Okafor, "A Sense of History in the Novels of Chinua Achebe," *Journal of African Studies* 8.2 (1981): 50-63; Margaret E. Turner, "Achebe, Hegel, and the New Colonialism," *Kunapipi* 12.2 (1990): 31-40.

12. Both Gikandi and Innes observe how Achebe's manipulation of time in the novel's opening scene points the reader toward issues of history and myth; see Gikandi, pp. 29-30 and C. L. Innes, *Chinua Achebe* (Cambridge Univ. Press, 1990), pp. 36-37.

13. I am of course referring to the fact that colonization destroyed the premodern culture described in Umuofia. Obviously the Igbo people survived the arrival of the British, but their ethical, social, and religious systems ceased to exist as they had in the nineteenth century.

14. Moses, pp. 110-11.

15. Rowell, "An Interview With Chinua Achebe," p. 97. Achebe's views on Okonkwo as an example of an Aristotelian tragic hero are complicated, suggesting that any single theory of tragedy is not adequate to describe how the novel handles its tragic material. Thus, while Achebe rejects the idea that Okonkwo is, *tout court*, an Aristotelian hero, he goes on to explain at length how *Things Fall Apart* can be read in Aristotelian terms: "Rowell: How do you respond to critics reading Okonkwo as a hero in terms of Aristotle's concept of tragedy?" "A: No. I don't think I was responding to that particular format. This is not, of course, to say that there is no relationship between these. If we are to believe what we are hearing these days the Greeks did not drop from the sky. They evolved in a certain place which was very close to Africa. . . . I think a lot of what Aristotle says makes sense" (p. 97). Achebe then proceeds to make the comment I quote in the body of this paper.

16. A number of critics, arguing against the tragic elements of *Things Fall Apart* and, reading the novel from a postheroic, Western perspective, contend that Okonkwo is not representative of his tribe—indeed, that he is fundamentally hostile to its interests and traditions; see, for example, Harold Scheub, "'When a Man Fails Alone,'" *Présence Africaine* 72.2 (1970): 61-89.

17. I agree with Moses when he maintains that Obierika's "assessment of Okonkwo's end is only partially correct" (p. 132); it is "correct" within the terms of the novel's first ending.

18. Kalu Ogbaa, "A Cultural Note on Okonkwo's Suicide," *Kunapipi* 2.3 (1981): 133-34.

19. See Kalu Ogbaa's "A Cultural Note on Okonkwo's Suicide," pp. 126-34, and Damian Opata's "The Sudden End of Alienation: A Reconsideration of Okonkwo's Suicide in Chinua Achebe's *Things Fall Apart*," *African Marburgensia* 22.2 (1989): 24-32.

20. Achebe offers a memorable example of the power-knowledge nexus in *Arrow of God* (New York: Anchor Books, 1989, [pp. 32-33]) when he shows a colonial officer reading *The Pacification of the Primitive Tribes of the Lower Niger* by George Allen, the District Commissioner in *Things Fall Apart*. For Michel Foucault's treatment of power-knowledge, see *Discipline and Punish: The Birth of the Prison*, trans. Alan Sheridan (New York: Vintage Books, 1979), and *Power/Knowledge: Selected Interviews and Other Writings 1972-1977*, ed. Colin Gordon (New York: Pantheon Books, 1980); for critiques of Foucault's application of this idea to Western democracies, see Richard Rorty, "Moral Identity and Private Autonomy: The Case of Foucault," *Philosophical Papers*, Vol. 2: *Essays on Heidegger and Others* (Cambridge: Cambridge Univ. Press, 1991), and Michael Walzer, "The Lonely Politics of Michel Foucault," *The Company of Critics: Social Criticism and Political Commitment in the Twentieth Century* (New York: Basic Books, 1988).

21. Robert M. Wren, *Achebe's World: The Historical and Cultural Context of the Novels* (Washington, DC: Three Continents, Press, 1980), pp. 17-20.

22. Achebe, *Hopes and Impediments: Selected Essays* (New York: Anchor Books, 1989), p. 71.

23. Achebe, "An Image of Africa: Racism in Conrad's *Heart of Darkness*," *Heart of Darkness: An Authoritative Text, Backgrounds and Sources, Essays in Criticism*, edited by Robert Kimbrough (New York: W.W. Norton and Company, 1988), p. 255.

24. *Ibid.*, pp. 251-52. As Simon Gikandi has written, "whenever [Achebe] looked around him, he was confronted by the overwhelming hegemony of colonialist rhetoric on Africa—what he called 'the sedate prose of the district-officer-government-anthropologist of sixty or seventy years ago'—which the African intellectual has had to wrestle, like Jacob and the angel, at almost every juncture of our contemporary history. To invent a new African narrative was then to write against, and decentre, this colonial discourse as a prelude to evoking an alternative space of representation"; *Reading Chinua Achebe*, p. 6.

25. Moses is the only critic who has argued that Achebe is not *simply* ironizing the District Commissioner: "While Achebe's irony invites us to dismiss the District Commissioner as the unfeeling and pompous representative of a racist and imperialist perspective, the novel ultimately *subsumes* rather than rejects the official British view" (p. 133).

26. Kalu Ogbaa, "An Interview with Chinua Achebe," *Research in African Literatures* 12.1 (1981): p. 6.

27. Interview with Serumaga, p. 13.

28. Achebe, *Hopes and Impediments*, p. 155.

29. See, for example, Achebe's interview with Serumaga, p. 16.

30. Achebe, *No Longer at Ease* (New York: Fawcett, 1969), pp. 43-44, my emphasis.

31. For a discussion of "contingency," see Rorty, *Contingency, Irony, and Solidarity* (Cambridge Univ. Press, 1989), especially Chapter One, "The Contingency of Language."

32. Achebe, "The Role of the Writer in a New Nation," p. 9.

33. Achebe, *Hopes and Impediments*, p. 34.

34. *Ibid.*

Okonkwo and His Mother:

Things Fall Apart and Issues of Gender in the Constitution of African Postcolonial Discourse

Biodun Jeyifo

In the oral tradition, we often do not know whether the storyteller who thought up a particular story was a man or a woman. Of course when one examines the recorded texts, one might wonder whether a myth or story doesn't serve particular interests in a given society.

—Mineke Schipper

The Chielo-Ezinma episode is an important sub-plot of the novel and actually reads like a suppressed larger story circumscribed by the exploration of Okonkwo's/man's struggle with and for his people. In the troubled world of *Things Fall Apart*, motherhood and femininity are the unifying mitigating principles, the lessons for Africa and the world.

—Carole Boyce Davies

So Okonkwo encouraged the boys to sit with him in his *obi*, and he told them stories of the land—masculine stories of violence and bloodshed. Nwoye knew that it was right to be masculine and to be violent, but somehow he still preferred the stories that his mother used to tell him, and which she no doubt still told to her younger children—stories of tortoise and his wily ways, and of the bird *eneke-nti-oba* who challenged the whole world to a wrestling contest and was finally thrown by the cat. . . . That was the kind of story that Nwoye loved. But he now knew that they were for foolish women and children, and he knew that his father wanted him to be a man. And so he *feigned* that he no longer cared for women's stories.

—Chinua Achebe, *Things Fall Apart* [my emphasis]

Okonkwo's *mother*? Within the total narrative space of *Things Fall Apart*[1] there is only one direct, substantive mention of our hero's mother. As far as I know, this has never been formally registered in the extensive discussions and commentaries on the novel, let alone critically explored, and this seems quite consistent with the author's more evident interest in the complex, tortured relationship of Okonkwo with his father and, later in the concluding sections of the novel, with his son Nwoye. As Carole Boyce Davies remarks in the article from which the second epigraph to this essay was extrapolated, in *Things Fall Apart* Achebe's "primary concern is woman's place within larger social and political forces" (247) which are, in the order of things, the spheres of male initiatives and control.

And yet the single, brief mention of Okonkwo's mother is extraordinarily suggestive both for reading Okonkwo's particular brand of misogyny and neurotic masculinist personality and for analyzing larger questions of the author's construction of male subjectivity and identity in the novel. This "new" reading would indeed be a *re-reading* whose condition of possibility derives from the manifold feminist project that is such a decisive, perhaps the most decisive current of postcolonial critical discourse at the present time.[2] In this short paper, I shall examine this one substantive reference to Okonkwo's mother in fairly close detail, hoping to deploy this close textual exegesis as a bridgehead to a more general discussion of gender-related issues in the constitution of a postcolonial African critical discourse. I shall be arguing in effect that between Achebe's "under-textualization" of Okonkwo's mother and a feminist re-reading of the novel which would foreground her and relocate the "motherlore" she represents in the intense gender politics of the novel, we encounter an instance of the fundamental challenge posed by issues of gender in postcolonial criticism and scholarship. The point has been repeatedly made that the *nationalist* "master texts" of African postcolonial literature, *needed*, as the basis of their self-constitution as *representative*, canonical works, to subsume gender difference under the putatively more primary racial and cultural difference of a resisting Africa from a colonizing Europe.[3] By this occlusion of gender difference, Okonkwo's mother, his wives and daughters recede into the *ground* which enables the *figure* of Okonkwo and his father and son to achieve their representational prominence. But beyond this "programmatic" under-textualization of Okonkwo's mother, *Things Fall Apart*, as a powerful work of realist fiction, could not fail to inscribe the effects of sexual difference and gender politics within the very "over-textualization" of "men's affairs" in the novel, this being the social totality of the precolonial order as it comes into contact with the invading colonial capitalism. This has an important *political* lesson: national liberation in Africa, as long as it remains a historic agenda enforced by neocolonial dependency and arrested decolonization,[4] and as it is profoundly inflected by new postnationalist discourses and cultural production, must reconfigure its founding moment as not irredeemably marked by an inevitable, *natural* sexism.

* * *

The allusion to Okonkwo's mother occurs in chapter nine of the novel; significantly, she is not named. The precise narrative moment seems, on the surface, of no particular thematic noteworthiness: three days after his participation in the ritual murder of the youth Ikemefuna, his "adopted" son, Okonkwo is just beginning to emerge from the emotional and spiritual trauma of that event. Characteristically, it irks him that he has indeed been weak and "unmanly" enough to have succumbed to the trauma. Indeed the whole episode lasts one short paragraph and can thus be quoted entirely:

> For the first time in three nights, Okonkwo slept. He woke up once in the middle of the night and his mind went back to the past three days without making him feel uneasy. He began to wonder why he felt uneasy at all. It was like a man wondering in broad daylight why a dream had appeared so terrible to him at night. He stretched himself and scratched his thigh where a mosquito had bitten him as he slept. Another one was wailing near his

right ear. He slapped the ear and hoped he had killed it. Why do they always go for one's ears? When he was a child his mother had told him a story about it.

But it was as silly as all women's stories. Mosquito, she had said, had asked Ear to marry him, whereupon she fell on the floor in uncontrollable laughter. "How much longer do you think you will live?", she asked. "You are already a skeleton." Mosquito went away humiliated, and anytime he passed her way he told Ear that he was still alive. (53, my emphasis)

It is significant that in the very next sentence after this recalled story we are told: "Okonkwo turned on his side and went back to sleep." Like the mosquito bite which presumably worried his brief wakeful moment within a restful sleep only as a very minor irritation, Okonkwo's memory of his mother's stories in his childhood is very easily suppressed; and it is easily consigned to the domain of "silly women's stories." This seems quite consistent with the larger pattern of intrafamilial and inter-generational conflicts elaborated in the novel: Okonkwo's relationship with his father, and later his relationship with his son, Nwoye, are foregrounded over relationships with his nameless mother, his wives, and his daughters. From a feminist perspective, this, more than anything else, reveals the male-centeredness of Achebe in this novel. While this is incontrovertible, it is only part of the story, and it barely scratches the surface of the complex and ambiguous gender politics of the text of *Things Fall Apart*. This point needs some elaboration.

As the third of the epigraphs to this essay indicates, Okonkwo's son, Nwoye, unlike his father, does not succeed in completely repressing either the memory of *his* mother's stories, or their powerful, subliminal hold on his imagination and psyche. Consequently, he has to *feign* a "manly" indifference to this motherlore. Okonkwo, by contrast, seems to have succeeded completely in a willed amnesia of his mother's creative role in the formation of his personhood, his sensibility. Indeed the precise nature of this willed amnesia is awesome: while his father,

Unoka, perpetually figures in both his psyche and his vigilant, conscious mind as an active, powerful (if negative) presence, Okonkwo's mother is assimilated into the neutral, abstract function of "mothers in general." For Okonkwo, his mother's stories and their significations evaporate into the generalized phallogocentric rubric of the "silliness" of motherlore. The catch in all of this is that neither this particular story, nor the many other women's stories given in *Things Fall Apart*, is silly; rather, in almost every instance, these stories are only deceptively simple and are usually of extraordinary emblematic, subversive resonance to the central narrative of Okonkwo's obsession with his father and his sons.[5] A close look at Okonkwo's mother's story and its narrative of the fractious, bitter liaison between Ear and Mosquito illustrates this point well.

Perhaps the most arresting detail in this story is the structure of reversals of gender hierarchy between the respective female and male personae in the tale. Thus Ear, the female persona, is the dominant, supercilious agent in the conflict. Mosquito, the male suitor, not only figures as an atrophied, diminished, "inadequate" phallus; the very manner and terms of his rejection strike deep: loss of vital powers unto death ("You are already a skeleton"!). Since this tale is told by Okonkwo's mother and thus belongs in *motherlore*, we can surmise that Mosquito here encodes the male's neurotic fear of female power as the nemesis of male potency and life-force. Putative female superiority in this vertical structure is compounded by Ear's additional figuration in traditional mythological anthropomorphism of the Body and its organs as *both* male and female, as Trinh T. Minh-ha tells us in her book *Woman, Native, Other*:

> . . . As a wise Dogon elder [Ogotemmeli] pointed out, "issuing from a woman's sexual part, the Word enters another sexual part, namely the ear" (the ear is considered to be bisexual, the auricle being male and the auditory aperture, female). (127)

The embodiment of abstract female power in this system of significations is particularly noteworthy in the way that it combines both "male" and "female" principles and their elaborated attributes and values. This, however, is a structure unperceived by Okonkwo and is indeed alien to his rigid, overliteral conceptions of the "masculine" ideals.

Is it of little or no consequence to the gender politics in the text of *Things Fall Apart* that abstract female power represented by the Ear and abstract male identity represented by the Mosquito are so vastly unequal in suppleness, vitality and resonance? In other words, is this story, told by Okonkwo's mother, and with all its powerfully resonating meanings, a mere narrative detail, a figural embellishment of the text bearing little relevance to the central conflict of Okonkwo's masculinist personhood which is lodged elsewhere, that is with the father and the Law of the Father?

There is absolutely no question that this tale of Okonkwo's mother, obviously drawn from the vast repository of motherlore, is centrally linked to Achebe's critical construction of Okonkwo's masculinist personality as this is conflictually played out, first with his father, then with his son. And this is all of one piece with the overabundant inscription in the novel of its protagonist's obsession with *maleness*, and his corresponding fear of, and suppression of *femaleness*. However, the major interpretive problem that we confront here seems to be that while *femaleness* as we encounter it in Okonkwo's mother's tale is a superior, stronger entity which confronts male identity with belittlement and insecurity, femaleness, as Okonkwo encodes it, is the exact opposite: weakness, fecklessness, cowardice, irresoluteness, sentimentality. In effect this means that in the light of Okonkwo's peculiar construction of "female" attributes, the personae of his mother's tale would be reversed: Ear would represent male superiority and Mosquito would represent female shrewishness. But this hardly resolves this issue, as long as Okonkwo operates as an isolated figure removed from the social context of his Umuofia community. Moreover, given Okonkwo's excessively literal phallocratic imagination, it would be as much of an absurdity to represent "maleness" by an orifice in the body as it would be to represent "femaleness" by the mosquito with its broomstick figure. Nothing reveals this crude, physical phallicism more than the fact that the gun, the machete, and the cudgel (for wife-beating and child beating), three over-literal extensions of an aggressive, neurotic masculinist identity, are Okonkwo's ultimate answers to any and all crises, and we see this in several incidents in the novel: the incident with the beating of his second wife during the peace week; the episode of the severe beating of his son, Nwoye, when the unhappy youth was spotted among the new community of Christian converts; and the climactic moment of the novel which results in Okonkwo's beheading of the first in the line of the advancing party of the hirelings of the colonial administration who had come to break up the village assembly at the end of the novel.

This problem of Okonkwo's negative transvaluation of female strength and superiority in his mother's tale to weakness and inferiority, however, disappears once we place Okonkwo in the context and nexus of his society's moral economy and symbolic codes.[6] This is a historically and culturally constructed context; it is a pre-capitalist, pre-feudal social formation in which, as amply demonstrated in Ifi Amadiume's *Male Daughters and Female Husbands*, "maleness" or "femaleness," the category "man" or "woman," do not operate as rigidly divided, biologically literal or ontological entities.[7] And Achebe's realist integrity renders this structure felicitously. Indeed *Things Fall Apart* not only has one of the most extensive and dense novelistic inscriptions of the *genderization* of subjectivity, signification and social space in postcolonial African fiction; the novel's overcoded inscription of the processes of en-gendering is massively fractured and ambiguous and cannot be read as a simple, unambiguous inscription of phallocratic dominance. Let me cite only one composite group of these ambiguous inscriptions of gender and gender relations in the present context. Thus, on the one hand, Okonkwo's representation of "femaleness" as weakness and irresoluteness seems to have validation in the system of division of cognitive and perceptual categories in his society which ascribes the designation "female" to smaller crops like the cocoyam and the designation "male" to bigger crops like the yam, a system which also describes an "ochu" (abomination) as either "female" or "male" depending on the degree of threat or destabilization to the social order that it poses. But on the other hand, the same panoply of symbolic values and cognitive codes describes as "female" the most important deity in the religion and sacred lore of the community (Ani), making her priest *male* (Ezeani); conversely, the important deity of the Oracle of the Hills and the Caves is "male" while his highest functionary is the *priestess* Chielo.

On a different but related note, it is important to stress the limits of a psychologistic reading of the relationship of Okonkwo to his parents and his sons and daughters which might fasten one-sidedly on his relations with his father and later with his son. It is indeed tempting to read an Oedipalization in the fact that almost everything that we are told about Unoka, Okonkwo's father, can be symbolically assimilated to the figure of the mosquito in the mother's story. By this reading, the driving fear of "femaleness" in Okonkwo's psyche is thus really both "guilt" for the father's fate of "mosquito" vitiation and eventual "death," and strong identification with and "possession" of the mother. But this is purely speculative and a rather sterile and fanciful, if fascinating, line of critical inquiry. Okonkwo both loathes the memory of his father and represses the lore of his mother; in the process he distorts both the "masculine" and the "feminine," by keeping them rigidly apart and by the ferocity of his war on the "feminine." His son, on the other hand, only *feigns* acceptance of this rigid masculinist code, but keeps alive the memory of motherlore in his conflicted, sorrowing consciousness. One crucial difference between father and son takes us beyond the purely psychologistic. This is the fact that the driving, all-consuming ambition of Okonkwo to be one of "the lords of the land," to take the highest title which only few men (and no women) ever manage to achieve within the course of several generations, this ambition in the service of material interests and social recognition of the highest kind, is absent in the son. Throughout the course of the novel, the evolving moral and spiritual sympathies of Nwoye move him away from such worldly sights to identification with the unprotected and "unprotectable" of his culture, those immiserated by the contradictory codes and practices of his society. We can indeed say that within the gendered scale of valuations and representations by which Okonkwo seeks to establish the greatest possible distance between himself and his father's "effeminacy," his son Nwoye is "feminized": he refuses Okonkwo's interpellative call to be a "man" contemptuous of "female" attributes. This important distance between father and son is eloquently but succinctly captured in the economy of the following short passage:

> The missionary ignored him and went on to talk about the Holy Trinity. At the end of it Okonkwo was fully convinced that the man was mad. He shrugged his shoulders and went away to tap his afternoon palm-wine. But there was a young lad who had been captivated. His name was Nwoye, Okonkwo's first son. It was not the mad logic of the Trinity that captivated him. He did not understand it. It was the poetry of the new religion, something felt in the marrow. The hymn about brothers who sat in darkness and fear seemed to answer a vague and persistent question that haunted his young soul in the question of twins crying in the bush and the question of Ikemefuna who was killed. He felt a relief within as the hymn poured into his parched soul. The words of the hymn were like the drops of frozen rain melting on the dry plate of the panting earth. Nwoye's callow mind was greatly puzzled. (103)

In the first epigraph to this essay, Mineke Schipper raises the important question of the gender(ed) provenience of stories and fictions in the precolonial oral traditions and the particular interests which such gender origins might serve. This question is at the heart of one of the major issues in African critical discourse at the present time: the project of reclaiming a separate, distinct tradition of African female writing and criticism which is not easily, indeed WILL NOT BE subsumed within the male-dominant tradition which, to date, has claimed to speak for the *whole* of African literary and critical traditions. It is impossible to take a full measure of this project without realizing that its objective is not merely to "correct" the stereotypes and misconceptions of the male-centered writers and critics, and not merely, in the words of the editor's comments in the *African Literature Today* issue on "Women," that African women now seek "to take their stand by their men,"[8] but rather to reclaim "women's stories" (herstory) from the void or repressed zones into which men and male-centeredness had consigned them. For just as the nationalist anti-colonial counter-discourse in literature and criticism once had to re-write and reinvent a *presence* that colonialist discourse, in its arrogance, imposture, and triumphalism, had theorized as absence, so also women writers and critics have to recover the submerged female tradition. What contemporary African feminist criticism at this level of self-authorization adumbrates is a return to *female* sources within Cabral's famous call for a return to "the source," or more radically, female sources as *the* source. In other words, the identification of creative female precursors or foremothers, and of discrete intertextual revision and influence between female and female-centered writers and critics, defines the most radical autonomization of gender difference in feminist African criticism at the present time. Particularly powerful instances of this expression are Chikwenye Okonjo's "The Dynamics of the Contemporary Black Female Novel in English," and an important essay by Florence Stratton which I now examine in the context of our reflections in this essay.

In "Periodic Embodiments: a Ubiquitous Trope in African Men's Writing," a trenchant critique of the male-dominant tradition of postcolonial African writing, Florence Stratton has uncovered, as few other feminist critical writings have done, the depth of the male-centeredness or phallocentrism of this tradition. According to Stratton, this male-dominant, male-centered tradition, given the fact and consequences of historic colonization, has been largely constructed around woman as the "embodiment" of the male writers' vision of the new African nation in all its changing historical experience, from colonial humiliations and anti-colonial struggles to the postcolonial agony of neocolonialism and virtual recolonization. Furthermore, Stratton avers that in making these "periodic embodiments" of woman as ideal symbol and representation of the nation, male writers have basically assumed that man is the visionary, the artist, the maker of the history of the nation, and woman the sign (of national or racial integrity, resistance and sovereignty) mobilized by male creativity, initiative, and revolutionary will. Perhaps the most telling point of Stratton's forceful argument in this article is the view that this deeply phallocratic assumption goes beyond its usual identification with the conservative current of the anti-colonial and postcolonial African male writer's idealization of woman as repository of cultural "essence" (what Stratton calls "the pot of culture" syndrome). Beyond this mostly Negritudist romantic-nostalgic idealization, Stratton also assimilates male writers of a more radical anti-imperialist, even anti-sexist vision and sensibility like Sembene or Ngugi, to this whole tradition of "periodic embodiment." This critique in effect implicates virtually *all* male African writers and critics.

What this line of polemic and projection indicates is, I believe, that feminist criticism, even when it critically engages and contests both imperialist domination and post-independence misrule in the context of the postcolonial state, will not be content with how women are positively depicted by certain "progressive" male writers, that is with regard to "accuracy," "sympathy," or "solidarity" with female oppression and resistance to it. The stakes, it seems, are much higher: women are no less visionary and creative, and no less makers of history and shapers of experience than men; "woman's issues" will no longer be subsumed into a supposed "broader" framework of national or racial collectivity defined and legitimated by men. And perhaps Stratton's most provocative thesis in this article is the implicit, sub-textual *uterocentrism* of her suggestion that men's denial or erasure of women's initiative and power is a product, and a projection, of a fundamental male anxiety and insecurity about femaleness and its putative *primal* connection to creativity.[9] By the light of this particular uterocentric critique of *all* male writers and critics, we have to look beyond the so-called strategic, programmatic suspension of gender difference in the name of a unified resistance to foreign *racial* domination for the deeper causes of that marginalization of women, as characters, writers, and critics, which enabled the constitution of postcolonial African literature and critical discourse as an engendered tradition. We also have to go beyond the excuse that colonial educational policies being what they were, women simply weren't there in that great moment of "awakening" when modern African literature and critical discourses began to stake their claims against outright European colonialist disavowals and "post-imperial" neo-liberal condescending universalism.[10] The deeper, more daunting cause, Stratton suggests, is perennial male anxiety and fear of femaleness as *the* source of creation and creativity. While I think we should ultimately reject this uterocentrism and the considerable obfuscations and mystifications to which it could give rise, I suggest that there are eminent political and hermeneutic considerations which demand that we do not simply dismiss it out of hand. Again let us turn to our re-reading of Okonkwo and his mother for a brief elaboration of this point.

Okonkwo's repression of motherlore that I have examined in this essay and the significations embedded in his mother's tale of the Ear and the Mosquito would seem to support this thesis of deep-rooted male insecurity about and fear of female power and creativity, with the corresponding need or will to tame it, domesticate it, marginalize it, and project it as the gift and vocation of a few "exceptional" women who are thus, like Chielo in *Things Fall Apart*, "honorary men." It would thus seem that the need and impulse for men to "colonize" women, to identify with the "master" subject position elaborated in Hegel's famous master-slave dialectic, runs very very deep and is reproducible across different social formations. It is in connection with this problem that the discourses of African feminist writing and criticism on "a double yoke" and "a double colonization," where African women's creativity is concerned, poses a great challenge to male writers and critics. We must remember that no colonization is ever given up easily, voluntarily, in "a fit of absent-mindedness."

It remains to state that for this radical feminist critique to be an effective intervention in postcolonial African critical discourse, it is important to disentangle biological, literal *maleness* from male-centeredness or phallocentrism as this involves elaborate signifying, perceptual and representational orders which make man the center and ground of reason, intellect, and will. One is born *into* and not *with* these codes already in place in the genes, and one has a choice either to, on the one hand, enter unproblematically, willingly, or opportunistically into them or, on the other hand, begin to study them, understand them ever more fully and consciously and help to destabilize or overthrow them. What Molara Ogundipe-Leslie once said about women and biology applies equally to men:

> True, the biological identity of a woman counts and is real. But woman, contrary to what some men [and most] think, is more than "a biological aperture," as Anaïs Nin said. Woman's biology is indeed an important and necessary aspect of her, but it is not all she is and it should not be used to limit her. (5)

The distinction that Lacan makes, as Gayle Rubin informs us, between the "function of the father" and a particular man who embodies that function is useful here: particular men may refuse to embody and actualize this function as phallocratic values define and consecrate that function.[11] If, as Nancy Chodorow has argued, "mothering" is reproduced by technologies of gender erected by patriarchy as it combines with different modes of production, no less is "fatherhood" so produced and reproduced, even if as the more privileged term of a patriarchal relational structure. Nwoye's memory of his mother's stories, his preference for "women's stories" and his merely feigned and not actual acceptance of a phallocratic erasure of motherlore all reveal the possibility of a breach between maleness as biology and maleness as either a consenting, or a resisting response to the interpellations of neocolonial, patriarchal neocapitalism.

This last point opens up for critical inquiry and research priorities the over-determined spaces in which both female creativity and transformative initiative, and the divergent male responses to them, are played out. Okonkwo, as we have seen, struggles against colonial conquest and a nascent imperialist domination, but with an aggressively masculinist personality and its deep alienations. Largely on account of this contradiction, his resistance is futile. This point has an emblematic pertinence to present antinomies of postcolonial critical discourse, for what Okonkwo could not have perceived we have inherited: colonial definitions and codifications of rights, duties and responsibilities not only divided colonizers from the colonized, but they also separated surrogate "native" rulers from their "native" subjects and "native men in general" from "native women in general." African male-centered writers and critics should take this lesson to heart as they create a "national" literature which, if not a mere appendage, a mere extension of metropolitan European traditions, is nonetheless imbricated in deeply gendered alienations and reifications whose genealogical roots go back to colonialism.

This lesson applies equally to Okonkwo's son, Nwoye, who, although he symbolically disavows the national-masculine ethic that is embodied in his father's personality and doomed resistance, nevertheless goes over to the colonizers and more or less embraces the colonialist ideology of the "civilizing mission." It is not overstating the case to observe that his "feminization" does not lead him to an adequate, critical comprehension of the invading colonial project: the historic separations consummated by colonial capitalism divided fathers and sons and "native" men from "native" women; but it also separated arriviste "assimiles" from the rest of the "native" population and a small but structurally significant group of middle-class women from their subaltern, disenfranchised "sisters."[12]

* * *

Even though its most important project lies elsewhere—in constructing a tradition of women's creativity in orature and literature with roots going back to precolonial society—it is a permanent task of feminist literary criticism and scholarship to contest and delegitimize the "under-textualization" of women and "women's affairs" in the mostly male-authored writings which claim to speak on behalf of the "nation," the continent, the "Black world." An ancillary task in this respect is the interrogation of the appropriation of "woman" as idealized "embodiment" of male-authored and male-centered myths and fictions of national resistance or racial pride: women's bodies will no longer passively bear the marks of opportunistic, mystifying idealizations which help to obscure the oppressions and wrongs done to real women. In this paper I have argued, rather self-consciously as a male, leftist critic, for a task to complement, not "complete," these projects of contemporary African literary-critical feminism(s): the uncovering of such divergent, conflicting constructions of "maleness" as we have identified in Okonkwo and his son, Nwoye, in *Things Fall Apart*. The motivation behind this enterprise bears restating: to reconfigure the nationalist silencing and repressing of gender difference as deeply fractured, bearing the very marks of this repression in the failures and contradictions of national liberation in the post-independence epoch in Africa. This reconfiguration allows us to re-write national liberation as a historic phenomenon with a greater complexity in issues of gender and gender politics than a benighted, categorical phallocentrism.[13] This is underscored by Carole Boyce Davies' words in the second epigraph to this essay: "In the troubled world of *Things Fall Apart*, motherhood and femininity are the unifying, mitigating principles, the lessons for Africa and the world."

This "lesson" apparently eluded Fanon's otherwise penetrating critique of the ideology of the national liberation movement in Africa as evidenced in the celebrated text titled "The Pitfalls of National Consciousness," the most widely debated chapter of *The Wretched of the Earth*. In that text, Fanon's desperate and prophetic warnings mostly addressed class and ethnic contradictions of nationalism, and it registered a deafening silence on questions of gender. But Fanon's critique does not exhaust the intellectual legacy of radical, insightful criticisms of national liberation in Africa. We have also, among others, the legacy of Cabral and the liberation movements of the Portuguese ex-colonies. Lars Rudebeck in his seminal work on Cabral and the PAIGC, *Guinea-Bissau: A Study in Political Mobilization*, has written:

> In the final analysis, Cabral seems to have viewed the anti-imperialist struggle very much as a cultural struggle—as a people's struggle to reconquer its right to a place in history. . . . The most important specific example of cultural struggle possible to discern within the total struggle and distinguishable from the school system is probably the systematic emphasis given by the PAIGC to the problem of female emancipation. This does not mean that the struggle for female emancipation is not integrated with the total struggle, nor does it mean that it is not an important part of the general educational task of the schools. It only means that this problem has been considered important enough in its own right to be singled out for specific attention in the concrete political practice of the PAIGC. (225)

Things Fall Apart occupies, if only in a fractured, ambiguous manner, a similar conceptual, ideological space of radical nationalist ideology in Africa. And it is a space which has been considerably expanded in postcolonial African fiction, by Achebe himself in *Anthills of the Savannah*, and by other male writers like Ousmane Sembene, Nuruddin Farah, Femi Osofisan and Ngugi wa Thiong'o. Indeed, it is the accumulated energy of this entire tradition that powers the savage satirical indictment of the sexual exploitation of women as a fundamentally constitutive part of the callow, boastful collective masculinist identity of the arriviste, compradorial bourgeoisie of neocolonial Kenya in Ngugi's *Devil on the Cross*. Male critics and theorists who wish to seriously engage feminism must critically reclaim this tradition.

From *Callaloo* 16, no. 4 (1993): 847-858. Copyright © 1993 by The Johns Hopkins University Press. Reprinted with permission of The Johns Hopkins University Press.

Notes

1. *Things Fall Apart* (Heinemann, 1958). All subsequent citations are from this edition and appear parenthetically in the text.

2. This is to be measured primarily in the number and quality of critical interventions by women in postcolonial debates of the last decade and a half. This "feminization" of the discipline, however, exceeds mere body count; its major effect has been to make us re-think some of the ruling concepts and paradigms of the field of postcoloniality: "nation" and "canon," representation and subjectivity. This essay is an initial attempt to productively engage aspects of these interventions.

3. On this point it is instructive to re-examine the documents of the two historic "Negro Writers Conferences," Paris, 1956, and Rome, 1959. Present at these conferences were the most prominent African, African-American and Afro-Caribbean writers and intellectuals, predominantly male, many of whom were later to become the core of the political and intellectual elites of Africa, the Caribbean and post-Civil Rights Afro-America. It is now widely accepted that the perspectives authorized and the agenda defined by these two conferences were decisive in the constitution of nationalist and Pan-Africanist postcolonial discourses, but with scant recognition of how deeply gendered and male-dominant these were. In the "Proceedings" of the Paris Conference there is a photograph of the participants; out of some fifty-five persons, only one is a woman. The "Proceedings" of the Rome Conference lists some sixty members of a rather large "Executive Council" (of the "Society of African Culture" instituted by the Conference) of which only three are women. The 1956 documents in fact contain a "Message from the Negro Women" which is remarkable only in how unremarkable it is. The strong suspicion that it was probably drafted by some of the male organizers of the conference is reinforced by the obvious factitiousness of sentiments in the "message" like the following: "Can you cite a single *Negro man of culture* who in his writings has not exalted the Negro woman, the Mother"? The *Negro man of culture* was the then current Francophone-derived term for the African, African-American and Afro-Caribbean artist and intellectual considered as a "representative" of the race. The

documents from these conferences and the tropes and topoi of discourse they inscribed and enshrined for a long time consolidated the "representative" figure of the post-colonial artist, intellectual or nationalist statesman as ineluctably male. See *Presence Africaine* (1956, 1959).

4. On the subject of arrested decolonization see Jeyifo, "The Nature of Things."

5. Barbara Harlow in *Resistance Literature* deploys one of these "women's stories" in *Things Fall Apart* as an "allegory for an African strategy for independence" (xv).

6. On the notion of a "moral economy" see James C. Scott (1976).

7. I hasten to add that this thesis is not uniformly applicable to all of precolonial African social formations. The feudal and semi-feudal centralized states of the Sahel and the Western Sudan obviously entailed considerable division and hierarchization of gender differences. Indeed Ifi Amadiume errs in more or less generalizing her thesis to all of African societies and cultures.

8. *Women in African Literature Today* (2).

9. There is of course an extensive, elaborate critical and theoretical discourse on the metaphorization of the womb as *the* ultimate site of creation and creativity, far more potent and superior to typical male-originated metaphors of creativity. The following exhortation from Anaïs Nin is representative: "All that happens in the real womb, not in the womb fabricated by man as a substitute . . . woman's creation far from being like man's must be exactly like her creation of children, that is, it must come out of her own blood, englobed by her womb, nourished by her own milk. It must be a human creation of flesh, it must be different from man's abstraction." Consider Trinh T. Minh-ha's comment on this statement of Anaïs Nin: "Man is not content with referring to his creation as his child, he is also keen on appropriating the life-giving act of child-bearing. Images of men 'in labor' and 'giving birth' to poems, essays and books abound in literature. Such an encroachment on woman's domain has been considered natural, for the writer is said to be either genderless or bisexual" (37). On this *utero-centrism* I have two comments to make, rather self-consciously as a male critic: First, uterocentrism courts, and even sometimes embraces, the occultation of gynocritics considered as a perceptible female aesthetic. Secondly, however, it is not impossible for this mystique to coexist with very progressive, socially conscious works of literature, theatre or film. Nana, the matriarch of Julie Dash's acclaimed *Daughters of the Dust*, says: "the ancestors and the womb, they are the same." This connects with the strain of the over-mythologization of history and memory in the film, a strain not incompatible with the film's equally powerful secular and de-mythologizing exploration of the violent clashes of the contending sacred narratives and epistemologies in the Gullah community.

10. Achebe's critique of neoliberal universalism in "Colonialist Criticism," dated as a timely response, a contextual intervention at the originary moment of the "Commonwealth Literature" rubric, remains pertinent. See his *Morning Yet on Creation Day.*

11. Gayle Rubin, "The Traffic in Women: Notes on the Political Economy of Sex."

12. On this point consider the fact that the "sisterhood" which binds the griot woman, Farmata, to Ramatoulaye, the middle-class protagonist of Mariama Ba's novel

So Long a Letter, is compounded by strong structures of class and caste inequalities. For the influence of colonial French education on Mariama Ba's views on women and education, see Riesz.

13. For very informative analyses of national liberation and gender politics in various locations in the Third World see Evelyne Accad, "Sexuality and Sexual Politics: Conflicts and Contradictions for Contemporary Women in the Middle East"; Angela Gilliam, "Women's Equality and National Liberation"; and Nayereh Tohidi, "Gender and Islamic Fundamentalism: Feminist Politics in Iran," all in Mohanty, Russo, and Torres, *Third World Women and the Politics of Feminism.* See also Cobham.

Works Cited

Accad, Evelyn. "Sexuality and Sexual Politics: Conflicts and Contradictions for Contemporary Women in the Middle East." *Third World Women and the Politics of Feminism.* 237-50.

Achebe, Chinua. *Things Fall Apart.* London: Heinemann, 1958.

_____. "Colonialist Criticism." *Morning Yet on Creation Day.* New York: Doubleday, 1975. 3-18.

Amadiume, Ifi. *Male Daughters, Female Husbands: Gender and Sex in an African Society.* London: Zed Books, 1989.

Chodorow, Nancy. *The Reproduction of Mothering: Psychoanalysis and the Sociology of Gender.* Berkeley: The University of California Press, 1978.

Cobham, Rhonda. "Boundaries of the Nation, Boundaries of the Self: African Nationalist Fictions and Nuruddin Farah's *Maps.*" *Research in African Literatures* 22.2 (Summer 1991): 83-98.

Davies, Carole Boyce. "Motherhood in the Works of Male and Female Igbo Writers: Achebe, Emecheta, Nwapa and Nzekwu." *Ngambika: Studies of Women in African Literature.* Ed. Carole Boyce Davies and Anne Adams Graves. Trenton, New Jersey: Africa World Press, 1986. 241-56.

Fanon, Frantz. "The Pitfalls of National Consciousness." *The Wretched of the Earth.* New York: Grove Press, 1968. 148-205.

Gilliam, Angela. "Women's Equality and National Liberation." *Third World Women and the Politics of Feminism.* 215-36.

Harlow, Barbara. *Resistance Literature.* London: Methuen, 1987.

Jeyifo, Biodun. "The Nature of Things: Arrested Decolonisation and Critical Theory." *Research in African Literatures* 21.1 (Spring 1990): 33-48.

Mohanty, Chandra T., Ann Russo, and Lourdes Torres, eds. *Third World Women and the Politics of Feminism.* Bloomington: Indiana University Press, 1991.

Ngugi wa Thiong'o. *Devil on the Cross.* London: Heinemann, 1982.

Ogundipe-Leslie, Molara. "The Female Writer and Her Commitment." *Women in African Literature Today.* London: James Currey, 1987. 5-13.

Ogunyemi, Chikwenye. "The Dynamics of the Contemporary Black Female Novel in English." *Signs* 2.1 (Autumn 1985): 63-80.

Présence Africaine. Nos. 8-10 (June-November 1956); Nos. 24-25 (February-May 1959).

Riesz, Janos. "Mariama Ba's *Une si longue lettre*." *Research in African Literatures* 22.1 (Spring 1991): 27-42.

Rubin, Gayle. "The Traffic in Women: Notes on the 'Political Economy' of Sex." *Toward an Anthropology of Women*. Ed. Rayna R. Reiter. New York: Monthly Review Press, 1975. 157-210.

Schipper, Mineke. "Mother Africa on a Pedestal: The Male Heritage in African Literature and Criticism." *Women in African Literature Today*. 35-54.

Scott, James C. *The Moral Economy of the Peasant: Rebellion and Subsistence in Southeast Asia*. New Haven: Yale University Press, 1976.

Stratton, Florence. "Periodic Embodiments: A Ubiquitous Trope in African Men's Writing." *Research in African Literatures* 21.1 (Spring 1990): 111-26.

Tohidi, Nayereh. "Gender and Islamic Fundamentalism: Feminist Politics in Iran." *Third World Women and the Politics of Feminism*. 251-67.

Trinh T. Minh-ha. *Woman, Native, Other*. Bloomington and Indianapolis: Indiana University Press, 1989.

Masculinity, Power, and Language in Chinua Achebe's *Things Fall Apart*_____

Ada Uzoamaka Azodo

> To recognize diversity in masculinities is not enough. We must also recognize the relations between the different kinds of masculinity: relations of alliance, dominance and subordination. These relationships are constructed through practices that exclude and include, that intimidate, exploit, and so on. There is gender politics within masculinity.
>
> —R. W. Cornell, *Masculinities* (Oxford: Polity Press, 1995, 32)

In issues of gender and language, discussions usually center around theories of dominance and difference, masculinity and language, power and identity, notions of competition and cooperation, and the fluidity of masculine subjectivity. It is from these points of view that Johnson and Meinhoff have attempted to theorize masculinity and language (1997). According to the two scholars, most of feminist criticism and critical theory, and studies in women's subjectivity and identity, engage in stereotyping of women and in lumping all men into a male-as-one, whereas they should be problematizing masculinity. Men are seen as the norm, at once the neutral and in the center. What is hardly ever taken note of is the variety of male identities, notwithstanding the reality that power is usually cited as the most important factor used by men to construct their own identities as the "ungendered representatives of humanity" (1997, 12). Johnson and Meinhoff have also raised the need to discuss masculinity in feminist studies, seen that "excessive preoccupation with male/female difference always has its root in essentialist notions of gender." Before Johnson and Meinhoff, Toril Moi and Chris Weedo had also indicated the same (12-15).

Comparing male and female speech patterns, Anthony Easthope states that male speech is seen as assertive whereas women's speech is seen as hesitant and indirect. We argue that it is merely trivializing issues if gender studies should always be reduced to comparing and con-

trasting masculinity and femininity. Gender differences, like class differences, are socially constructed and endowed with different values
and qualities. Men are as prone to differences as women. Since much
of gender is about power relations, there is need to challenge openly
and problematize the status quo, rather than condone inequality by le-
gitimizing the norm. Our goal, therefore, is primarily to embrace the
anti-essentialist approach to masculinity by deconstructing the notion
of uni-masculinity. We intend to show that male power, prestige and
dominance differ according to a man's temperament, personality and
uniqueness for, according to Jack Saltlel: "the starting point for understanding masculinity lies, not in its contrast with femininity, but in the
asymmetric dominance and prestige which accrue to males in . . . society" (1995, 119). Secondly, we intend to demonstrate how men use language, ranking in social structures, and hegemonic gatherings to en-
trench men as the powers of the day in their communities. According to
the concept of hegemony expounded by the Italian Marxist philosopher Antonio Gramsci, a precursor of Althusser's theories on ideology,
men in power do not always use direct coercion to rule. Men can use indirect coercion to exercise leadership in their groups. In Althusser's
Ideological State Apparatuses, people become inadvertently conspira-
tors in their own subordination and exploitation. Gramsci, for his part,
has stressed the role of culture in contributing to how people view
themselves in their communities. Even commonplace activities such as
leisure contribute to the people's sense of self and world view, unwittingly reinforcing and perpetuating the status quo. Being thus im-
mersed in ideology in their day-to-day lives, people imbibe cultural
practices as normal and natural (Webster, 1996, 63-64). Finally, because the construction of identity is a creative enterprise, rather than
something that just happens, we mean to see how group ideology and
male language forge different identities. The pertinent questions to ask
are: How do men construct their identities through language? What are
the different kinds of power? How do they work with men when they
gather or meet in palaver groups to discuss issues?[1]

We shall adopt the investigative method for the study of four selected dialogues in Chinua Achebe's *Things Fall Apart*, in order to gain insights into how male hegemonic cults achieve, construct and prolong patriarchal traditions that ensure male superiority. In the Umuofia community of *Things Fall Apart*, Igbo men are constrained to achieve and flaunt it, in order to be seen and respected. To be able to draw upon divergent types of power, men apply different resources during discussions, including the use of irony, riddles, proverbs, sarcasm, jokes, oratory, voice and status, to mention only these few. The Umuofia community of *Things Fall Apart* being a close-knit one, each man is known along with his foibles, weaknesses and strengths, all of these attributes and qualities force the kind of personality and/or power he can muster at any gathering. When he speaks, such a man by his gestures, stance, posture and gaze is forced to live up to community expectations without appearing strange or incoherent to himself or his community.

The plan of this paper imposes the following three imperatives: theoretical exploration of the ideological framework of the study; practical discussion of particular ideologies of masculinity and power in *Things Fall Apart*, and finally, a discussion of the ideology of power among a selected number of men in the village of Umuofia. We shall conclude by pulling together salient aspects of our arguments to illustrate how men construct different types of identities and power.

* * *

Theoretically, at the forefront of studies in masculinity should be a consideration of men's speaking patterns, not only to show how they use language in oral and written texts but also how males, *ad infinitum*, construct their subjectivity through hegemonic discourses. According to the French theorist Michel Foucault, in *The Subject and Power* (1982), power is essentially an action which modifies another action immediately or mediately, indirectly or directly, in an unreal or real manner. People show their power when they deem it necessary to counter an action with another action. For power to be effective, it must be appropriate to the situation and the subjects so acted upon must sense it and accept it as such. To this end, illusions can have the same effect as actions which motivate the subject to counter a situation with other actions, when such a subject deems it necessary to do so to avoid some serious consequences. To the observer, certain actions might appear illogical and irrational, but that is only because the reasons behind the actions are not known or are not clear to the observer. A few examples might suffice to illustrate this point. Power show, to avoid emotion of fear or lack of self-esteem, might appear incomprehensible to the observer. Actions, to avoid being seen as weak or ineffective, could also appear illogical to the Other, though rational and logical to the subject. In the final analysis, it is the values of the community as well as their perception of power which are valid in determining what constitute serious consequences when certain actions are not taken in the presence of other actions or appear illogical to the one who has not the wherewithal to make a full and informed judgment. Therefore, our present study necessarily has to delve into the values and ideologies of the Umuofia community in *Things Fall Apart*, just as should any analysis of issues of power and masculinity.

Practically speaking, people in powerful positions act many roles at different times. This is the reason why successful politicians seem to do well, for they know how to play different roles at different times, as the occasion demands. Such power is usually constructed through the medium of language because only particular ways of speaking are appropriate to particular roles, situations and circumstances. A personality might be dominated by one role, but more often than not, such a personality is made of other aspects of roles which come together on occasion to define such a personality. To determine these roles and demonstrations of power, we seek to understand how a masculine and/or powerful discourse is affected by formal or informal community structures.

In the manner that Scott Fabius Kiesling has done it (Johnson and Meinhoff, 1997, 67-79), we have identified seven processes in *Things Fall Apart* from which individual men construct their identities: physical (coercive and ability); economic; knowledge; structural; nurturing, demeanor, and ideological. The agents of the British colonial administration show *coercive physical power* when they punish and beat up the indigenous population of Umuofia at the slightest provocation or transgression of their stringent rules. Okonkwo, the protagonist of the novel, shows coercive power when he beats up his wives. On the other hand, Okonkwo shows *ability physical power*, which is a combination of skill and ability power, when he beats the community expert wrestler, Amalinze, otherwise known as the Cat, who had not been beaten for seven years. In the sports calendar of Umuofia, seven years is equivalent to a lifetime. With that singular feat, Okonkwo's "fame had grown like bush-fire in the harmattan" (1959: 1). He won the heart of the village beauty, Ekwefi, who would later become his second wife and the mother of his precocious daughter Ezinma. Even "the old men agreed it [the fight] was one of the fiercest since the founder of their town engaged a spirit of the wild for seven days and seven nights" (1). Again we see the symbolism of the number seven as equivalent to the Jewish "forty days and forty nights," which Jesus Christ spent in the wilderness being tempted by the devil. Later, we learn that the extremely male Okonkwo "ruled his household with a heavy hand" (13). Needless to add that it is the values and ideologies of the community which have given birth to the stuff of which Okonkwo is made. We also note that another wrestler, Okafor, "quick as the lightning of Amadiora," threw his opponent, Ikezue, again demonstrating *ability physical power* which prompted his supporters to carry him shoulder high, bursting into this antiphonal song, constructed on the spur of the moment, and accompanied with the clapping of hands:

Who will wrestle for our village?
Okafor will wrestle for our village.
Has he thrown a hundred men?
He has thrown four hundred men.
Has he thrown a hundred Cats?
He has thrown four hundred Cats.

Wrestling, in the view of this community, although a source of entertainment, is a masculine competitive sport. Women are excluded from it, though they may attend as spectators and fans.

Economic power is seen in Okonkwo's enterprising spirit. He borrows a hundred seed yams, toils hard on his farm and realizes a bountiful harvest. He doubles his barn, accumulates his own seed yams and is able to return what he had borrowed as capital (18-25). Even in the year of the horrible harvest when there was not enough rain for the crops, thanks to the climatic inconsistencies of the moving Intertropical Convergence Zone,[2] Okonkwo survives by sheer will power in the face of great odds. Soon, he is able to marry three wives, a sign of affluence in his community. He supports his family and controls his women as he is expected to do, his achievements having gone into his head to a lesser or greater extent. Later he takes titles, aiming for the fourth and the ultimate, the *Ozo* title. Title taking is an expensive undertaking which is possible only with men of a certain ease of living. That Okonkwo was finally unable to attain his ambition, due to his encounters with the British administration, was a mortal blow.

Power from *knowledge* is the process of acquiring knowledge in order to perform some specific functions. For example, even lazy Unoka, Okonkwo's father, though he did not take any title, for indeed in the eyes of the community he was nothing more than an *agbala* (a woman), was an accomplished flutist who thrilled gatherings and functioned as emissary in gay and sorrowful community gatherings (6-7).

Structural power is seen in the power accorded an individual in the hierarchy of the village system. Ogbuefi Ezeudu, the oldest man in

Umuofia "who had been a great and fearless warrior in his time, . . . was now accorded great respect in all the clan" (57). It was on that authority and power that he advised Okonkwo, out of sight and earshot of all and sundry, not to be involved in the murder of the unfortunate youth, Ikemefuna, billed to be sacrificed to the Earth goddess, Ani, as atonement for the murder of a daughter of a contiguous clan:

> That boy calls you father. Do not bear a hand in his death. . . .
>
> Yes, Umuofia has decided to kill him. The Oracle of the Hills and the Caves has pronounced it. They will take him outside Umuofia as is the custom, and kill him there. But I want you to have nothing to do with it. He calls you father. (57)

When Ogbuefi Ezeudu chooses to say to Okonkwo, "I *want* you to" (my emphasis) rather than "I *would like you* to" (again, my emphasis), he demonstrates his authority and power as an elder who has seen many moons and has become very wise. Words proffered from such a man should never have been disregarded by Okonkwo. And Okonkwo paid dearly for his transgression with his exile and dispossession by the community. Okonkwo's fate took a downward turn from this point on in the plot of the novel. He goes from isolation and exile to suicide and interment in the evil forest reserved only for the dregs and other never-do-wells of the village community. That his cadaver was refused an abode with Mother Earth is the highest insult that he could have been given in death. He was left to rot on the surface of the earth under the elements or to be devoured by preying beasts of the wild.

Nurturing power is of two types—feeding and teaching—and is seen as the power that an individual wields over another or a group in the process of rendering help. Such a power is demonstrated by male heads of households who could hold up family cooking as women of the household and their children waited for the common husband and father to dole out rations of yam, the king and male crop. According to Achebe's narrator during the New Yam Festival (37-45):

Early that morning, as Okonkwo offered a sacrifice of new yam and palm oil to his ancestors he asked them to protect him, his children and their mothers in the new year. (39)

A little further, Achebe explains thus the significance of the New Yam Festival, the mark of a new beginning in Igbo mythology, during which each male leader of a household officiated practically as a priest:

The New Yam Festival was thus an occasion for joy throughout Umuofia. And *every man whose arm was strong*, as the Ibo [sic] people say, was expected to invite large numbers of guests from far and wide. Okonkwo always asked his wives' relations, and since he now had three wives his guests would make a fairly big crowd. (37) (my emphasis)

In another sense, a great nurturer was he who, like Achebe's proverbial Igbo strong man, "set before his guests a mound of foo-foo so high that those who sat on one side could not see what was happening on the other" (37). Without taking into account the obvious hyperbole or overstatement inherent in the citation, it is evident that a provider could have an enormous power on the people who look up to him.

Nurturing power in form of teaching is seen in Uchendu, Okonkwo's aged maternal uncle who, during Okonkwo's exile, tried to alleviate his depression and despair by recalling the connotation of the name, Nneka, as maternal home of refuge. This is perhaps one singular point in the novel when a man actually lauded the female element in Igbo cosmology, destroying once and for all the myth that all men hold all women in total disregard:

It's true that a child belongs to its father. But when a father beats his child, it seeks sympathy in its mother's hut. A man belongs to his fatherland when things are good and life is sweet. But when there is sorrow and bitterness he finds refuge in his motherland.

Your mother is there to protect you. She is buried there. And that is why we say that mother is supreme. . . . If you think you are the greatest sufferer in the world ask my daughter, Akueni, how many twins she has borne and thrown away. Have you not heard the song they sing when a woman dies?

> For whom is it well, for whom is it well?
> There is no one for whom it is well.
> I have no more to say to you. (135)

Demeanor power is the power of solidarity by which one is seen as a good person with whom people would like to be associated. Such a person is a good friend with high moral values, even in the face of adversity. A classical example is Obierika, whose name actually signifies his attributes, that of "a man with a very large heart." He is one who can always be depended upon. The day that Okonkwo's compound was sacked, following a community decree at the heels of the manslaughter of a citizen at the funeral of the old man Ezeudu, it was Obierika who alone, single-handedly, even though he participated in the macabre cleansing of the land, "with no hatred in his heart for Okonkwo" (125), had followed him into exile, bringing him money he had collected from the sale of his yams which he, Obierika, had saved before a mighty conflagration engulfed Okonkwo's compound, razing it to the ground. Obierika's commitment to a man he regards as a friend, even though he sanctioned his punishment for his misdeeds, is very touching:

> That is money from your yams. . . . I sold the big ones as soon as you left. Later on I sold some of the seed yams and gave out others to share croppers. I shall do that every year until you return. But I thought you would need the money now and so I brought it. Who knows what may happen tomorrow? Perhaps green men will come to our clan and shoot us. (142)

It might be problematic to see *demeanor* as power, because the subject acts from emotions of love, fraternity, friendship or other, which in general are viewed as weak emotions. Yet, because Okonkwo feels happy, respectful and grateful, it can be said that Obierika exerted a *demeanor power* over Okonkwo. It is Obierika's kindness in this instance which constitutes his power over Okonkwo who, by his nature, is not known to brook any nonsense or allow himself to be put in a weak and disadvantageous position by anyone. Even Okonkwo was overwhelmed with emotion, and as he put it, even killing one of his (Okonkwo's) sons for Obierika would not have compensated adequately for the latter's kindness and generosity (142).

Lastly, the most important of powers, as we have inferred above, is *ideological power*. In the words of Kiesling, it is "the power whereby ways of thinking about the world are naturalized into a community's behavior" (Johnson and Meinhoff 1997: 68). The ideological process defines and ratifies certain traits as powerful and determines which of the other processes are available, that is, identifies the role in the community. Put simply and differently, the ideological process determines what is or is not powerful in all the other six processes.

Suffice it to say that even though we have separated all the seven power processes for the practical ease and purpose of analysis and explication, all are intertwined, as Foucault would say, in "a net-like organization . . . , something which circulates, or rather something which only functions in the form of a chain" (1980: 98). Umuofia community's dominant ideology thus appears to be that of extreme masculine competition and systematic hierarchy, where the world is really male. Even a pubescent male adolescent appears more important than a woman old enough to be his mother. This ideology affects men's demeanor, title-taking culture, occupations (such as hunting and farming), pastime and recreational activities (such as games, palm-wine drinking, goat-meat pepper soup eating, and wrestling), roles of the male household head (who invariably officiates also as priest in the family shrine and is the chief nurturer of the family). The list could go on and on. In this community, "Age was respected . . . but achievement was revered. As the elders said, if a child washes his hands he could eat with kings" (12). A man has made it when he wields physical, economic, knowledge, structural, nurturing and demeanor processes of power. It is for this reason that the eventual fall of Okonkwo makes *Things Fall Apart* a classical Igbo tragedy, approaching the dimensions of classical Greek tragedy, such as *Oedipus Rex*.

The local show of power in Umuofia then is a miniature of power processes in world communities. This singular comparison makes Achebe's *Things Fall Apart* still one of the most important African literary texts in the new millennium. From our angle of vision, power is constructed, defined and ratified by the Umuofia community's parameters of values, constraining them to fit themselves into not only sex roles, but indeed also into gender roles at any given time. It is either you are male or you become a female even when you have the male sex but are unable to attain the expectations of the community. Unoka, in the eyes of Umuofia, was a woman, *agbala* (13). This notoriety would eternally plague his son, Okonkwo, driving him to vaunt his exploits by running other less achieving men down (28), and imbuing himself with such an extreme and destructive paranoia of failure, which would later become his Achilles' Heel, his dark shadow, his sore-spot and the primary cause for his down-fall:

> With a father like Unoka, Okonkwo did not have the start in life which many young men had. He neither inherited a barn nor a title, nor even a young wife. But in spite of these disadvantages, he had begun even in his father's lifetime to lay the foundations of a prosperous future. It was slow and painful. But he threw himself into it like one possessed. And indeed he was possessed by the fear of his father's contemptible life and shameful death. (21)

But what roles and/or identities do men fall into as they create power in encounters with other men? How do we compare Umuofia with contemporary society? We turn to ideology of power among a selected number of male characters in *Things Fall Apart* as we attempt to respond to these questions.

How does a man, following his initial socialization into the community at puberty, gain status and, in the several roles available to him, project the kind of identity expected of him?

As a full-fledged adult member of the community, a man is expected to build and own his own hut, marry a wife and have children, preferably male children. He is expected to work hard daily on his farm, without feeling fatigue or, if he does, not show it. He should have several rows of yam in his barn (86). He should be seen to provide adequately for his family. Any deviation from the norm earned such a man an inability to become titled. He would not become an ancestor on his death for none of the living would like to put him up as a mentor and guide for the next generation to come. So difficult and expensive was title-taking that "only one or two in any generation ever achieved the fourth and highest" (123), the *Ozo* title. The wise old man, Ezeudu, managed to take only three of the four titles. Holders of *Ozo* title are forbidden to climb the palm tree, though they may tap it standing on the ground (169). The men institute measures geared towards conferring prestige, esteem and dignity to the title, which is signified by a thin thread worn around the ankle. At death, the high-ranking persons are "buried after dark with only a glowing brand to light the sacred ceremony" (123). Men take care of themselves in death in this way, seeing to it that death does not expose the corpse of a male to ridicule.

Moreover, real men are prosperous. This is visible in their households with a large compound secured by a high brick wall. The head of the household, the man, is everything for his family. His hut or his *obi*, as it is known in Umuofia, sits prominently close to the gate of the compound, a vantage point from which he investigates all the goings-in and comings-out of his compound. Long stalls of yam bespeak his affluence (25), even as animals (goats for the man and chickens for the woman) and coco yam of his wives attest further to his economic vigor. The man has a personal shrine where he worships his personal deity, his *Chi* (14). His relationship with his wives and children is that of fear of his wrath. Hence Okonkwo's frequent outbursts of anger are likened to the claps of thunder. A "real" man shuns the company of women. A man romantically involved with his wife is seen as weak and not at all the stuff of which real men are made (68).

The legislative arm of the village system of government is exclusively in the hands of men. Elders of the community, who are invariably titled men, make up the group, "the most powerful and most secret cult in the clan" (88). They deliver justice according to the dictates of tradition, social harmony and peace expectations of the community. It is for this reason that the *Egwugwu*, the community of masked spirits, is treated with utmost sanctity, that is, as the spirits of the ancestors, when they sit in judgment over the living. They are held to be sacrosanct and women and children view them from the fringes, from the periphery, while the center is reserved and occupied by the men. Four selected dialogues involving some of the more notable characters in the novel would help us understand better the dynamics of power in the community of Umuofia.

Power Ideology 1: Unoka and Okoye

Background information on Unoka as a youth and an old man reveals that, in contrast to his son, Okonkwo, even as a youth, Unoka was "lazy and imprudent and was quite incapable of thinking about tomorrow" (8). He spent the meager money he had drinking palm-wine and making merry. He was, therefore, a debtor who was despised by his community. His demeanor reflects his good-for-nothing life, for he wore a "haggard and mournful look," except when he was playing his flute (8). He was thus a "failure" as a grown-up. He was "poor and his wife and children had barely enough to eat." He was a "loafer" and a "coward."

The encounter between wily Unoka and dignified Okoye, who "had a large barn full of yams and had three wives" and was about to take the "idemili title," the third highest title in the land, sways the reader inadvertently to Okoye's side (10). Human beings are such that with conditioning they imbibe the values of the community and culture they live in. A well-entrenched and established citizen is certainly more beneficial to a community than a loafer and a drunkard. However, by the end of their encounter, Unoka had succeeded in turning the table against Okoye, making him out as silly and ineffective at best, at worst a Shylock, the proverbial oppressor, who has come to demand his "pound of flesh":

> As soon as Unoka understood what his friend was driving at, he burst out laughing. He laughed loud and long and his voice rang out clear as the ogene, and tears stood in his eyes. His visitor was amazed, and sat speechless. At the end, Unoka was able to give an answer between fresh outbursts of mirth.
>
> "Look at that wall," he said. . . . "Look at those lines of chalk." . . . Unoka had a sense of the dramatic and so he allowed a pause, in which he took a pinch of snuff and sneezed noisily, and then he continued: "Each group there represents a debt to someone, and each stroke is one hundred cowries. You see, I owe that man a thousand cowries, but he has not come to wake me up in the morning for it. I shall pay you, but not today. Our elders say that the sun will shine on those who stand before it shines on those who kneel under them. I shall pay my big debts first." And he took another pinch of snuff, as if that was paying the big debts first. Okoye rolled his goatskin and departed. (11)

Unoka outwitted Okoye by exercising physical ability power through the length and timber of his outbursts of laughter, the ring of his voice, his dramatic presentation of the case and above all the clinching of the whole episode with a very apt proverb. It is important to recall that among the Igbo, proverbs are "the palm-oil with which words are eaten" (13).

Power Ideology 2: Mr. Smith and the Elders of Umuofia

Compared to his predecessor, Mr. Brown, the new white, British administrator, Mr. Smith, is not liked, because he treats Africans and their gods with contempt. Some overzealous converts to the new Christian religion unmask the *egwugwu* in protest against African religion. When the group of six men destroy the new Christian church building in retaliation, they are invited into the presence of the District Commissioner, ostensibly for dialogue. But, the cunning administrator tactically "disarms" the community leaders before they have a chance to unsheathe their machetes, that is assuming they are even in the disposition to wage a battle against the administrator. Here is the process of his display of power. First of all, the Commissioner gets the group of six men to trust him and so put down their guard by coming in alone and sitting down. Secondly, he invites their spokesperson to tell him the group's version of what had happened between the villagers and the agents of the British colonial administration. As Ogbuefi Ekuweme, the leader of the group, rises to his feet to give his deposition, the Commissioner interrupts him, thus stressing that he, the Commissioner, is the power broker. He gives power of speech and takes it back at will. It turns out he wants to bring in his men at that point, again ostensibly to be privy to the dialogue, so that there would be no further mistakes. How would the group of six men have known that his real intention was to have them bound up and that he had no need to hear their side of the case? All becomes clear to them when they are surrounded and hand-cuffed. To hand-cuff a man is to impose one's ultimate physical power on his person. He loses all ability to use his limbs. Even running any great distance in hand-cuffs is a near impossibility. Then the administrator moves methodically to the next stage. Having emasculated the men, he is no longer pleading, or feigning to plead. He is again the agent of the Queen of England whose Britannica rules the waves:

We shall not do you any harm . . . , if only you agree to cooperate with us. We have brought a peaceful administration to you and your people so that you may be happy. If any man ill-treats you we shall come to your rescue. But we will not allow you to ill-treat others. We have a court of law where we judge cases and administer justice just as it is done in our own country under a great queen. I have brought you here because you joined together to molest others, to burn people's houses and their place of worship. That must not happen in the dominion of the queen, the most powerful ruler in the world. I have decided that you will pay a fine of two hundred bags of cowries. You will be released as soon as you agree to this and undertake to collect that fine from your people. What do you say to that?

The six men remained sullen and silent and the Commissioner left them for a while. (178)

The District Commissioner finishes his address by imposing a fine on the six men, which he expects them to collect from their people by themselves or face worse treatments. The six are undoubtedly dumbfounded at the realization, in the end, of how a single man has been able to overpower a group. His African agents, the court messengers, follow up on their master's footsteps, confirming Gramsci's and Althusser's ideologies on how members of a group embrace the tactics of the oppressor and inadvertently foster his aggression even against themselves as a distinct group. They shaved the men's hair, beat them and taunted them: "Who is the chief among you? . . . We see that every pauper wears the anklet of title in Umuofia. Does it cost as much as ten cowries?" (178). The group's only recourse was silence and hunger strike. Even when they are left alone by the Commissioner's men "they found no words to speak to one another" (179), until they were tired and had to give in to save themselves further torture. When the ordeal of the six finally filtered down to their subjects, "Umuofia was like a startled animal with ears erect, sniffing the silent, ominous air and not knowing which way to run" (180). It is significant that even the community's reaction was only defensive, not aggressive. They were minded only to see "which way to run." By subduing the leaders of the group, the Commissioner has subdued the entire community of Umuofia.

The Commissioner was able to exercise power and control by using a varied strategy in dealing with his victims. He exercised coercive power and ability to use it indirectly by getting his agents to do his dirty job. He had knowledge of the gullibility of the populace and used it to his advantage. Structurally speaking, he is the "white man," the servant of the Queen of England, the Lord administrator of her overseas dominion of Africa. His predecessors sacked the whole town of Abame for killing a single white man, the narrator of *Things Fall Apart* tells us. So, even before the community had to deal with the District Commissioner, this community was already in awe of his powers. He had economic power, for his administration had made it possible for the local people to earn money for the first time in their lives from the sale of palm fruits and palm-oil. From this angle of vision, he was an employer who could hire and fire. He was therefore a nurturer. He tells the men he "shall" protect them against their oppressors. The peculiar use of "shall" is very poignant when compared to his assertion later that he "will" not tolerate any dissidence. Ideologically, the six men were already defeated before the Commissioner came into their presence after a long delay.

Power Ideology 3: Okika, the Orator

Following the detention of the group of six, Okika, one of them, seethes with anger. This opportunistic emotion transforms his words into a veritable fire of words, as he breathes fire and promises death to the perpetrators of the heinous misdeed. Okika, unlike Egonwanne, the oldest man of the village who would have toed the path of compromise, wanted to match power with power, might with might. Onyeka, who had a "booming voice," was asked to clear the stage for him, for even though he was a great orator, he was not blessed with a booming voice.

Okika's speech is a veritable classic of rhetoric, and we see the need to cite it in its entirety, so that the stages of his power of language on the people may become clear:

'You all know why we are here, when we ought to be building our barns or mending our huts, when we should be putting our compounds in order. My father used to say to me: "Whenever you see a toad jumping in broad daylight, then know that something is after its life." When I saw you all pouring into this meeting from all the quarters of our clan so early in the morning, I knew that something was after our life.' He paused for a brief moment and then began again:

'All our gods are weeping. Idemili is weeping, Ogwugwu is weeping, Agbala is weeping, and all the others. Our dead fathers are weeping because of the shameful sacrilege they are suffering and the abomination we have all seen with our eyes.' He stopped again to steady his trembling voice.

'This is a great gathering. No clan can boast of greater numbers or greater valor. But are we all here? I ask you: Are all the sons of Umuofia with us here?' A deep murmur swept through the crowd.

'They are not. . . . They have broken the clan and gone their several ways. We who are here this morning have remained true to our fathers, but our brothers have deserted us and joined a stranger to soil their fatherland. If we fight the stranger we shall hit our brothers and perhaps shed the blood of a clansman. But we must do it. Our fathers never dreamed of such a thing, they never killed their brothers. But a white man never came to them. So we must do what our fathers would never have done. Eneke the bird was asked why he was always on the wing and he replied: "Men have learned to shoot without missing their mark and I have learned to fly without perching on a twig." We must root out this evil. And if our brothers take the side of evil we must root them out too. And we must do it *now*. We must bale this water now that it is only ankle-deep. . . .' (186-187)

Having sensitized the gathering to the emergent nature of the situation, Okika does not waste time but goes on, employing run-on phrases. Then the first pause. He allows the people to internalize what he just told them. When he begins to speak again, he bemoans the sacrilegious nature of the offense, adding that in the face of adversity, the community has not seen it fit to stand together. The inference is that a house divided unto itself cannot stand. He intones that the forefathers whose presence is eternally with the living would not have condoned such an act. As worthy descendants of the ancestors, they should do what their forebears would have done. It is significant that most Igbo proverbs begin with "As our fathers say." At this stage, Okika begins to lay the ground rules for action. It is almost as if he was saying, "But we must do it," "So we must do what our fathers would have done," "We must root them out too."

Okika has a lot of ability power, power of demeanor and knowledge. He knows how to pick the right words and work effectively on the psychology of his audience. When five court messengers of the British administration showed up to interrupt the gathering, charging that, "The white man whose power you know too well has ordered this meeting to stop," Okonkwo was ready for action, to counter indirect coercive power with direct coercive power:

> In a flash Okonkwo drew his machete. The messenger crouched to avoid the blow. It was useless, Okonkwo's machete descended twice and the man's head lay beside his uniformed body. (188)

Power Ideology 4: Obierika and the District Commissioner

The four escaping agents of the British Commissioner report to their master the murder of one of them by Okonkwo. Enraged, the Commissioner comes down from Government Hill to seek redress:

'Which among you is called Okonkwo?' he asked through his interpreter.

'He is not here,' replied Obierika.

'Where is he?'

'He is not here!'

The Commissioner becomes visibly angry. In spite of the apparent dichotomy in the degree of social power, in the end, we can say that it is a perfect power match. First of all, Obierika refuses, right from the start, to volunteer more information than is necessary to respond to the Commissioner's question without appearing to be disrespectful. This tactic is not lost on the Commissioner, who begins to be irritated: "Where is he?" he asks in reply to Obierika's non-committal first response: "He is not here." Following the repeat of this same statement, the Commissioner loses total control of his temper. He warns that there will be adverse consequences to disobedience of his orders. At that point, Obierika recognizes the danger in prolonging his register. He thus changes his strategy, although still determined to match power with power. "We can take you where he is, and perhaps your men will help us" (189). The British commissioner finds Obierika's circumlocution very annoying. Beaten in his own game, he leads a band of men into the bush where he finds Okonkwo hanging on his suicide rope. It is a total defeat for the Commissioner, who would never get to arrest his victim and punish him at will. Obierika feels triumphant, for he recognizes that Okonkwo, his friend, has escaped the commissioner's wrath through suicide. He rubs salt into injury when he asks the commissioner and his men, lumping them together as strangers to the land and instruments of the oppression of the people, to help them take down the dead body:

Perhaps your men can help us bring him down and bury him. We have sent for strangers from another village to do it for us, but they may be a long time coming. (190)

By casting the commissioner and his men as the Other, Obierika has de-centered power, moving it to the margin. He has successfully negotiated ideological power, turning it on its head. With great ability, knowledge and demeanor, Obierika has reversed the roles of the master and the subaltern, putting the subaltern, albeit temporarily, over the master.

* * *

We have tried to depart from the norm of discussing masculinity in opposition to femininity, but rather see men's shows of power, privilege and force in its variety, through language in force, language foregrounded, back-grounded, presupposed or absent in Chinua Achebe's *Things Fall Apart*. Through the study of four pieces of communication between a man and a group, an African and a European, and two men, one on one, we have been able to identify a variety of masculinity and powers of men through language. First, a man or a group of men can be cowered when that man or the group of men feels less powerful than the opponent, the Other. On an individual basis, a man can achieve superiority with silence, by merely refusing to respond when he thinks it is below his dignity to respond to the Other he considers inferior to him. On a group basis, we find that even a whole community can be routed by a powerful man, due to his position in the group and because of the perception of this group of his power. Second, a good speaker can sway or "conquer" a whole community by his sheer artistry in the manipulation of language. Third, two men can do a war of words with no one having a clear upper hand in the dialogue, due to the tenacity of purpose of both interlocutors. Anyone desirous of being taken seriously can gain insights from this study and also learn to avoid being made out as a victim. Chinua Achebe's *Things Fall Apart* has lent itself to the exploration of how in a traditional and patriarchal community, African men manifest a variety of identity and subjectivity. Perhaps, it is about time gender studies shifted from sheer comparison of femininity and masculinity alone to studies about how masculinity is initiated and fostered in society.

Notes

1. It is important to note that in African palaver groups, men discuss important issues facing the people before making far-reaching decisions. It is typically, formally and informally, the structure around which the village government thrived. A corollary could be women's groups on the farm or cooking or fetching water or firewood, or even the *Umuada* group. With male informal groups, such as the age-grade, the sole criterion for entry seems to be age within two to four years of one another. For more formal groups, like the *egwugwu*, the *ndichie* or the council of elders, entrance into the group is more selective and restricted. First of all, a member has to be titled and be one of the most highly regarded in the ward or canton or clan. Each member has to be initiated into the cult of the spirits and will remain a member, an elder of some sort, so long as he has not done anything to tarnish his name. He must always be aboveboard and be a mentor and an example to the young ones and future generations born and yet unborn. April A. Gordon and Donald L. Gordon, *Understanding Contemporary Africa* (second edition), Boulder and London: Lynne Rienner Publishers, 1996, 8-9.

2. "The ITCZ (Intertropical Convergence Zone) represents a meteorological phenomenon whereby large scale airflows from generally opposite directions converge or meet, creating a relatively constant updraft of displaced air. The vertical movement is supplemented by buoyant heated air from the sun-soaked, warm surface conditions of the tropical regions. The rising air cools off rapidly, causing atmospheric water vapor (if present) to condense into droplets first, then precipitation. At least this is the ideal chain of events, and the ITCZ is the primary rainmaking mechanism not only in Africa but throughout the tropical world. Rainfall often occurs as daily thunderstorms and can be torrential during the rainy season. . . . Sometimes the ITCZ 'misbehaves' and does not shift when it's normally expected to or move where it usually should, bringing stress to the life that depends on it."

Works Cited

Achebe, Chinua. *Things Fall Apart*. New York: Fawcett Crest, 1959.
Cahn, Victor L. *Gender and Power in the Plays of Harold Pinter*. New York: St. Martin's Press, 1993.

Cornell, R. W. *Gender and Power*. Stanford: Stanford University Press, 1987.

_____. *Masculinities*. Oxford: Polity Press, 1995, 37.

Easthope, Anthony. *What a Man's Gotta Do: The Masculine Myth in Popular Culture*. Boston: Unwin Hyman Press, 1986.

Foucault, Michel. *The Subject and Power*. In: *Critical Inquiry* 8. 777-795.

Gordon, April A., and Donald L. Gordon. *Understanding Contemporary Africa* (second edition). Boulder and London: Lynne Rienner Publishers, 1996.

Johnson, Sally, and Ulrike Hanna Meinhoff. *Language and Masculinity*. Cambridge, MA: Blackwell Publishers, 1997.

Kaye/Kantrowitz, Melanie. *The Issue Is Power: Essays on Women, Jews, Violence and Resistance*. San Francisco: Aunt Lute Books, 1992.

Kiesling, Scott Fabius. "Power and Language of Men." In: Sally Johnson and Ulrike Hanna Meinhoff. *Language and Masculinity*. Cambridge, MA: Blackwell Publishers, 1997.

Lang, Hermann. *Language and the Unconscious: Jacques Lacan's Hermeneutics of Psychoanalysis* (translated from the German by Thomas Brockelman). New Jersey: Humanities Press, 1997.

Obelitala, Alphonse. *L'initiation en Afrique noire et en Grece: Confrontation de quelques rites de passage*. Brazzaville: P. Kivaiva Verlag, 1982.

Poole, Adrian. *Tragedy: Shakespeare and the Greek Example*. New York: Basil Blackwell, Inc., 1987

Pucci, Pietro, Ed. *Language and the Tragic Hero: Essays on Greek Tragedy in the Honour of Gordon M. Kirkwood*. Atlanta: Scholars Press, 1988.

Saltlel, Jack. "Men, Inexpressiveness, and Power." In: B. Thorne, C. Kramarae and N. Henley, Eds. *Language, Gender and Society*. Cambridge, MA: Newbury House, 1995. 119-124.

Segal, Erich, Ed. *Greek Tragedy: Modern Essays in Criticism*. Cambridge and London and Mexico City: Harper and Row Publishers, 1983.

Thorne, B., C. Kramarae, and N. Henley, Eds. *Language, Gender and Society*. Cambridge, MA: Newbury House, 1995.

Webster, Roger. *Studying Literary Theory: An Introduction* (second edition). London/New York/Sydney/Auckland: Arnold Publishers, 1990.

Weigman, Robyn, and Elena Glasberg. *Literature and Gender: Thinking Critically Through Fiction, Poetry, and Drama*. New York/Sydney/Amsterdam: Longman. 1999.

The Plight of a Hero in Achebe's *Things Fall Apart*[1]

Patrick C. Nnoromele

Although *Things Fall Apart* remains the most widely read African novel, the failure of its hero continues to generate haunting questions in the minds of some of its readers, especially among those who seem to identify with the hero's tragedy. Central to this discomfort is the question: why did Achebe choose as his hero an aspiring but brutal young man who ultimately took his own life? The author himself acknowledges that he has "been asked this question in one form or another by a certain kind of reader for thirty years" (Lindfors 1991, 22).[2] According to Achebe, these readers wanted to know why he allowed a just cause to stumble and fall? Why did he let Okonkwo (the hero of the novel) fail?

Several commentators have argued that Okonkwo's failure is due to his individual character weaknesses. Many blame it on the fragmentation of the Umuofia society and the destruction of its cultural values by the colonial powers. Yet others stress both.[3] There is no doubt that these things played a role in the suffering mind of the hero, but to argue that they are the reason for his failure is, in my opinion, too limited. Hence, I want to argue, contrary to popular views, that Okonkwo's downfall is not necessarily due to weaknesses in character or departed African glories but rather is a function of heroism in the cultural belief systems of the Igbos. As Okhamafe aptly noted, perhaps "things begin to fall apart in this nine-village Umuofia clan long before a European colonialist missionary culture inserts itself there" (Okhamafe 1995, 134).

Things Fall Apart is not a novel without a cultural context. It is a text rooted in the social customs, traditions, and cultural milieu of a people. The characters and their actions are better understood when they are examined in that light. To do otherwise not only denies the novel a full measure of appreciation, it also renders vague and imprecise the significance of certain events, actions, and actors in the story.

What we have in this novel is a vivid picture of the Igbo society at the end of the nineteenth century. Achebe described for the world the positive as well as the negative aspects of the Igbo people. He discussed the Igbos' social customs, their political structures, religions, even seasonal festivals and ceremonies. He provided the picture without any attempt to romanticize or sentimentalize it. As he said on another occasion, "the characters are normal people and their events are real human events" (Lindfors 1991, 21).[4] Achebe told the story as it is.

The fact of his account is that the Igbo clan (of which I am a member) is a group of African people with a complex, vigorous, and self-sufficient way of life. Prior to the invasion of their land and the eclipse of their culture by foreign powers, they were undisturbed by the present, and they had no nostalgia for the past. In the novel, Achebe portrayed a people who are now caught between two conflicting cultures. On the one hand, there is the traditional way of life pulling on the Umuofia people and one man's struggle to maintain that cultural integrity against an overwhelming force of the colonial imperialism. On the other hand, we have the European style which, as presented, seems to represent the future, a new community of the so-called "civilized world." It now appears this African man, Okonkwo, and the entire society of Umuofia must make a choice between the old and the new—if they have the power. The desire to become a member of European-style society has its attraction. For one, it is conveyed to the Umuofia people, including Okonkwo, as a means of enjoying the spoils of twentieth-century civilization. But Okonkwo refused to endorse the appeal. He recognized that accepting the invitation is done at the expense of the things that comprised his identity and defined his values.

So when some members of the Umuofia community unwittingly accepted the invitation and endorsed "a strange faith," things fell apart for the Igbo people in Achebe's novel. Umuofia's integrated, organic community was irreparably fractured. Their gods were blasphemed and their hero disabled. Their customs were desecrated and shattered. The people were divided or put asunder. The British District Commissioner took charge and controlled the people. So we have what seems like a total imposition of one cultural, social, and political structure upon another. The hero of the novel found himself plunged into disaster. He had to kill himself. Obierika, one of the characters in the novel, expressed it this way: "That man [Okonkwo] was one of the greatest men in Umuofia. You drove him to kill himself and now he will be buried like a dog" (1996, 147). This was a tragic act, leading to the exacerbating question of why did Achebe let the hero fail, especially among those who have experienced or confronted the harsh face of colonialism. However, Okonkwo's calamitous act was not unexpected. All that happened to him and the fact that he had to take his own life were primarily the function of the Igbo's conception of a hero and, perhaps, the rift within the clan brought about by foreign domination.

A hero, in the Igbo cultural belief system, is one with great courage and strength to work against destabilizing forces of his community, someone who affects, in a special way, the destinies of others by pursuing his own. He is a man noted for special achievements. His life is defined by ambivalence, because his actions must stand in sharp contrast to ordinary behavior. So a hero is not made in isolation; rather he is a product of the social matrix within which he operates. The person's determination to pursue his individual interest concomitantly with that of the society is a constant source of dynamic tensions because his obligations to his society can become an impediment to his individual quest for fame and reputation. However, this impediment must be overcome if he is to be a hero. Paradoxically, a hero becomes both the disrupting and integrating principles of the community. Okonkwo, the central character in *Things Fall Apart*, is the epitome of this complex concept and the personification of the cultural ambiguity of the Igbo people.

In *Things Fall Apart*, Achebe made it clear that Okonkwo's single passion was "to become one of the lords of the clan" (1996, 92). According to Achebe, it was Okonkwo's "life-spring." Okonkwo wanted to be a hero. Unfortunately, the road to heroism in the Igbo's belief system is chronically fraught with difficulties of varying degrees.

The first challenge Okonkwo was expected to overcome was his father's reputation—in this case his father had none. However, he was determined to succeed in whatever respect his father had failed, knowing full well that among his "people a man was judged according to his worth and not according to the worth of his father" (1996, 6)—a juxtaposition of opposing claims about which the narrator (quite understandably) made no attempt to reconcile.[5] His father, Unoka, enjoyed gentleness and idleness. He "was lazy and improvident and was quite incapable of thinking about tomorrow" (3). Unoka was said to rejoice in song, dance, and drinking of palm-wine as his way of avoiding responsibility. In fact, he preferred these things to tending his yam-field. He was a man without title in the village of Umuofia, and he could not endure the sight of blood (8). Biologically, he was a male, but among the Igbo, he was never a man. So people laughed at him. In order to become a hero, Okonkwo felt he must overcome this public estimation of his father. At the outset of the novel, Achebe made the following remarks about Okonkwo: "His fame rested on solid personal achievements." "He had no patience with unsuccessful men" (3). "His whole life was dominated by fear, the fear of failure and of weakness" (9). So Okonkwo hated what his father was and became the opposite.

Not only is a hero expected to overcome the reputation of his father, he is also expected to surpass the reputations of his peers. In other words, he must outperform people in his age group or those he grew up with. Among the Igbos good effort is respected, "but achievement was revered" (1996, 6). Okonkwo must achieve concrete things to be a hero and he did. Here is Achebe's account of his achievement:

> If ever a man deserved his success, that man was Okonkwo. At an early age, he had achieved fame as the greatest wrestler in all the land. That was not luck At the most, one could say that his chi or personal god was good. But the Igbo people have a proverb that when a man says yes, his chi says yes also. Okonkwo said yes very strongly: so his chi agreed. And not only his chi, but his clan too, because it judged a man by the work of his hands.

That was why Okonkwo had been chosen by the nine villages to carry a message of war to their enemies unless they agree to give up a young man and a virgin to atone for the murder of Udo's wife. (Achebe 1996, 19-20)

Okonkwo's accomplishments in Umuofia earned him the respect and honor of the elders and the people. He defeated Amalinze the Cat and was proclaimed the greatest wrestler in Umuofia and Mbaino. He demonstrated exceptional skills as a warrior of the clan by bringing home five heads during inter-tribal conflicts. Achebe portrayed him as a man with "incredible prowess" and passion to conquer and subdue his enemies (1996, 6). He was a successful farmer and married three wives—clear evidence among the Igbos of a strong and wealthy man. The ultimatum of war that he delivered to the enemy of Umuofia yielded immediate results. Achebe wrote: "When Okonkwo of Umuofia arrived at Mbaino as the proud and imperious emissary of war, he was treated with great honor and respect, and two days later he returned home with a lad of fifteen and a young virgin. The lad's name was Ikemefuna, whose sad story is still told in Umuofia unto this day" (9). Okonkwo started with nothing, but through hard work and determination he became successful.

Another barrier one is expected to overcome in the quest for heroism is the person's obligation to the society, which, of course, may adversely affect his individual quest for reputation. The nature of the dynamic tensions this can create was evident in Okonkwo's lifestyle. Perhaps this accounts for the reason some interpreters of *Things Fall Apart* think that Achebe paints "a paradoxical portrait of a protagonist who is both a typical Igbo man as well as an individual" (Lindfors 1991, 17).[6]

Among the Igbos, a person's obligation to the society calls for cooperation. It calls for submission to the counsel of elders, the precepts, and laws of the land, which are established for the good of the society. I think the most difficult aspect of it all is the subordination of one's own interest to that of the group or society. Okonkwo had a scrupulous desire to fulfill his obligation to the society, but he often realized that it only brought him to a crossroad of conflicting loyalties. A typical example of this happened on the night when the Priestess of Agbala came to take Ezinma, Okonkwo's daughter, for Agbala's blessing. In spite of his inexorable commitment to support and defend the laws of the land, Okonkwo felt the natural pull to resist established social order. He was expressively unapproving of the untimely visit by the Priestess. He perceived her arrival as an intrusion to his family's domestic life. However, his insistent but unsuccessful protestations only elicited a scream from the Priestess of Agbala, who warned: "'Beware, Okonkwo!' 'Beware of exchanging words with Agbala. Does a man speak when a god speaks? Beware!'" (Achebe 1996, 96). Albeit, the Priestess took Ezinma to the Oracle of the Hills and Caves and returned her safely to Okonkwo's family the following day. But we learned from the narrator that Okonkwo was noticeably worried, and wondered about these conflicting loyalties.

Even Obierika, who seemed to disapprove of Okonkwo's commitment to the central doctrines of his culture, observed and agonized over the lack of equilibrium between the pull of private values and public expectations. The force of this pull is succinctly captured in the following passage:

He remembered his wife's twin children, whom he had thrown away. What crime had they committed? The Earth had decreed that they were an offense on the land and must be destroyed. And if the clan did not exact punishment for an offense against the great goddess, her wrath was loosed on all the land and not just on the offender. As the elders said, if one finger brought oil it soiled the others. (Achebe 1996, 88)

Obierika, like Okonkwo, felt the endemic tensions of conflicting cultural values—the incessant discord between public loyalty to the goddess of the clan and private loyalty to the family. But the difference between Okonkwo and Obierika was, Okonkwo was a man of few words.

He allowed his actions to speak for him. However, the cumulative effects of all these things led to his eventual suicide. This is the kind of dilemma one confronts on the road to heroism and it can be overwhelming. A hero, in Okonkwo's world, must face (it seems) a constant strife between two sets of values, the societal and the personal, but he never can find the equilibrium. It is, therefore, not a surprise to see Okonkwo take his own life. I believe this was precisely what Sarr observed when he critically remarked that at times, the reader of Achebe's novel, is faced with contradictions. "Ibo society" he added, "is full of contradictions." "It is a male-dominated society, in which the chief goddess is female and in which proverbial wisdom maintains 'Mother is supreme'"—a sustained duality in belief systems common to much of Africa (1993, 349).[7] Central to this observation is the fact that the Igbo community is a society that is at once communal and individualistic. Such a worldview or ambiguous value system reveals, Sarr properly concluded, "the dilemma that shapes and destroys the life of Okonkwo" (349).

Although Okonkwo expressed rigidity and inflexibility in his life, Achebe told us that down in his heart Okonkwo was not a cruel man. I believe the most charitable way to understand this is by looking briefly at different manifestations of Okonkwo's esoteric life. For example, when he violated the peace week by beating his youngest wife, which was an offense to the goddess, Okonkwo agreed to make offerings as demanded by the custom of Umuofia. In fact, he offered an additional pot of palm-wine, which was a distinct indication of genuine repentance and cooperation for the good of the community. Achebe had Ezeani say to Okonkwo:

> You know as well as I do that our forefathers ordained that before we plant any crops in the earth we should observe a week in which a man does not say a harsh word to his neighbors. We live in peace with our fellows to honor our great goddess of the earth without whose blessing our crops will not grow. You have committed a great evil. [As Okonkwo heard this] He

brought down his staff heavily on the floor. Your wife was at fault, but even if you came into your Obi and found her lover on top of her, you would still have committed a great evil to beat her. [As soon as Okonkwo heard this] His staff came down again. The evil you have done can ruin the whole clan. The earth goddess whom you have insulted may refuse to give us her increase, and we shall all perish. His tone now changed from anger to command. You will bring to the shrine of Ani tomorrow one she-goat, one hen, a length of cloth and a hundred cowries. He rose and left the hut. (Achebe 1996, 22)

Okonkwo made the sacrifices to the earth goddess.

In another occasion, we learn that Okonkwo breathed a heavy sigh of relief when he found out that his wife, Ekwefi, was unharmed after he had fired at her in a fit of rage. Thus, we observe within some of these occasional flashes of cruelty, a rare manifestation of tenderness. Similarly, on the night when the priestess of Agbala carried Ekwefi's daughter off to the Oracle of the Hills and Caves for the young girl to pay homage to her god, Ekwefi followed in terror for her child. Cognizant of his wife's state of terror, Okonkwo joined Ekwefi to provide re-assurance. When Ekwefi noticed Okonkwo's presence, "Tears of gratitude filled her eyes" (Achebe 1996, 106). As both of them waited outside their home in the dawn, Achebe said, Ekwefi remembered the generous love with which Okonkwo had taken her at the moment she became his wife. Perhaps Okonkwo was not a cruel man. For these occasional episodes are seemingly indications of a kind-hearted man.

Paradoxically, Okonkwo would never achieve heroism among the Igbos if he totally subordinated his interest to that of the society at large. Hence, it was incumbent on him to exhibit other qualities that might be perceived as a threat to social order. "And he did pounce on people quite often" (Achebe 1996, 3). As Achebe said, Okonkwo made people wonder whether he respected the gods of the clan. He "was popularly called the 'Roaring Flame'" (108). "Okonkwo was not the man to stop beating somebody halfway through, not even for fear of a goddess" (21). In his culture, a man who was unable to rule his own family was not considered a real man, not to mention a hero. So Okonkwo "ruled his household with a heavy hand" (9) and made people afraid of him. A hero should be impervious to emotions. The narrator told us that Okonkwo expressed no emotion, except anger. He was stoical to the harsh realities of life and appeared immune to problems. This is the life of a hero, a self-made man. Sometimes Okonkwo acted as if he was answerable to no one, and at other times he was the opposite. Obierika (Okonkwo's closest friend) pointed to this cultural ambiguity in the system when he sought (as he always did) a compromise from Okonkwo between conflicting loyalties. But Okonkwo responded impatiently, "The Earth (goddess) cannot punish me for obeying her messenger" (47). It would seem, for the Igbos, a hero must lead a life of self-contradiction; and Okonkwo was one primary example. It is, therefore, not surprising why contemporary commentators like Wasserman and Purdon contended that "Okonkwo represents a type of selfish individualism that is in essence a threat to Ibo notions of clan, and culture" (1993, 327).

In the opening lines of chapter seven, the narrator said, it seemed the elders of Umuofia had forgotten Ikemefuna (the lad who was entrusted to Okonkwo's care) but not the oracle. For three years Ikemefuna lived in Okonkwo's household. He was wholly absorbed into the family and Okonkwo became fond of him. Suddenly, the announcement came from the Oracle that Ikemefuna must be killed according to the tradition of Umuofia. The boy at this point regarded Okonkwo as a father. So, Ogbuefi Ezeudu specifically warned Okonkwo to stay at home. "The Oracle of the Hills and the Caves has pronounced it. They will take him (Ikemefuna) outside Umuofia as it is the custom, and kill him there. But I warn you to have nothing to do with it. He calls you father" (Achebe 1996, 40).

The cultural practice was that when the gods or goddesses demanded anyone for sacrifice, the family must be excluded because the Umuofia people believed that the emotional attachment the family might have for that individual would interfere with the process or the obligation to execute the demands of the Oracle. Hence, Ogbuefi Ezeudu sought for at least a passive compromise from Okonkwo. Since Okonkwo's passion was to be a hero, he felt his manliness might be called into question; therefore, he defied his friend's admonition and accompanied the procession into the forest.

What happened next would be used in the novel partly for the downfall of Okonkwo. Ikemefuna had to die. The values of the whole clan of Umuofia would be tested, if not forever, by this journey in which Ikemefuna would be killed. Achebe explained the episode in these words:

> As the man who had cleared his throat drew up and raised his machet, Okonkwo looked away. He heard the blow The pot (of palm-wine) fell and broke in the sand. He heard Ikemefuna cry, "My father, they have killed me!" as he ran towards him. Dazed with fear, Okonkwo drew his matchet and cut him down. He was afraid of being thought *weak*. (Achebe 1996, 43; emphasis is mine)

The death of Ikemefuna invoked varying or contrasting emotional reactions from both Okonkwo and Nwoye (Okonkwo's son) which dramatizes what Okonkwo apprehended as a dichotomy between strength and gentleness. Achebe said, as "soon as his father walked in, that night, Nwoye knew that Ikemefuna [someone he had come to know and treat as a friend] had been killed, and something seemed to give way inside him, like the snapping of a tightened bow. He did not cry. . . . He just hung limp" (1996, 43). Nwoye would have loved to cry, but couldn't, because Okonkwo had tried to raise him up like himself. In Okonkwo's world, real men do not show effeminate emotion. Crying is not a masculine attribute.

In Chapter Eight, we are told that Okonkwo himself could not sleep. He was distraught and deeply affected by the death of Ikemefuna and his son's reaction to it. As Achebe told us, Okonkwo was not a man of many words (something traditionally viewed as a masculine quality in the Umuofia's belief system), so he bottled his feelings within his heart. For two whole days he ate nothing as he struggled to erase the memory of killing a child who called him father. It was the cumulative effects of these things, including the impact the death of Ikemefuna had on his son, that paved the way to Okonkwo's eventual suicide. But the death of Ikemefuna had no immediate impact on the Umuofia people. It was, however, definitely an apocalyptic step towards things that were yet to come.

Later at the funeral of Ogbuefi Ezeudu, Okonkwo's gun accidentally discharged and killed the son of Ezeudu. Even though this was an accident, it was viewed as an abomination in the land, for under no circumstances would someone kill a clansman. Okonkwo and family had to flee the land before the cock crowed. They found refuge in his mother's village, Mbanta. He and his family endured seven years in exile. In the meantime, offerings were made in Okonkwo's compound, after their departure, to cleanse the land and placate the gods. Okonkwo saw this sojourn to Mbanta as a training experience in the wilderness. While he was in the village, he found out that the Mbanta clan was allowing missionaries to establish Christian churches and make converts especially among the untouchable. He saw how the missionaries defied the power of the local gods. His son, Nwoye, who suffered from inner turmoil as a result of the death of Ikemefuna,[8] decided to attend the mission school. He left his father's house and joined the Christian church. This was the straw that broke the camel's back. Okonkwo was furious and disappointed. He tried unsuccessfully to get the Mbanta clan to chase the missionaries out. When they couldn't get the missionaries out, Okonkwo sighed heavily and longed for his father's land, where according to him, men were men, bold, and war-like (Achebe 1996, 141).

When he finally returned to his fatherland, little did he know that the missionaries had penetrated his father's land too and made converts of different categories of Umuofia clan, ranging from the lowborn and the outcast to the men of title and stature. They also established white government with a courthouse where "the District Commissioner judged cases in ignorance" (Achebe 1996, 123). Obierika explained it this way: "The white man is very clever. He came quietly and peaceable with his religion. We were amused at his foolishness and allowed him to stay. Now he has put a knife on the things that held us together and we have fallen apart" (125). Fallen apart indeed! "Okonkwo's return to his native land was not as memorable as he had wished" (129). He never received the hero's welcome he dreamed of. He returned to a different Umuofia from the one he had known. In the present Umuofia, "men [have] unaccountably become soft like women" (129). He wanted to fight, but Obierika said to him: "It is already too late. . . . Our own men and our sons have joined the ranks of the strangers. They have joined his religion and they help to uphold his government. . . . How do you think we can fight when our own brothers have turned against us?" (124).

Okonkwo left and killed himself, not because of character weakness, or the departed African glories. Rather, it was the inevitable consequence of the Igbos' complex concept of a hero. As Sarma keenly pointed out:

> One cannot some-how lay the blame on Okonkwo. His action at the end, hasty though it was, was quite in accordance with the traditional values. It was an act of conviction, almost religious, and the end vindicated the character of Okonkwo, who emerges as the lone representative of the Igbo value system while the entire community lay around him in a shambles. (Sarma 1993, 69)

Okonkwo, who had a resolute hunger to become a hero, was not afraid of the forces that surrounded him. However, he was so overwhelmed by the cumulative effects of his experiences on the road to heroism that he felt the only thing left to do was to commit suicide. Okonkwo had to maintain his integrity as a hero. The truth of this profound but ambivalent act is reflected in the Igbo proverb that says: "The thought that led a man to truncate his own existence was not conceived in a day." It was not just one single thing or event that forced Okonkwo to kill himself. His suicidal act was an ultimate expression of the compound effects of his own experiences in his unflinching desire to become a hero. Okonkwo was a hero. Hence, he had to depart from the battlefield as one. A hero would rather die than be captured and/or humiliated by the enemy. Okonkwo's death cheated his enemies, the European colonizers, of their revenge. But to the Umuofia people, it was unambiguously imprinted in their minds that there had been an irreversible break with the past. Umuofia would never again be what it was.

Contrary to the charge that the author of the novel allowed Okonkwo to stumble and fall, Achebe did not cause the hero's downfall. He was not responsible for Okonkwo's tragedy. Achebe saw his role as that of a neutral narrator. Thus, he presented, in a non-committal fashion, the tensions and conflicts between traditional values and alien culture, the "private self" and "public man" and their attendant consequences in a pre-colonial society.

From *College Literature* 27, no. 2 (2000): 146-156. Copyright © 2000 by *College Literature*. Reprinted with permission of *College Literature*.

Notes

1. Special thanks to all my colleagues and students in the Honors Program whose thoughtful questions stimulated and sustained my interest in writing this article. I am also grateful to the following reviewers, Michael H. Bright, Ronald J. Messerich, and Salome C. Nnoromele, whose valuable suggestions and useful criticisms helped shape this essay.

2. Achebe did respond to the question (without sufficient elaboration) by saying: "the concepts of success and failure as commonly used in this connection are inadequate. Did Okonkwo fail? In a certain sense, he did, obviously. But he also left behind a story strong enough to make those who hear it . . . wish devoutly that things had gone differently for him" (Achebe 1991, 22-23).

3. For this and other contemporary interpretations of the novel, see Lott and Lott (1993). This volume contains an extensive bibliographic essay on *Things Fall Apart*. See also McDougall (1986, 24-33).

4. The characters in this novel, including the gods or divinities, ancestors, and the events, are actual representations of the Igbo people and their cultural belief systems.

5. Among the Umuofia people, a hero is expected to overcome the reputation of his father. Yet the society maintains that one is not judged by the worth of one's father. This is a contradiction, an unresolved discrepancy so indicative of the Igbo traditional values. Achebe made no effort to reconcile or extract a true version from these conflicting accounts, because he was writing from the standpoint of a neutral narrator.

6. See also Devi (1993, 79-86).

7. See, for instance, Adams (1982).

8. Nwoye could not express his emotion as felt, because his father, Okonkwo, reacting to his own father's effeminacy, had taught Nwoye to believe that the expression of effeminate emotion was a sign of weakness. Thus, Nwoye tried to bottle his feelings in his heart. The unavoidable consequence of this was the despair and inner turmoil he suffered in his life.

Works Cited

Achebe, Chinua. 1991. "Teaching *Things Fall Apart*." In *Approaches to Teaching Achebe's "Things Fall Apart,"* ed. Bernth Lindfors. New York: The Modern Language Association of America.

_____. 1996. *Things Fall Apart*. Portsmouth: Heinemann.

Adams, Monni. 1982. *Designs for Living: Symbolic Communication in African Art*. Cambridge: Harvard University, Carpenter Center for the Arts.

Devi, N. Rama. 1993. "Pre- and Post-Colonial Society in Achebe's Novels." In *Indian Response to African Writing*, ed. A. Ramakrishna Rao and C. R. Visweswara Rao. New Delhi: Prestige Books.

Lindfors, Bernth, ed. 1991. *Approaches to Teaching Achebe's "Things Fall Apart."* New York: The Modern Language Association of America.

Lott, John, and Sandra Lott. 1993. "Approaches to *Things Fall Apart*." In *Global Perspectives on Teaching Literature*, ed. Sandra Ward Lott, Maureen S. G. Hawkins, and Norman McMillan. Urbana, Illinois: National Council of Teachers of English.

McDougall, Russell. 1986. "Okonkwo's Walk: The Choreography of Things Falling Apart." *World Literature Written in English* 26.1: 24-33.

Okhamafe, Imafedia. 1995. "Genealogical Determinism in Achebe's *Things Fall Apart*." In *Genealogy and Literature*. Ed. Lee Quinby. Minneapolis: University of Minnesota Press.

Sarma, S. Krishna. 1993. "Okonkwo and His *Chi*." In *Indian Response to African Writing*, ed. A. Ramakrishna Rao and C. R. Visweswara Rao. New Delhi: Prestige Books.

Sarr, Ndiawar. 1993. "The Center Holds: The Resilience of Ibo Culture in *Things Fall Apart*." In *Global Perspectives on Teaching Literature*, ed. Sandra Ward Lott, Maureen S. G. Hawkins, and Norman McMillan. Urbana, Illinois: National Council of Teachers of English.

Wasserman, Julian, and Liam O. Purdon. 1993. "If the Shoe Fits: Teaching *Beowulf* with Achebe's *Things Fall Apart*." In *Global Perspectives on Teaching Literature*, ed. Sandra Ward Lott, Maureen S. G. Hawkins, and Norman McMillan. Urbana, Illinois: National Council of Teachers of English.

Okonkwo's Suicide as an Affirmative Act:
Do Things Really Fall Apart? _____

Alan R Friesen

Okonkwo in Achebe's *Things Fall Apart* has long been considered a tragic figure who is caught up in events that he cannot overcome, a victim *of* rather than an active participant *in* his own fate. Many critics have understood the novel to be "the tragic story of Okonkwo's rise and fall among the Igbo people, concluding with that least ambiguous of all endings, the death of the hero" (Begam 397) without fully examining the ramifications of Okonkwo's suicide upon both the colonial and Igbo cultures. These critics assume that the story follows the mode of tragedy (whether Aristotelian, modern or Igbo) and conclude that his suicide is the end product of his inability to control his own fate; however, this interpretation of Okonkwo's suicide as the final failure of an ill-fated man is simply not consistent with the rest of the text. On the other hand, if we assume that Okonkwo's suicide was an affirmative act, that is, a conscious decision to promote a positive ideal instead of an act of failure, then another interpretation presents itself. Rather than a tragic act, Okonkwo's suicide can be seen as his last attempt to remind the Igbo people of their culture and values in the face of impending colonisation.

The whole interpretation of Okonkwo's suicide hinges on the concept of fate: despite his strength and heroic qualities, is he really in control of his life? Most of the critics who call Okonkwo a tragic figure do so because they believe that he cannot overcome his fate, or *chi* as it is referred to in Igbo culture. *Chi* "is a very enigmatic entity, and this accounts for the diversity of opinions as to its nature. But hardly any opinion contradicts the Igbo peoples belief that *chi* is an entirely personal deity, if it can be called a deity" (Ebeogu 74). Moreover

[i]t is entirely responsible for the fortunes or misfortunes of the individual while on earth, and nothing happens to the individual except his *chi* con-

sents. But, paradoxically, the Igbo folk think that the individual can somehow manipulate this personal enigmatic force called *chi*, and that one's *chi*
is always inclined to consent to one's wishes. The relationship between the
individual and his *chi* is thus manipulative. (74)

So, then, what is Okonkwo's *chi*? Is it, as some critics have claimed,
"determined to lead him into disaster and shame," necessitating Okonkwo's suicide in order to "concede defeat to this enigmatic entity" (77),
or is it determined to bring Okonkwo to a position in which he will sacrifice his own life in order to inspire resistance against the colonial oppressors? In other words, is Okonkwo in control of his *chi*, or does his
chi control him? Let us look at several key events leading up to
Okonkwo's suicide to see if we can gain an insight into this event.

From the novel's opening, "Okonkwo was well known throughout
the nine villages and even beyond" (Achebe 1), it is apparent that
Okonkwo's *chi* is very strong. With no pejoratives to indicate that this
fame is the result of some infamous act, we can only assume that he is
respected throughout these nine villages. Indeed, his first measurable
achievement is the defeat of Amalinze the Cat in a wrestling match, described as "one of the fiercest since the founder of their town engaged a
spirit of the wild for seven days and seven nights" (1).

This description is important to the narrative for two reasons. First
of all, it links Okonkwo with the progenitor of his village, implying a
connexion reminiscent of that between Grecian kings and their gods.
Not only is Okonkwo famous, but he is now associated with the super-
natural. Second, Okonkwo defeats the undefeatable wrestler, which
again reinforces this notion of divinity and sets up the claim that
Obierika makes at the end of the novel, that Okonkwo is "one of the
greatest men in Umuofia" (191). From the onset, therefore, we are
meant to believe that there is nothing that Okonkwo cannot overcome,
that his *chi* is heroic.

Certainly, his first year as a farmer confirms that his *chi* is heroic. To
begin with, due to the fact that his father was more concerned with mu-

sic than farming, Okonkwo was not able to inherit anything from him (21) and so had to borrow the seeds for his first crop. Unfortunately, the terrible weather during this year almost caused him to lose everything. Instead of simply giving up and becoming an *agbala* like his father, he says that "[s]ince I survived that year, I shall survive anything" (27).

But not only did he survive, he rises "from great poverty and misfortune to be one of the lords of the clan" (28). He starts out in life with nothing, but through hard work he becomes a great leader. If his *chi* was inclined to point him towards disaster, thus far it seems that his "inflexible will" has illustrated the precept that "one's *chi* is always inclined to consent to one's wishes" (Ebeogu 74). With this new rank comes responsibility, and he is soon given the duty of looking after Ikemefuna, the war-ransom from Mbaino given to Umuofia in exchange for the murder of Ogbuefi Udo's wife. For three years Ikemefuna lives in Okonkwo's village, but eventually the elders of the clan decide to execute Ikemefuna for his clan's involvement in the aforementioned murder. Even though Okonkwo is warned by Ogbuefi Ezeudu to "not bear a hand in [Ikemefuna's] death" because the "boy calls [Okonkwo] father" (Achebe 55-56), ultimately Ikemefuna is slain at Okonkwo's hand.

Of this incident, there seems to be a general consensus among critics. Shelton says that "Okonkwo severely antagonized the *ndichie* (ancestors) and *Chukwu* (the High God, Creator, and Giver of all life and power) by killing Ikemefuna . . . [and] alienated his *chi*" (36). He goes on to claim that Okonkwo's family is cursed, tracing the effects of this through *Things Fall Apart* and its sequel *No Longer at Ease*. Iyasere is a bit more forgiving, saying that "Okonkwo is in competition with the gods and [kills Ikemefuna] out of his pathological fear of being thought weak—his fear of being perceived as like his father Unoka" (Iyasere 306). Both authors concur on one point: Okonkwo acts wrongly and is ultimately punished for his actions.

However, this conclusion is contrary to the text itself. Even though Obierika says that "if the Oracle said my son should be killed I would neither dispute it nor be the one to do it" (Achebe 64-5), Okonkwo's earlier claim that "[t]he Earth cannot punish me for obeying her messenger" (64) is absolutely true. His statement is not contradicted in the text, nor is it opposed in any of the critical readings that have been published in the past fifty years, despite the abundance of statements such as "Okonkwo broke the law of the gods . . . [when] he killed Ikemefuna" (Okpala 562). First of all, Ikemefuna's execution is legally sanctioned: "Umuofia has decided to kill him. The Oracle of the Hills and the Caves has pronounced it" (Achebe 56). Second, Ezeudu only *wants* Okonkwo to abstain from becoming involved in his "son's" death; he is not ordered, in other words, to stay out of it, and so cannot be faulted for disobeying an elder by landing the fatal blow.

From an emotional viewpoint, however, we are deeply shocked when we see that Okonkwo does indeed kill his son instead of letting somebody else commit the act. Why would he do such a thing? To be sure, Okonkwo is widely regarded as impulsive and rarely thinks before he acts (Macdonald 51), but when we take a closer look at the scene we realise that Okonkwo's actions were not brutal, but were instead relatively humane. The execution has been ordered, without any possibility of reprieve; the novel is clear in this regard. As the execution party marches out of the village, Ikemefuna becomes aware of what is about to happen and runs towards Okonkwo, shouting "My father, they have killed me!" At this point, we have Okonkwo at the rear of the party with the other members ostensibly moving toward Okonkwo; had Okonkwo defended his son as we wish he would have done, not only would Ikemefuna's fate be cruelly postponed, but Okonkwo would have gone against the will of the Oracle, which is tantamount to turning his back on the clan himself. Shelton's claim, then, that Okonkwo and his family are cursed because of Ikemefuna's murder makes no sense—how much more cursed would Okonkwo's family had been if he had instead defended his son against the Oracle?

By not only killing his son, an act that we have already established as inevitable, but also by doing it swiftly, Okonkwo saves Ikemefuna from the cruel fate of being run to the ground by the other executioners. An image of Ikemefuna trying to escape from a group of men with machetes is much more brutal than a sudden blow that kills him. Not only did Okonkwo obey the Earth's messenger, but he did so in the most humane and logical way possible. Although the narrator does note that Okonkwo was "[d]azed with fear" and was "afraid of being thought weak" (59) when he killed Ikemefuna, there is no doubt that Okonkwo could not have thought of a better way to handle the situation under the circumstances. Okonkwo is not the victim of tragedy in this scene, but the architect of his own *chi*.

The killing of Ezeudu's son, however, is slightly more problematic. On the surface, there is no way that Okonkwo could have purposefully forced the gun to explode, consciously or unconsciously, nor could the immediate effects of this be seen as anything other than tragic. By way of punishment for accidentally killing another member of the clan, Okonkwo is forced to leave the village and live in Mbanta for seven years. This not only takes away his status as a lord of a clan and ruins his carefully planted farm, but it also robs his son Nwoye of the chance of taking a title and becoming a prominent member of their society. At the same time, the fact that Okonkwo is removed from the village shortly before the arrival of the missionaries is somewhat fortuitous.

Over the course of the seven years that Okonkwo is in exile, major changes occur in Umuofia, beginning with the slaughter of the village of Abame. A white man comes to the village and tries to communicate with the villagers, but ostensibly since he cannot communicate with them, the villagers kill him. In retribution, the white men's fellows wait until the villagers are all at the market and then kill them. Okonkwo says of the incident that "they were fools" and since they "had been warned that danger was ahead[,] [t]hey should have armed themselves with their guns and their machetes even when they went to market" (130).

Two years later, when the missionaries have established a mission in Mbanta, he discovers that his son has converted to this new religion and has forsworn the customs of his ancestors. When Okonkwo considers this new situation, "[a] sudden fury rose within him and he felt a strong desire to take up his machete, go to the church and wipe out the entire vile and miscreant gang" (Achebe 142). At first, Okonkwo dismisses the villagers of Abame as foolish for not being prepared for an ambush, but after seeing the "demasculating" effects of the white man first-hand he realises that the situation is much more grave than he at first believes. Had Okonkwo first experienced the missionary-invaders in Umuofia, it is certain that he would have done as his fury had dictated and attempt to directly fight back against the white man. Furthermore, Okonkwo is not as concerned since this all takes place in Mbanta and not in his own village; Okonkwo already thinks that the people of Mbanta are weak, so he is not surprised when they allow the missionaries to gain inroads in the village. Although he is not fully in control of the events that lead to his exile, we can attribute the accidental killing of Ezeudu's son to his fortuitous *chi* which saves his life at this point so that he can sacrifice it at a later point for a greater gain. The fact that he prospers while in exile seems to support this, that "his *chi* might now be making amends for the past disaster" (Achebe 158).

This sacrifice comes immediately following the slaying of the messenger, an event that again shows Okonkwo to be in control of his *chi*. After Okonkwo returns from exile, he learns that the missionaries have further encroached into his culture than he could have believed. He is saddened because his people have "so unaccountably become soft like women" (168) and have lost their martial spirit. Tension between the church and the village escalates until finally Enoch, a convert, tears off the mask of an *egwugwu*, killing an ancestral spirit (171). The village retaliates by burning the church to the ground, which redeems the village in Okonkwo's eyes: "[i]t was like the good old days again, when a warrior was a warrior" (176). With Okonkwo back in the village, it seems as if the clan is returning to its war-like state, and he has reason to hope that the village might actually gain enough courage to "kill the missionary and drive away the Christians" (176).

This hope is important to the scene in which Okonkwo kills the messenger, which takes place shortly after Okonkwo and several of his peers are tricked into captivity as retribution for the destruction of the church. In the meeting that follows, it appears as if the village has had enough. Okika, one of the "great men" of the village, gives this speech:

> If we fight the stranger we shall hit our brothers and perhaps shed the blood of a clansmen. But we must do it. Our fathers never dreamed of such a thing, they never killed their brothers. But a white man never came to them. So we must do what our fathers would never have done. . . . We must root out this evil. And if our brothers take the side of evil we must root them out too. And we must do it *now*. (187)

Okika's speech is then interrupted by an Igbo messenger who tells the assembly that "[t]he white man whose power you know too well has ordered this meeting to stop" (188), at which point Okonkwo kills the messenger, his "machete descend[ing] twice and the man's head lay beside his uniformed body" (188).

Unlike the accidental killing which led to Okonkwo's exile, this murder is specifically designed to incite the village to revolt against the white man. Everything up to this point indicates that Okonkwo's actions are "correct": the village "listened to him with respect" when he urges action against the church, joins him as they burn down the chapel, and takes Okika's speech to be dogma—in other words, there was no other response for Okonkwo to take without it being completely out of character. If Okonkwo had *not* killed this messenger, Okika's speech would have been meaningless—what would have been the point of an immediate call to action if the men of the village had meekly shuffled off at the first sign of trouble? His *chi* was not against him when he killed the messenger; he killed him because he was attempting to uphold the culture of his people in the face of the impending colonisation by the white men and their collaborators.

When Okonkwo discovers, then, that his village does not in fact support his actions because they "had let the other messengers escape," he does not rave, he does not go out and attack the court, but he contemplatively "wip[es] his machete on the sand and [goes] away" (188). We discover shortly thereafter that Okonkwo has hung himself on a tree behind his compound. This act of suicide is what has troubled and confused critics; despite the fact that we have seen that Okonkwo has been in control of his *chi* thus far, Ebeogu claims that "he suddenly realises that his *chi* is determined to lead him into disaster and shame. So he takes his own life in order to end it all" (77). Macdonald says that "Okonkwo knows they will never go to war and that his act of hope has now sealed his destruction because he is completely alone in his opposition to the new authority. The only alternative to the ignominy of hanging in the white man's gaol is to take his own life, ironically an abomination to all he stood for in the past" (59). In other words, Macdonald claims that Okonkwo kills himself because the only other option is his execution at the hands of the white man.

However, this runs contrary to Igbo beliefs on suicide. Ukwu and Ikebudu say that suicide is

> considered an "*nso ani*," a sin against the Earth. The Igbos do not concede to the difficulties of life or to the demands of everyday life. They do not accept suicide, in any form and at any age, as a solution to any problem regardless of the complexities. Suicide is believed to be a terrible and evil way to die. The Igbos strongly believe in reincarnation. Reincarnation is one of the ways they share their love with their loved ones who have passed. Consequently, death by suicide is believed to be an evil and "a bad death." If one committed suicide, that person was never (and never will be) at peace with him/herself, the community (i.e. village), relatives, and most importantly the gods.

As we can see, suicide is one of the worst acts that an Igbo person can commit as it is both a crime against the individual and against the village. Macdonald claims that Okonkwo commits suicide because it is better than dying at the hands of the white man, but being murdered, it seems, is infinitely more desirable than taking one's own life. A murdered clan member at the very least would be able to join their ancestral spirits or be reincarnated, but for somebody who commits suicide there is nothing beyond life. There is no other alternative, then, than the interpretation that Okonkwo chooses to commit suicide rather than being executed by the white man.

However, as the above passage illustrates, this opens up a multitude of problems. I have claimed that Okonkwo's act of suicide is a positivity rather than the end result of some tragic flaw, and we have seen that throughout the entire novel that, at the very least, Okonkwo and his *chi* seem to be working together towards a positive end. What, then, was Okonkwo hoping to achieve from such a "terrible and evil" act? I believe that Okonkwo is lamenting the village's turn away from their traditional customs, and by committing the worst possible offence in Igbo culture, he hopes to turn back the overwhelming tide of movement towards the white man's ideology.

The progression of the novel makes it clear that the village is moving further and further away from their traditional customs. After Okonkwo kills Ikemefuna, a rift appeared between Okonkwo and Nwoye; Nwoye had already questioned the killing of Ikemefuna and the traditional custom of leaving twin newborns in the forest to die, but it is not until he hears the missionaries singing that he feels "relief within as the hymn poured into his parched soul" (137). We sympathise with Nwoye because we too as readers feel uncomfortable over these acts in the novel, but Okonkwo does not feel the same way: after thinking about Nwoye's act of leaving his house and becoming a Christian, he realises that

> his son's crime stood out in stark enormity. To abandon the gods of one's father and go about with a lot of effeminate men clucking like old hens was the very depth of abomination. Suppose when he died all his male children decided to follow Nwoye's steps and abandon their ancestors? Okonkwo

felt a cold shudder run through him at the terrible prospects, like the prospect of annihilation. He saw himself and his fathers crowding round their ancestral shrine waiting in vain for worship and sacrifice and fording nothing but ashes of bygone days, and his children the while praying to the white man's god. (142)

Okonkwo is caught in a difficult situation: if he allows the white man to influence Nwoye and the rest of the village, then there will be nobody left to worship him or his ancestors when he dies, leading to the situation as described in the above passage.

The scene in which Enoch unmasks an *egwugwu* and kills an ancestral spirit also exemplifies this slide into colonisation. Such an act was absolutely unheard of; after he had killed the spirit,

the Mother of the Spirits walked the length and breadth of the clan, weeping for her murdered son. It was a terrible night. Not even the oldest man in Umuofia had ever heard such a strange and fearful sound, and it was never to be heard again. It seemed as if the very soul of the tribe wept for a great evil that was coming—its own death. (171-2)

Certainly Okonkwo hears this portent, which again echoes his previous thoughts on Nwoye and the slow movement of the clan towards Christianity. Not only are its children becoming Christians, but the converts are committing gross acts of sacrilege. As we have already seen, the chapel is torn down in retribution, but the chapel can be rebuilt, whereas nothing can bring that ancestral spirit back to life.

So when faced with the choice of either humbly going home at the messenger's request or attacking him for his disrespect, to Okonkwo there is no other choice: he must act, and he must kill. But when he realises that he is alone and that Umuofia will not go to war to fight for their customs and traditions that are slowly slipping away, Okonkwo has another choice to make. He could allow himself to be killed, thus assuring his reincarnation or his enshrinement along with his ancestors, but as we have already seen this would be a futile act: being ignored while their children are worshipping the white man's God (which would happen if Umuofia loses more converts and traditions) is exactly "the prospect of annihilation" (142) that Okonkwo fears.

If Okonkwo wishes to try to save his culture, then, it seems as if there is only one other plausible option: suicide. He could have gone on a rampage and attempted to take on the white men himself, but then his village too would be destroyed like Abame, which would have negated any attempt to move the villagers back towards their traditions. If he commits suicide instead, at the very least his people would survive to feel the effects of his act.

Ukwu and Ikebudu have already made it clear that suicide for the Igbo people is a terrible act, and as such it is likely that it is an extremely rare event. Certainly, suicide is not mentioned anywhere else in the novel. On the other hand, the arrival of the white man and Christianity is a singular event, one that by definition cannot be repeated. It is understandable that the people of Umuofia are swayed by the novelties of the white man, including Christianity and the trading store, which is why Okonkwo undertook such a drastic step in order to force his people to remember and consider the customs that they are throwing away. If they were swayed at first by the prospect of merely selling palm-oil and kernels, then how much more would they be concerned over the suicide of one of their clansmen, especially one who is "one of the greatest men in Umuofia" (191)?

This act is perhaps not the most prudent, especially considering that Okonkwo would essentially cease to exist according to what Ukwu and Ikebudu tell us about Igbo culture, but given the situation it is the most effective. Influential men, including Nwoye, the son of one of the greatest men in Umuofia, have left the clan in order to become Christians. The missionaries built their chapel in the Evil Forest, which instead of destroying them only showed that the white men's medicine was strong. Enoch kills an ancestral spirit. Finally, when Okonkwo kills a messenger and all but starts a war between the white men and

Umuofia, his peers prove to be too "womanly" to do what is necessary: "kill the missionary and drive away the Christians." Okonkwo is faced with a singular event that is much too large for him to effectively combat with outward violence alone, so he turns the violence inwards and kills himself; in other words, he fights the singularity of the white men with the singularity of suicide in Igbo culture.

The suicide in and of itself achieves nothing, but since it is such a rare event in Igbo culture it compels the villagers to recollect the customs and rites associated with it. It forces them to think about Okonkwo, once a great man, who has been driven to suicide by the arrival of the white man. It would provoke thought and discussion in Umuofia about Igbo culture and values and perhaps even beyond, as he would be remembered for his infamous act rather than his fame as a mere wrestler in his youth. I would contend that the very act of remembering these values presents a powerful affront against the missionaries, who encourage Umuofia to forget their culture and history and join with them in worshipping a god who has not even existed for them until just recently. Moreover, in the language of the church, Okonkwo has become a "martyr" for his beliefs, and as the church well knows, once dead, martyrs cannot be silenced.

But Ukwu and Ikebudu tell us that suicide is "an '*nso ani*,' a sin against the Earth." Would Okonkwo really commit such a grievous act against the gods in order to turn the people back towards the gods? First, throughout the novel it is apparent that Okonkwo is not exactly concerned with what the gods think. During the Week of Peace, Okonkwo beats his wife Ojiugo because she forgets to cook the afternoon meal. Although such an act is forbidden during the Week of Peace and his wives remind him of this, "Okonkwo was not the man to stop beating somebody half-way through, not even for fear of a goddess" (31). Although he is concerned with the culture of his people (as evidenced by the fact that the offering he makes to Ani, the earth goddess, is more than what is required), it is apparent that he shows this concern in his own way and by his own time.

Second, although the act of suicide is fairly rare, the fact that the Igbo culture in Umuofia is slipping away is a brand new concept in the clan. Up until this point, Okonkwo's clan was protected by not only a complex system of beliefs but a system of inter-tribal warfare: if one clan has offended another (as in the case of the murder of Ogbuefi Udo's wife) and if no peaceful arrangement can be achieved, then the two clans go to war. Okonkwo is fully aware of this system, having shown "incredible prowess in two inter-tribal wars" (12), but with the arrival of the white man and their ability to kill an entire village without even being seen, the balance of power has shifted. The entire system of peace was dependent on the threat of war; with such a threat being impotent against the interlopers, the concept of peace is now meaningless. This might be assuming a bit much, but surely Umuofia's gods would not want their worshippers to go to war against the white people with the end result of being completely obliterated. Surely it would be much more reasonable for one man to sacrifice his life in order for others to have the chance to realise their mistake and turn back to their gods. We cannot know for sure how the gods would react to this situation, but reason would seem to dictate that one life sacrificed for the greater good is infinitely better than a total loss of worshippers to either death or Christianity. In a sense, not to take action would be suicidal for the Igbo people.

Third, putting aside the issue of the gods completely, it is also apparent that Okonkwo is more concerned about the lack of ancestor worship than the fact that the gods will not receive as much adulation. He mentions the image of him and his ancestors huddling over their cold ancestral shrine, whereas when "things" start to "fall apart" he shows no interest in how the gods would view the situation. He might, therefore, be willing to grieve the gods if his ancestors receive the worship that they deserve.

We cannot be certain, but it is more likely that Okonkwo would risk angering the gods by committing suicide in order to bring his people back to the traditions that he considers to be important rather than doing nothing, resulting in total colonisation or launching a one-man attack on the Christians, which would lead to total annihilation. However, was his attempt in vain? It is a bit difficult to measure the effects of Okonkwo's suicide given the fact that the novel ends a page after we discover his death, but there is one significant statement made just before the novel closes: Obierika ferociously says to the commissioner that "[Okonkwo] was one of the greatest men in Umuofia. You drove him to kill himself and now he will be buried like a dog" (Achebe 191). Throughout the entire novel, Obierika is "the conscience of the clan" (Champion 274), the voice of reason that stands in contrast to Okonkwo's own words and actions. Obierika questions some of the traditions of the clan, asking at one point "[w]hy should a man suffer so grievously for an offense he had committed inadvertently?" (118) and later grieves for his twin children that he himself had thrown into the Evil Forest (118). It is fitting that this man, both progressive and yet remaining true to his culture, would give Okonkwo's benediction of being "one of the greatest men in Umuofia."

Furthermore, the fact that Achebe uses the literary technique of inclusion ("one of the greatest men of his time/in Umuofia") indicates that he too agrees with Obierika's pronouncement. At the beginning of the novel, at the height of his fame the narrator says that "although Okonkwo was still young, he was already one of the greatest men of his time" (12). The fact that Obierika repeats this phrase almost word-for-word validates Okonkwo's suicide: even after killing himself and performing one of the most heinous acts an Igbo man could think of undertaking, he is still "one of the greatest men in Umuofia." His suicide could not, then, have been merely the result of a tragic flaw or *hamartia*; would a fatal flaw and a useless death be so celebrated by the novel's most rational character? At the beginning of the novel, Okonkwo is a great man because he is wealthy, he has achieved fame, and he has taken two wives. At the end of the novel, after he commits suicide, he is a great man because he has made the ultimate sacrifice of his immortality (in Igbo fashion), his honour and the honour of his family and village in order to remind his people of what they would lose if they turned away from their past and instead looked towards the white man's God.

Finally, if we see Okonkwo's suicide as a failed act, then we can only assume that Achebe supports the act of colonisation as described in the novel. If Okonkwo really does "function as the true representative of his people . . . [by] committing what is a form of collective suicide by submitting to the British . . . [and preceding] his people in their communal destruction" (Begam 400), then either Achebe is giving us the novel in order to lament the death of the Igbo people or he tacitly supports the transformation of the Igbo people from proud and self-dependent to "improved specimens." If, on the other hand, Okonkwo's suicide is a positive act designed to immortalise the traditions that his people are so close to throwing away, then Okonkwo's death is not a "form of collective suicide" but is instead the transference of Igbo culture from the physical to the mythic. As reflected in his ties to divinity in the opening passage, Okonkwo is no longer a mere mortal who is powerless to act against the colonisers, but is a symbol of anti-colonialism to rally around, a martyr for the Igbo people.

Although *Things Fall Apart* can be interpreted in the tragic mode, the novel is much more meaningful if we interpret Okonkwo's suicide as an act of wilful resistance rather than an act of shame and dishonour. Within the text itself, the effects of Okonkwo's suicide are barely felt in the colonial world; the commissioner is still planning on writing his study, Nwoye is still lost to Igbo culture, and even Obierika's fierce words fall upon deaf ears. But on the other hand, if we consider Okonkwo's suicide to be a positivity rather than an act of defeat, then in a sense Igbo culture still lives on; perhaps things do not fall apart after all.

From *Postcolonial Text* 2, no. 4 (2006): 1-11. Copyright © 2006 by Postcolonial Press. Reprinted with permission of the author.

Works Cited

Achebe, Chinua. *Things Fall Apart*. New York: Fawcett Crest, 1959.

Begam, Richard. "Achebe's Sense of an Ending: History and Tragedy." *Studies in the Novel* 29 (1997): 396-411.

Champion, Ernest A. "A Story of a Man And His People: Chinua Achebe's *Things Fall Apart*." *Negro American Literature Forum* 8 (1974): 272-277.

Ebeogu, Afam. "Igbo Sense of Tragedy: A Thematic Feature of the Achebe School." *The Literary Half-Yearly* 24 (1983): 69-86.

Irele, Abiola. "The Tragic Conflict in the Novels of Chinua Achebe." *Critical Perspectives on Chinua Achebe*. Eds. C. L. Innes and Bernth Lindfors. Washington, DC: Three Continents Press, 1978. 10-21.

Iyasere, Solomon O. "Okonkwo's Participation in the Killing of His 'Son' in Chinua Achebe's *Things Fall Apart*: A Study of Ignoble Decisiveness." *CLA Journal* 35 (1992): 303-15.

Macdonald, Bruce F. "Chinua Achebe and the Structure of Colonial Tragedy." *The Literary Half-Yearly* 21 (1980): 50-63.

Okpala, Jude Chudi. "Igbo Metaphysics in Chinua Achebe's *Things Fall Apart*." *Callaloo* 25 (2002): 559-566.

Sarr, Ndiawar. "The Center Holds: The Resilience of Igbo Culture in *Things Fall Apart*." *Global Perspectives on Teaching Literature*. Eds. Sandra Ward Lott et al. Urbana, IL: National Council of Teachers of English, 1993. 347-355.

Shelton, Austin J. "The Offended *Chi* In Achebe's Novels." *Transition* 13 (1964): 36-37.

Ukwu, Dele Chinwe, and Anthony I. Ikebudu. *Igbo People (Nigeria) & Their Beliefs or Views About Suicide*. Long Beach City College. 2 Dec. 2004. http://lib.lbcc.edu/chiamaka/IgbosSuicide.htm.

RESOURCES

1930	Albert Chinualumogu Achebe is born on November 16 in Ogidi, in Eastern Nigeria.
1944-1948	Achebe attends Government College, Umuahia.
1948-1953	Achebe attends University College, Ibadan, focusing on medicine before pursuing a bachelor's degree in literature.
1954	Achebe begins working as a journalist for the Nigerian Broadcasting Corporation.
1956	Achebe trains with the British Broadcasting Corporation in London.
1958	*Things Fall Apart* is published by Heinemann, a British publisher.
1959	*Things Fall Apart* wins the Margaret Wrong Memorial Prize.
1960	Nigeria gains independence on October 1. *No Longer at Ease* is published. Achebe receives a Rockefeller Fellowship and tours Africa for six months.
1961	Achebe marries Christie Chinwe Okoli.
1962	*The Sacrificial Egg, and Other Stories* is published. Achebe becomes founding editor of the Heinemann African Writers Series. Daughter Chinelo is born.
1963	Nigeria becomes a republic, and Nnamdi Azikiwe is elected its first president.
1964	*Arrow of God* is published; it receives the *New Statesman* Jock Campbell Award. Son Ikechukwu is born.
1966	*A Man of the People* is published. Massacres of Igbo in the North cause Achebe to leave Lagos and return to Eastern Nigeria.
1967	Biafra secedes from Nigeria, triggering civil war. Achebe's son Chidi is born.

1970	Biafra surrenders, and the Nigerian civil war ends. Achebe's daughter Nwando is born.
1971	Achebe becomes founding editor of *Okike: An African Journal of New Writing*. The poetry collection *Beware, Soul Brother, and Other Poems* is published.
1972	*Girls at War, and Other Stories* is published. *Beware, Soul Brother, and Other Poems* wins the Commonwealth Poetry Prize.
1972-1975	Achebe serves as Visiting Professor of Literature at the University of Massachusetts at Amherst.
1975	Achebe delivers his famous lecture "An Image of Africa," which criticizes Joseph Conrad's *Heart of Darkness*. *Morning Yet on Creation Day* is published.
1975-1976	Achebe serves as Visiting Professor of Literature at the University of Connecticut, Storrs.
1976	"An Image of Africa" is published in the *Massachusetts Review*. Achebe returns to Nigeria and becomes Professor of Literature at the University of Nigeria, Nsukka.
1979	Achebe receives the Nigerian National Merit Award and the Order of the Federal Republic. He is elected chairman of the Association of Nigerian Authors.
1982	*Aka weta*, a volume of Igbo-language verse edited by Achebe and Obiora Udechukwu, is published.
1983	*The Trouble with Nigeria* is published. Achebe is elected Deputy National President of the People's Redemption Party.
1987	*Anthills of the Savannah* is published and short-listed for the Booker Prize.
1987-1988	Achebe serves as Visiting Fellow at the University of Massachusetts at Amherst.
1988	*Hopes and Impediments*, a book of essays, is published.

1989	Achebe serves as Distinguished Visiting Professor at the City College of New York. He is nominated for the presidency of PEN International.
1990	*Arrow of God* is adapted as a play by Emeka Nwabueze. A celebration of Achebe's sixtieth birthday is held at Nsukka. Achebe is badly hurt in a near-fatal car accident that leaves him paralyzed from the waist down. He accepts a position as Charles P. Stevenson Professor of Languages and Literature at Bard College in New York.
1993	The Everyman's Library series of world classics adds *Things Fall Apart* to its list of titles.
1998	Achebe delivers the McMillan-Stewart Lectures at Harvard University.
1999	Elections install a new civilian government in Nigeria.
2000	*Home and Exile*, a book of essays, is published.
2005	*Collected Poems* is published.
2007	Achebe is awarded the Man Booker International Prize, an award presented every two years for an author's body of fiction.
2009	Achebe joins Brown University as the David and Marianna Fisher University Professor of Africana Studies.

Works by Chinua Achebe

Long Fiction
Things Fall Apart, 1958
No Longer at Ease, 1960
Arrow of God, 1964
A Man of the People, 1966
Anthills of the Savannah, 1987

Short Fiction
"Dead Men's Path," 1953
The Sacrificial Egg, and Other Stories, 1962
Girls at War, and Other Stories, 1972

Poetry
Beware, Soul Brother, and Other Poems, 1971, 1972 (published in the United States as
    Christmas in Biafra, and Other Poems, 1973)
Collected Poems, 2004

Children's Literature
Chike and the River, 1966
How the Leopard Got His Claws, 1972 (with John Iroaganachi)
The Drum, 1977
The Flute, 1977

Nonfiction
Morning Yet on Creation Day, 1975
An Image of Africa, 1977
The Trouble with Nigeria, 1983
Hopes and Impediments, 1988
Conversations with Chinua Achebe, 1997 (Bernth Lindfors, editor)
Home and Exile, 2000
The Education of a British-Protected Child, 2009

Edited Texts

Don't Let Him Die: An Anthology of Memorial Poems for Christopher Okigbo, 1932-1967, 1978 (with Dubem Okafor)

Aka weta: Egwu aguluagu egwu edeluede, 1982 (with Obiora Udechukwu)

African Short Stories, 1985 (with C. L. Innes)

Beyond Hunger in Africa, 1990 (with others)

The Heinemann Book of Contemporary African Short Stories, 1992 (with C. L. Innes)

Miscellaneous

Another Africa, 1998 (poems and essay; photographs by Robert Lyons)

Bibliography

Achebe, Chinua. *Things Fall Apart: Authoritative Text, Contexts, and Criticism*. Ed. Francis Abiola Irele. New York: W. W. Norton, 2008.

Bascom, Tim. "The Black African and the 'White Man's God' in *Things Fall Apart*: Cultural Repression or Liberation?" *Commonwealth Essays and Studies* 11.1 (1988): 70-76.

Bloom, Harold, ed. *Chinua Achebe's "Things Fall Apart."* Philadelphia: Chelsea House, 2002.

Booker, M. Keith. *The African Novel in English: An Introduction*. Portsmouth, NH: Heinemann, 1998.

_____, ed. *The Chinua Achebe Encyclopedia*. Westport, CT: Greenwood Press, 2003.

Bottcher, Karl H. "The Narrative Technique in Achebe's Novels." *Journal of the New African Literature and the Arts* 13/14 (1972): 1-12.

Carroll, David. *Chinua Achebe*. New York: St. Martin's Press, 1980.

_____. *Chinua Achebe: Novelist, Poet, Critic*. 2nd ed. New York: Macmillan, 1990.

Champion, Ernest A. "The Story of a Man and His People: Chinua Achebe's *Things Fall Apart*." *Negro American Literature Forum* 8.4 (Winter 1974): 272-77.

Cobham, Rhonda. "Problems of Gender and History in the Teaching of *Things Fall Apart*." *Matatu: Journal for African Culture and Society* 7 (1990): 25-39.

Cook, David. *African Literature: A Critical View*. London: Longman, 1977.

Counihan, Clare. "Reading the Figure of Woman in African Literature: Psychoanalysis, Difference, and Desire." *Research in African Literatures* 38.2 (Summer 2007): 161-80.

Ebeogu, Afam. "Igbo Sense of Tragedy: A Thematic Feature of the Achebe School." *Literary Half-Yearly* 24.1 (1983): 69-86.

Egar, Emmanuel Edame. *The Rhetorical Implications of Chinua Achebe's "Things Fall Apart."* Lanham, MD: University Press of America, 2000.

Ekwe-Ekwe, Herbert. *African Literature in Defence of History: An Essay on Chinua Achebe*. Dakar, Senegal: African Renaissance, 2001.

Emenyonu, Ernest N., ed. *Emerging Perspectives on Chinua Achebe*. 2 vols. Trenton, NJ: Africa World Press, 2004.

Ezenwa-Ohaeto. *Chinua Achebe: A Biography*. Bloomington: Indiana University Press, 1997.

Gikandi, Simon. "Chinua Achebe and the Invention of African Literature." *Things Fall Apart*. By Chinua Achebe. 1958. Portsmouth, NH: Heinemann, 1996. ix-xvii.

_____. *Reading Chinua Achebe: Language and Ideology in Fiction*. Portsmouth, NH: Heinemann, 1991.

Glenn, Ian. "Heroic Failure in the Novels of Chinua Achebe." *English in Africa* 12.1 (1985): 11-27.

Greenberg, Jonathan Daniel. "Okonkwo and the Storyteller: Death, Accident, and Meaning in Chinua Achebe and Walter Benjamin." *Contemporary Literature* 48.3 (Fall 2007): 423-50.

Innes, C. L. *Chinua Achebe.* New York: Cambridge University Press, 1990.

Innes, C. L., and Bernth Lindfors, eds. *Critical Perspectives on Chinua Achebe.* Washington, DC: Three Continents Press, 1978.

Iyasere, Solomon O. *Understanding "Things Fall Apart": Selected Essays and Criticism.* Troy, NY: Whitston, 1998.

JanMohamed, Abdul R. "Sophisticated Primitivism: The Syncretism of Oral and Literate Modes in Achebe's *Things Fall Apart.*" *Ariel* 15.4 (1984): 19-39.

Johnson, John. "Folklore in Achebe's Novels." *New Letters* 40.3 (1974): 95-107.

Jones, Eldred D. "Language and Theme in *Things Fall Apart.*" *Review of English Literature* 5.4 (1964): 39-43.

Killam, G. D. *The Writings of Chinua Achebe.* New York: Africana, 1969.

Kortenaar, Neil ten. "Chinua Achebe and the Question of Modern African Tragedy." *Philosophia Africana* 9.2 (Aug. 2006): 83-100.

Landrum, Roger. "Chinua Achebe and the Aristotelian Concept of Tragedy." *Black Academy Review* 1 (1970): 22-30.

Laurence, Margaret. *Long Drums and Cannons: Nigerian Dramatists and Novelists, 1952-1966.* Edmonton: University of Alberta Press, 2001.

Leach, Josephine. "A Study of Chinua Achebe's *Things Fall Apart* in Mid-America." *English Journal* 60.8 (Nov. 1971): 1052-56.

Lindfors, Bernth, ed. *Approaches to Teaching Achebe's "Things Fall Apart."* New York: Modern Language Association of America, 1991.

Macdonald, Bruce F. "Chinua Achebe and the Structure of Colonial Tragedy." *Literary Half-Yearly* 21.1 (1980): 50-63.

Moses, Michael Valdez. *The Novel and the Globalization of Culture.* New York: Oxford University Press, 1995.

Muoneke, Romanus Okey. *Art, Rebellion, and Redemption: A Reading of the Novels of Chinua Achebe.* New York: Peter Lang, 1994.

Niven, Alastair. "Chinua Achebe and the Possibility of Modern Tragedy." *Kunapipi* 12.2 (1990): 41-50.

Njoku, Benedict Chiaka. *The Four Novels of Chinua Achebe.* New York: Peter Lang, 1984.

Nwahuananya, Chinyere. "Social Tragedy in Achebe's Rural Novels: A Contrary View." *Commonwealth Novel in English* 4.1 (1991): 1-13.

Obiechina, Emmanuel. *Culture, Tradition, and Society in the West African Novel.* New York: Cambridge University Press, 1975.

_____. "Narrative Proverbs in the African Novel." *Research in African Literatures* 24.4 (1993): 123-40.

Ogbaa, Kalu. *Understanding "Things Fall Apart": A Student Casebook to Issues, Sources, and Historical Documents.* Westport, CT: Greenwood Press, 1999.

Ogede, Ode. *Achebe and the Politics of Representation.* Trenton, NJ: Africa World Press, 2001.

_____. *Achebe's Things Fall Apart: A Reader's Guide.* London: Continuum, 2007.

Okafor, Clement A. "A Sense of History in the Novels of Chinua Achebe." *Journal of African Studies* 8.2 (1981): 50-63.

Okechukwu, Chinwe Christina. *Achebe the Orator: The Art of Persuasion in Chinua Achebe's Novels.* Westport, CT: Greenwood Press, 2001.

Okpala, Jude Chudi. "Igbo Metaphysics in Chinua Achebe's *Things Fall Apart.*" *Callaloo* 25 (2002): 559-66.

Okpewho, Isidore, ed. *Chinua Achebe's "Things Fall Apart": A Casebook.* New York: Oxford University Press, 2003.

Olorounto, Samuel B. "The Notion of Conflict in Chinua Achebe's Novels." *Obsidian II* 1.3 (1986): 17-36.

Opata, Damian. "Eternal Sacred Order Versus Conventional Wisdom: A Consideration of Moral Culpability in the Killing of Ikemefuna in *Things Fall Apart.*" *Research in African Literatures* 18.1 (1987): 71-79.

_____. "The Structure of Order and Disorder in *Things Fall Apart.*" *Neohelicon* 18.1 (1991): 73-87.

Pandurang, Mala, ed. *Chinua Achebe: An Anthology of Recent Criticism.* Delhi: Pencraft International, 2006.

Petersen, Kirsten Holst, and Anna Rutherford, eds. *Chinua Achebe: A Celebration.* Portsmouth, NH: Heinemann, 1991.

Rhoads, Diana Akers. "Culture in Chinua Achebe's *Things Fall Apart.*" *African Studies Review* 36.2 (1993): 61-72.

Shelton, Austin J. "The Offended Chi in Achebe's Novels." *Transition* 13 (1964): 36-37.

_____. "The 'Palm-Oil' of Language: Proverbs in Chinua Achebe." *Modern Language Quarterly* 30.1 (1969): 86-111.

Smith, Angel. "The Mouth with Which to Tell of Their Suffering: The Role of Narrator and Reader in Achebe's *Things Fall Apart.*" *Commonwealth Essays and Studies* 11.1 (1988). Rpt. in *Understanding "Things Fall Apart": Selected Essays and Criticism.* Ed. Solomon O. Iyasere. Troy, NY: Whitston, 1998. 8-26.

Taylor, Willene P. "The Search for Values Theme in Chinua Achebe's Novel *Things Fall Apart*: A Crisis of the Soul." *Griot* 2.2 (1983): 17-26.

Turkington, Kate. *Chinua Achebe: "Things Fall Apart."* London: Arnold, 1977.

Udumukwu, Onyemaechi. "The Antinomy of Anti-colonial Discourse: A Revisionist Marxist Study of Achebe's *Things Fall Apart.*" *Neohelicon* 18.2 (1991): 317-36.

Walder, Dennis. *Post-colonial Literatures in English: History, Language, Theory.* Malden, MA: Blackwell, 1998.

Whittaker, David, and Mpalive-Hangson Msiska. *Chinua Achebe's "Things Fall Apart."* New York: Routledge, 2007.

Wise, Christopher. "Excavating the New Republic: Post-colonial Subjectivity in Achebe's *Things Fall Apart.*" *Callaloo* 22.4 (1999): 1054-70.

Wren, Robert M. *Achebe's World: The Historical and Cultural Context of the Novels.* Washington, DC: Three Continents Press, 1980.

CRITICAL
INSIGHTS

About the Editor_____

M. Keith Booker is the James E. and Ellen Wadley Roper Professor of English and Director of the Program in Comparative Literature and Cultural Studies at the University of Arkansas. He is the author or editor of nearly forty books on literature, film, television, and literary theory. He has worked extensively with postcolonial literature and is the coauthor of *The African Novel in English: An Introduction* (1998) and *The Caribbean Novel in English: An Introduction* (2000). He is the editor of *Critical Essays on Salman Rushdie* (1999) and *The Chinua Achebe Encyclopedia* (2003).

About *The Paris Review*_____

The Paris Review is America's preeminent literary quarterly, dedicated to discovering and publishing the best new voices in fiction, nonfiction, and poetry. The magazine was founded in Paris in 1953 by the young American writers Peter Matthiessen and Doc Humes, and edited there and in New York for its first fifty years by George Plimpton. Over the decades, the *Review* has introduced readers to the earliest writings of Jack Kerouac, Philip Roth, T. C. Boyle, V. S. Naipaul, Ha Jin, Ann Patchett, Jay McInerney, Mona Simpson, and Edward P. Jones, and published numerous now classic works, including Roth's *Goodbye, Columbus*, Donald Barthelme's *Alice*, Jim Carroll's *Basketball Diaries*, and selections from Samuel Beckett's *Molloy* (his first publication in English). The first chapter of Jeffrey Eugenides's *The Virgin Suicides* appeared in the *Review*'s pages, as well as stories by Rick Moody, David Foster Wallace, Denis Johnson, Jim Crace, Lorrie Moore, and Jeanette Winterson.

The Paris Review's renowned Writers at Work series of interviews, whose early installments include legendary conversations with E. M. Forster, William Faulkner, and Ernest Hemingway, is one of the landmarks of world literature. The interviews received a George Polk Award and were nominated for a Pulitzer Prize. Among the more than three hundred interviewees are Robert Frost, Marianne Moore, W. H. Auden, Elizabeth Bishop, Susan Sontag, and Toni Morrison. Recent issues feature conversations with Salman Rushdie, Joan Didion, Norman Mailer, Kazuo Ishiguro, Marilynne Robinson, Umberto Eco, Annie Proulx, and Gay Talese. In November 2009, Picador published the final volume of a four-volume series of anthologies of *Paris Review* interviews. *The New York Times* called the Writers at Work series "the most remarkable and extensive interviewing project we possess."

The Paris Review is edited by Philip Gourevitch, who was named to the post in 2005, following the death of George Plimpton two years earlier. A new editorial team has published fiction by André Aciman, Colum McCann, Damon Galgut, Mohsin

Hamid, Uzodinma Iweala, Gish Jen, Stephen King, James Lasdun, Padgett Powell, Richard Price, and Sam Shepard. Poetry editors Charles Simic, Meghan O'Rourke, and Dan Chiasson have selected works by John Ashbery, Kay Ryan, Billy Collins, Tomaž Šalamun, Mary Jo Bang, Sharon Olds, Charles Wright, and Mary Karr. Writing published in the magazine has been anthologized in *Best American Short Stories* (2006, 2007, and 2008), *Best American Poetry, Best Creative Non-Fiction*, the Pushcart Prize anthology, and *O. Henry Prize Stories*.

The magazine presents two annual awards. The Hadada Award for lifelong contribution to literature has recently been given to Joan Didion, Norman Mailer, Peter Matthiessen, and, in 2009, John Ashbery. The Plimpton Prize for Fiction, awarded to a debut or emerging writer brought to national attention in the pages of *The Paris Review*, was presented in 2007 to Benjamin Percy, to Jesse Ball in 2008, and to Alistair Morgan in 2009.

The Paris Review was a finalist for the 2008 and 2009 National Magazine Awards in fiction, and it won the 2007 National Magazine Award in photojournalism. The *Los Angeles Times* recently called *The Paris Review* "an American treasure with true international reach."

Since 1999 *The Paris Review* has been published by The Paris Review Foundation, Inc., a not-for-profit 501(c)(3) organization.

The Paris Review is available in digital form to libraries worldwide in selected academic databases exclusively from EBSCO Publishing. Libraries can contact EBSCO at 1-800-653-2726 for details. For more information on *The Paris Review* or to subscribe, please visit: www.theparisreview.org.

M. Keith Booker is the James E. and Ellen Wadley Roper Professor of English and Director of the Program in Comparative Literature and Cultural Studies at the University of Arkansas. He is the author or editor of nearly forty books on literature, film, television, and literary theory.

Norbert Mazari is a musician who was previously affiliated with Sonoma State University in California.

Petrina Crockford lives and writes in Colorado. She has studied and taught fiction in Nigeria, including in the Niger Delta, not far from where Chinua Achebe's Okonkwo would have lived.

Joseph McLaren is Professor of English at Hofstra University, where he teaches courses in African, Caribbean, and African American literature. He is the author of *Langston Hughes: Folk Dramatist in the Protest Tradition, 1921-1943* (1997) and has edited two volumes of *The Collected Works of Langston Hughes*. He is also the coeditor of *Pan Africanism Updated* (1999).

Amy Sickels is an MFA graduate of Pennsylvania State University. Her fiction and essays have appeared or are forthcoming in *DoubleTake*, *Passages North*, *Bayou*, the *Madison Review*, *LIT*, *Natural Bridge*, and the *Greensboro Review*.

Thomas Jay Lynn is Associate Professor of English at Penn State Berks, where he began teaching in 1999 and where he is the Coordinator of the Associate Degree in Letters, Arts, and Sciences. His scholarly and teaching interests include African literature, postcolonial literature, ancient literature, and folklore, and he has published on African literature in a variety of journals. He previously taught for five years at Greenhills School in Ann Arbor, Michigan. He has volunteered with numerous groups and has led book discussions through the Pennsylvania Humanities Council and the Reading Public Library.

Matthew J. Bolton is Professor of English at Loyola School in New York City, where he also serves as Dean of Students. He received his doctor of philosophy degree in English from the Graduate Center of the City University of New York (CUNY) in 2005. His dissertation at the university was titled "Transcending the Self in Robert Browning and T. S. Eliot." Prior to attaining his Ph.D. at CUNY, he also earned a master of philosophy degree in English (2004) and a master of science degree in English education (2001). His undergraduate work was done at the State University of New York at Binghamton, where he studied English literature.

Margaret Laurence is considered one of Canada's most influential and successful writers of the twentieth century. A novelist and short-story writer, she is best known for her novel *The Stone Angel* (1964). She received many awards for her work, most notably the Governor General's Award for both *The Diviners* (1974) and *A Jest of God* (1966).

David Cook was Professor of English and Head of the Department of Modern European Languages at the University of Ilorin in Nigeria. He served as Dean of the Faculty of Arts between 1967 and 1969. He is the author of *African Literature: A Critical View* (1977) and coeditor of *Poems from East Africa* (1971).

David Hoegberg is Associate Professor of English at Indiana University-Purdue University. His lectures center on the roles of power, negotiation, and community in literature. He has published numerous papers on authors such as Earl Lovelace, Derek Walcott, Athol Fugard, and Chinua Achebe, and he has received seven fellowships in the past sixteen years, most recently the 2007 New Frontiers in the Arts and Humanities Fellowship.

Carey Snyder is Associate Professor of English and Scholarship Committee Chair at Ohio University. Specializing in British and American modernism and the Victorian novel, she has published articles for such scholarly publications as *Modern Fiction Studies*, *College Literature*, and *Woolf Studies Annual*. In 2008 she published her first book, *British Fiction and Cross-Cultural Encounters: Ethnographic Modernism from Wells to Woolf*.

B. Eugene McCarthy is Professor Emeritus of English at the College of the Holy Cross and cofounder of the African American Studies Program. He is the editor of *From Bondage to Belonging: The Worcester Slave Narratives* (2007) and author of *William Thomas Gray: The Progress of a Poet* (1997) and *Wycherly: A Biography* (1980).

Richard Begam is Associate Professor of English at the University of Wisconsin, where he lectures primarily in twentieth-century British, Anglophone, and Irish literature. He is the author of two books: *Modernism and Colonialism: British and Irish Literature* (2007) and *Samuel Beckett and the End of Modernity* (1996). He is currently working on several books, one of which ties Samuel Beckett to philosophical ideas and another of which examines modernity in James Joyce's *Ulysses*.

Biodun Jeyifo is Professor of African and African American Studies and of Comparative Literature at Harvard University. He has published nine books on the topics of African culture and literature, including *Wole Soyinka: Politics, Poetics, Postcolonialism* (2004), *Modern African Drama* (2002), and *The Truthful Lie: Essays in a Radical Sociology of African Drama* (1985).

Ada Uzoamaka Azodo is Associate Faculty in Minority Studies and Women's Studies at Indiana University Northwest. He is the editor of several volumes, including *Emerging Perspectives on Ken Bugul: From Alternative Choices to Oppositional Practices* (2008), *Gender and Sexuality in African Literature and Film* (2007), and *Emerging Perspectives on Ama Ata Aidoo* (1999).

Patrick C. Nnoromele is Associate Professor of Philosophy and Religion at Eastern Kentucky University. He is the author of *Rationality, Justification, and Truth of Religious Beliefs: The Philosophy of William James* (1989).

Alan R Friesen earned his master's degree from the University of Regina in 2006. His dissertation was titled "Demonic Possession, Spirit Possession, and Soul-Loss in William Gibson's 'Sprawl Trilogy.'"

Acknowledgments

"Chinua Achebe" by Norbert Mazari. From *Dictionary of World Biography: The 20th Century*. Copyright © 1999 by Salem Press, Inc. Reprinted with permission of Salem Press.

"The *Paris Review* Perspective" by Petrina Crockford. Copyright © 2011 by Petrina Crockford. Special appreciation goes to Christopher Cox, Nathaniel Rich, and David Wallace-Wells, editors at *The Paris Review*.

"*Things Fall Apart*" by Margaret Laurence. From *Long Drums and Cannons: Nigerian Dramatists and Novelists, 1952-1966* (2001), pp. 91-97. Copyright © 2001 by the University of Alberta Press. Reprinted with permission of the University of Alberta Press.

"Chinua Achebe: *Things Fall Apart*" by M. Keith Booker. From *The African Novel in English: An Introduction* (1998), pp. 65-83. Copyright © 1998 by Heinemann Educational, Ltd. Reprinted with permission of Pearson Education, Ltd.

"The Centre Holds: A Study of Chinua Achebe's *Things Fall Apart*" by David Cook. From *African Literature: A Critical View* (1977), pp. 65-81. Copyright © 1977 by Longman Group, Ltd. Reprinted with permission of Longman Group, Ltd.

"Principle and Practice: The Logic of Cultural Violence in Achebe's *Things Fall Apart*" by David Hoegberg. From *College Literature* 26, no. 1 (1999): 69-79. Copyright © 1999 by *College Literature*. Reprinted with permission of *College Literature*.

"The Possibilities and Pitfalls of Ethnographic Readings: Narrative Complexity in *Things Fall Apart*" by Carey Snyder. From *College Literature* 35, no. 2 (2008): 154-174. Copyright © 2008 by *College Literature*. Reprinted with permission of *College Literature*.

"Rhythm and Narrative Method in Achebe's *Things Fall Apart*" by B. Eugene McCarthy. From *Novel* 18, no. 3 (1985): 243-256. Copyright © 1985 by Novel, Inc. All rights reserved. Reprinted by permission of the publisher, Duke University Press.

"Achebe's Sense of an Ending: History and Tragedy in *Things Fall Apart*" by Richard Begam. From *Studies in the Novel* 29, no. 3 (Fall 1997): 396-411. Copyright © 1997 by the University of North Texas. Reprinted with permission of the University of North Texas.

"Okonkwo and His Mother: *Things Fall Apart* and Issues of Gender in the Constitution of African Postcolonial Discourse" by Biodun Jeyifo. From *Callaloo* 16, no. 4 (1993): 847-858. Copyright © 1993 by The Johns Hopkins University Press. Reprinted with permission of The Johns Hopkins University Press.

"Masculinity, Power, and Language in Chinua Achebe's *Things Fall Apart*" by Ada Uzoamaka Azodo. From *Emerging Perspectives on Chinua Achebe*, vol. 1, *Omenka: The Master Artist*, edited by Ernest N. Emenyonu (2004), pp. 49-65. Copyright © 2004 by African World Press. Reprinted with permission of African World Press.

Gem of the Ocean, The (Wilson), 82

Gikandi, Simon, 23, 41, 47, 61, 119, 166, 169, 175, 222

Glenn, Ian, 41

Graff, Gerald, 4

Green, Margaret, 91

Heart of Darkness (Conrad), 3, 20, 33-34, 55, 59, 70, 165, 214

Homeric influences, 70, 73, 100, 126, 209

Hopes and Impediments (Achebe), 119

Igbo; language, 5, 27, 46, 53, 60, 73, 98; massacres, 10, 113; rituals, 156, 173; warfare, 29, 62

Ikemefuna (*Things Fall Apart*), 87, 102, 139, 149, 191, 276; sacrifice, 26, 62, 92, 103, 132, 147, 150, 251, 277, 285

"Image of Africa, An" (Achebe), 3, 55, 81

Innes, C. L., 20, 40, 98, 104, 106, 119, 173

Irele, Francis Abiola, 41, 45, 120, 124, 132, 207

Irony, 92, 139, 148, 215, 217

Italie, Hillel, 66

Iyasere, Solomon O., 48, 97-98, 190, 285

Jahn, Jahnheinz, 188

JanMohamed, Abdul R., 98, 104, 106, 119, 176

Jeyifo, Biodun, 48, 105

Johnson, John, 38

Johnson, Sally, 245

Jones, Eldred D., 40, 141

Kellogg, Robert, 188

Kiesling, Scott Fabius, 249, 254

Killam, G. D., 41, 104, 119, 125, 181

King Solomon's Mines (Haggard), 20, 55

Kortenaar, Neil ten, 161, 170, 175

Landrum, Roger, 41

Larson, Charles R., 11, 42-43, 180

Laurence, Margaret, 39, 138

Lindfors, Bernth, 38, 40, 46, 119

McCarthy, B. Eugene, 40

Macdonald, Bruce, 207, 290

Malinowski, Bronislaw, 166, 168, 170

Man of the People, A (Achebe), 10, 117, 137, 185

Meinhoff, Ulrike Hanna, 245

Mercy, A (Morrison), 82

Miri, Angela F., 173

Missionaries. *See* Christian missionaries

Mister Johnson (Cary), 20, 33, 57, 70, 161

Modernism, 70, 78, 81, 97

Moore, Gerald, 124, 137, 140

Morning Yet on Creation Day (Achebe), 34, 119, 180, 242

Morrison, Toni, 82

Moses, Michael Valdez, 28, 100, 103, 110, 209, 222

Mphahlele, Ezekiel, 127

Msiska, Mpalive-Hangson, 48

"Named for Victoria, Queen of England" (Achebe), 116

Names and naming, 27, 53, 153, 197-198, 227, 252

Nance, Carolyn, 38

Narayan, Kirin, 171, 178

Narration and narrators, 27, 46, 55, 59, 63, 65, 104, 163, 168, 173-175, 177, 186, 192, 202, 205, 280

Ngara, Emmanuel, 40

Ngugi wa Thiong'o, 44, 235, 241